# SPARKNOTES

# 101

## U.S. History

### 1865 through the 20th Century

SPARK PUBLISHING

SPARKNOTES is a registered trademark of SparkNotes LLC

Spark Educational Publishing
A Division of Barnes & Noble Publishing
120 Fifth Avenue
New York, NY 10011
www.sparknotes.com

ISBN 1-4114-0336-3

Please submit changes or report errors to
*www.sparknotes.com/errors.*

Printed and bound in the United States.

*Library of Congress Cataloging-in-Publication Data*

SparkNotes 101 U.S. history.
    v. cm.
  Includes bibliographical references and index.
  Contents: [1] From the precolonial period to 1865 -- [2] 1865 to
    modern times.
  ISBN 1-4114-0335-5 (v. 1) -- ISBN 1-4114-0336-3 (v. 2)
  1. United States--History--Outlines, syllabi, etc. 2. United States
  --History--Examinations--Study guides. I. Title: SparkNotes
  101 United States history. II. Title: SparkNotes one hundred
  one U.S. history. III. Title: SparkNotes one hundred and one
  U.S. history.
  E178.2.S695 2005
  973--dc22
                        2005009726

# Contents

# *Acknowledgments*

SparkNotes would like to thank the following writers and contributors:

**Greg Cantrell, Ph.D.**
Professor of History and Erma and Ralph Lowe Chair in Texas History, Texas Christian University

**Ashley Laumen**
Teaching Assistant, Department of History, Texas Christian University

**Sean Taylor, Ph.D.**
Visiting Assistant Professor of History, Minnesota State University Moorhead

**Timothy Buckner**
Teaching Assistant, Department of History, University of Texas at Austin

**Paul Rubinson**
Teaching Assistant, Department of History, University of Texas at Austin

**Josh Cracaft**
A.B., Government, Harvard University

**Christian Lorentzen**
A.B., Classics, Harvard University

**Anaxos, Inc.**

# A Note from SparkNotes

Welcome to the *SparkNotes 101* series! This book will help you succeed in your introductory college course for U.S. History: 1865 through the 20th Century.

Every component of this study guide has been designed to help you process your course material more quickly and score higher on your exams. You'll see lots of headings, lists, charts, maps, and, most important, no long blocks of text. This format will allow you to quickly situate yourself and easily get to the crux of your course. We've organized the book in the following manner:

**Introduction**: Before diving in to the major chapters, you may want to get a broader view of the themes that will be covered in more detail later on. Remember, it is these overarching themes that are usually tested on exams.

**Chapters 1–9:** Each chapter provides a clarification of material included in your textbook. Key features include:

- **Sidebars:** Throughout the text, these call out main points and relate material to major themes.

- **Key Terms:** Important names, events, amendments, treaties, etc., are bolded throughout each chapter for quick scanning and reviewing.

- **A+ Student Essay:** It's the real thing. Each chapter contains a typical essay prompt with a response that will show you how to pull together the facts from the chapter and use them in a compelling argument. At the same time, the essays delve more deeply into particular topics in history, enriching the content of each chapter.

- **Sample Test Questions:** These show you the kind of questions you are most likely to encounter on a test. Bulleted points follow each question and clarify the kind of information you need to include in your answers.

- **Timeline:** This end-of-chapter outline provides an at-a-glance recap of major events.

- **Major Figures:** This section provides a summary of the major figures presented in the chapter, along with their significance.

- **Suggested Reading:** This list makes recommendations for enhancing your knowledge with further research in notable books.

**Index:** Use the index at the back of the book to make navigation easier or to look up specific events, people, documents, treaties, and other topics.

We hope *SparkNotes 101: U.S. History: 1865 through the 20th Century* helps you, gives you confidence, and occasionally saves your butt! Your input makes us better. Let us know what you think or how we can improve this book at **www.sparknotes.com/comments**.

# *Introduction*

An analysis of American history between 1865 and the present reveals some major themes that provide an interpretive framework for understanding America's past:

- The Contested Terrain of the Capitalist Economy
- The Transformative Power of War
- A World Power
- A Land of the Free
- The Changing American Identity
- Waves of Reform
- The Rise and Fall of Liberalism

## *The Contested Terrain of the Capitalist Economy*

The Union's victory in the Civil War ensured that the northern characteristics of free enterprise, industrialization, and capitalism would quickly become the driving forces of the U.S. economy. As the United States expanded westward across the continent, American business also expanded overseas. But many Americans challenged the U.S. business ethos. In the wake of a series of catastrophic economic downturns, capitalism's role in American society underwent reassessment by workers and owners alike. Would America reflect unfettered competitive enterprise? Or would the government limit capitalism and protect workers? These are among the economic questions that have remained contested since Reconstruction. Some examples of influential events that changed the direction of American capitalism include:

- **The Gilded Age.** In the late nineteenth century, huge corporations grew to dominate the U.S. economy.

1

- **Workers' rights.** As the economy grew, workers organized in order to protect their rights.

- **The prosperity of the 1920s.** A booming economy ushered in a new economic era, introducing Americans to consumer credit and mass-produced consumer goods.

- **Periodic depressions.** In the late nineteenth and twentieth centuries, periodic economic depressions created drastic shifts in American policy, including the search for an overseas empire and the birth of the liberal state.

- **The New Deal.** When Roosevelt became president in 1933, he quickly implemented a variety of programs known as the New Deal. These programs stimulated economic recovery for the United States.

- **End of liberal reforms.** An economic downturn in the 1970s helped bring about a speedy end to the liberal reforms of the 1960s. With the economy in shaky territory, Americans shifted their focus from securing civil liberties to securing their own economic well-being.

# The Transformative Power of War

The United States changed drastically after every war it fought. Modern America often found itself at war during the late nineteenth and twentieth centuries, and these wars always had consequences. Some examples of major post-Reconstruction wars that shaped U.S. society include:

- **The Indian Wars** of the 1870s, 1880s, and 1890s cleared the great western plains of Native Americans, opening up a vast frontier to settlement and development.

- **The Spanish-American War** of 1898 turned the United States into a world power with colonies overseas.

- **World War I** forced the United States into Europe's affairs for the first time since the early nineteenth century.

2

- **World War II** launched the United States into a position of world leadership.

- **The Korean War** encouraged the militarization and mobilization of U.S. society during the Cold War.

- **The Vietnam War** revealed the limits of American power and threatened to divide the nation along racial, economic, and generational lines.

# A World Power

At the beginning of the twenty-first century, America stands alone as the world's only superpower. This ascendance began in 1898, when America defeated Spain and took control of Cuba, the Philippines, and other island holdings. Then, after World War II, America's powerful military and capitalist economy transformed it into a world power. Foreign affairs played a pivotal role in shaping the development of the American nation. Some of these events include:

- **The founding of an American empire** in 1898 introduced the United States as an influential power in global politics.

- **A culture of isolationism** after World War I withdrew the nation from Europe's affairs, creating a soured political climate that encouraged a second world war.

- **The emergence of the United States as a world leader.** After World War II, the United States accepted its position of dominance in global affairs.

- **The Cold War rivalry** with the Soviet Union forced the United States to extend its influence around the globe in efforts to spread democracy and stop communism.

- **Anticommunism.** Throughout the Cold War, U.S. policy-makers viewed every event in terms of the Cold War rivalry. Anticommunism dominated aspects of U.S. foreign and domestic policy between 1940 and 1970.

# A Land of the Free

The revolutionary changes of Reconstruction granted the freedoms of the U.S. Constitution and the Bill of Rights to African Americans. But the abrupt halt of Reconstruction in 1877 ushered in a new era of oppression. Over the next 100 years, African Americans and other groups waged a constant struggle for their rights. Gradually, those opposing change and progress gave way to the forces of justice and equality. The more significant events in the struggle to make America a more perfect union include:

- **The landmark constitutional amendments.** Slavery was finally ended and African Americans were granted full citizenship.

- **The creation of the NAACP.** The late nineteenth and early twentieth centuries saw the birth of many organizations that fought for the rights of the oppressed, including the NAACP (National Association for the Advancement of Colored People).

- **A massive population shift among the nation's African Americans.** During World War I, a vast number of African Americans moved from the rural South into the cities of the North.

- **Amendment XIX.** For decades, American women had fought for suffrage, and after World War I, they won the right to vote.

- **The Civil Rights movement.** This quest was at its peak from 1955–1965, seeking basic civil rights for all Americans.

# The Changing American Identity

Although the United States had long been considered a nation of immigrants, most of the immigrants who arrived before the Civil War came from western and northern Europe. After the war, the origins of immigrants began to change. Eventually, immigrants, many of them nonwhite, began to arrive from all over the globe. With this influx of ethnic groups, existing notions of American identity and the very concept of national identity became matters of debate. New arrivals sought to assert their own values as part of the American character. Some of the factors that changed American identity include:

- **Increased immigration** from Eastern and Southern Europe, Latin America, and Asia

- **The Cold War era**, when Americans came to define themselves in contrast to communism

- **The Sixties,** when a "generation gap" began to widen between young people in America and their parents, leading to a real sense of division in the country.

- **The culture wars** of the 1980s and 1990s. The 1980s witnessed the decline of the middle class in America. This economic trend persisted in the 1990s and enhanced the sense of divide among American citizens.

# Waves of Reform

While not always successful, reform movements have forced Americans to reconsider the ways they see the economy and government. Reform has a long tradition in American society, often working to curb the excesses of unfettered capitalism. Some of the more notable reform movements from after the Civil War include:

- **The Populist movement** of the 1880s, which began as a revolt against the excesses of the Gilded Age.

- **The Progressive movement** of the early 1900s, which worked within the major parties and advanced a slew of reforms, including suffrage, Prohibition, child labor laws, and antimonopoly laws.

- **The New Deal** of the 1930s, which not only provided relief, recover, and reform but also drastically changed the federal government's role in politics and society.

# The Rise and Fall of Liberalism

Since the founding of the United States, Americans have been conflicted over the role of the federal government in the economy. Some have argued that the government should stay out of the economy altogether, in favor of free enterprise. Others have countered that the government should regulate the economy in order to redistribute wealth across society. After the Civil War, American policy leaned toward the free-enterprise side of the argument. However, following the Great Depression, many Americans embraced Liberalism. In hard economic times, Liberalism argues that the government should provide an economic safety net for the public. In good economic times, the government should help provide for the poor and needy. Liberalism dominated American politics for decades until the conservative revolution of the early 1980s. Some of the pivotal events in the rise and fall of Liberalism include:

- **Franklin D. Roosevelt's New Deal** of the 1930s, which transformed Democrats into social-welfare advocates.

- **The Great Society** of the 1960s, which spent more than $2 billion in social-welfare reform and promised the beginning of a new age.

- **The Vietnam War**, which drastically divided American society.

- **The Conservative Revolution** of the 1980s, in which Americans elected Ronald Reagan, a diehard conservative who abandoned most social-welfare programs, to the presidency.

These major themes provide a basic structure upon which to build your knowledge of American history. You may find it helpful to return to this section of the book periodically and organize what you are learning in terms of these themes.

# Reconstruction: 1862–1877

- Wartime Reconstruction
- Presidential Reconstruction
- Radical Reconstruction
- Reconstruction in the South
- Grant's Presidency
- The End of Reconstruction

Despite the Union's victory on the battlefield, sectional differences between North and South still seethed, and the prospect of rebuilding and healing the United States amid such chaos and destruction was daunting. The competing needs of southern blacks and whites—as well as those of northern emigrants to the region—made the challenges of reestablishing the United States as a cohesive and functional country largely insurmountable. This process, which came to be known as Reconstruction, proved virtually endless for those involved. Local, state, and national leaders wrestled with complex questions, such as how to mend the broken South and how a new society would embrace both Confederate elites and former slaves.

Modern historians regard Reconstruction as a failure. Although Radical Republicans restored the Union politically, they failed to protect African Americans from abuse by white southern elites. By the end of the 1870s, former Confederates had reclaimed power in the southern states and virtually reinstated slavery.

# Wartime Reconstruction

Historians refer to efforts to reunite and reform the nation during the Civil War as a dress rehearsal for Reconstruction. During this phase, President **Abraham Lincoln**, Congress, and military leaders issued a number of proclamations, acts, and field orders related to the ongoing war. Such actions fueled ongoing conflicts over issues including:

- Emancipation and the rights of African Americans
- The fate of the Confederacy
- Landownership in the South
- The transformation of the southern labor system and economy

## LINCOLN'S PROCLAMATIONS

President Lincoln wanted to win the war without annihilating the Old South, whereas Congress wanted to dramatically transform southern society. Still, Lincoln's ultimate goal was to reunite the nation. He wanted to abolish slavery because he knew that this would cripple the southern economy; on the other hand, Lincoln believed emancipation should unfold gradually so as not to alienate the proslavery border states in the Union. Lincoln issued two proclamations during the war addressing reunification and emancipation: the **Emancipation Proclamation** and the **Proclamation of Amnesty and Reconstruction**.

### Emancipation Proclamation

Lincoln earned the moniker "the Great Emancipator" for the **Emancipation Proclamation** he issued on January 1, 1863. Despite the nickname, Lincoln's proclamation only liberated slaves in the states at war with the Union. Not surprisingly, months passed before many of those slaves found out they were free. The proclamation did *not* free any slaves in the border states or in areas of the Confederacy occupied by the Union. Nonetheless, Lincoln's proclamation made slavery a central issue of the war.

The proclamation deprived the Confederacy of its labor force and thus crippled the region's economy. It also legalized the enlistment of freedmen, who wanted to fight to keep their freedom.

This influx of men reinvigorated the Union military and greatly contributed to the defeat of the Confederate forces.

### SECEDED STATES

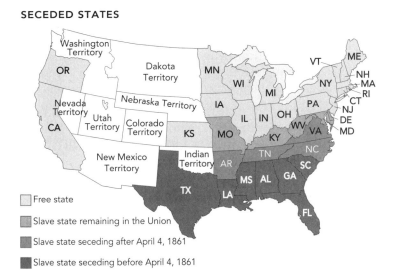

- Free state
- Slave state remaining in the Union
- Slave state seceding after April 4, 1861
- Slave state seceding before April 4, 1861

> In September 1862, Lincoln issued an ultimatum to the Confederacy after a major Union victory at Antietam. After only one day of fighting, a cumulative total of 23,000 soldiers lay dead or wounded. Lincoln told the Confederacy to either return to the Union by January 1, 1863, or all women, men, and children enslaved in rebellious states would be "forever free."

### Proclamation of Amnesty

Lincoln outlined his postwar vision for reunification when he issued the **Proclamation of Amnesty and Reconstruction** in December 1863. More commonly known as **Lincoln's Ten-Percent Plan**, the proclamation promised the following:

- The pardoning of all Confederates who signed an oath of allegiance to the United States, excluding government and military leaders.

- The recognition of any southern state government, provided that 10 percent of the state's voters in the election of 1860 pledged their allegiance to the United States. Arkansas, Louisiana, and Tennessee reorganized under these terms in 1864 but were not recognized by Congress.

- The protection of lower-ranking Confederate officers from trial and execution for treason

- The return of political rights and land confiscated by the federal government to the Confederates after they received pardons and accepted the emancipation of black people.

- The prosecution of Confederate military and civilian officials and others who left federal positions to join the Confederacy. Ex-Confederates who killed or tortured Union soldiers, both black and white, would also be denied amnesty.

## CONGRESS'S ACTS

Congress favored a more aggressive approach to freeing the slaves than President Lincoln. Even though Republicans in Congress never completely agreed on any issue during Reconstruction, almost all of them wanted to punish the South.

### Freeing Slaves in the District of Columbia

In April 1862, Congress passed legislation to free enslaved African Americans in Washington, D.C. Lincoln consented, but only reluctantly, as the **First Confiscation Act** of 1861, guaranteed compensation to the District's slave owners. In July 1862, Congress also passed the **Second Confiscation Act**, which freed all blacks enslaved by government officials in Confederate states. The Confiscation Act of 1862 also freed all southern slaves who sought refuge behind Union lines.

### The Wade-Davis Bill

Republicans in Congress led by **Thaddeus Stevens** and **Benjamin Wade** opposed Lincoln's Ten-Percent Plan because they wanted to punish the southerners who had caused the war. Furthermore, they sought to pass additional legislation to protect free blacks. In response to Lincoln's Proclamation of Amnesty and Reconstruction, Wade and Congressman **Henry Winter Davis** of Maryland sponsored the **Wade-Davis Bill** to appoint provisional military

Some 180,000 African Americans served in the Union forces
during the Civil War. Perhaps the most famous of these was
**Harriet "the Moses of Her People" Tubman**, who personally
led as many as 300 slaves to freedom via the Underground
Railroad. Recruited by military officials in 1862, she taught survival
skills to black refugees in the South Carolina Sea Islands. Tubman
also nursed wounded soldiers, served as a spy, and even led
troops into battle. Despite her commitment, Tubman never
received pay for her services.

governors in the former Confederate states. The bill also required
that more than 50 percent of white men in each state take an
oath of allegiance to the Union before a new constitution could
be drafted. Additionally, this new constitution would have to
renounce both slavery and secession and disenfranchise all
former Confederate leaders.

Although Congress passed the Wade-Davis Bill in July 1864, Lincoln thought it too radical and refused to sign it. Hoping to avoid
the controversy of an outright veto, he simply **"pocket vetoed"** the
bill by withholding his signature until Congress adjourned for the
year. Without Lincoln's signature, the Wade-Davis Bill died.

### UNION MILITARY LEADERS' ACTIONS

At the beginning of the Civil War, many Union commanders
supported slavery. Some even returned escaped slaves to their
Confederate owners, reasoning that they were fighting to preserve the Union, not to free black people. But over time, a number
of northern military officers began to advocate emancipation. Many
petitioned for emancipation in order to rid themselves of the
responsibility for the thousands of black refugees, or **"contraband
of war,"** that flooded Union camps. Consequently, commanders
often issued special field orders to help them defeat the Confederacy by depriving the South of its slaves. After the war and the
end of slavery, these generals led the way in redefining the status of
blacks in the South. Military leaders also made decisions regarding
southern landownership and helped establish a free labor system.

### The Port Royal Experiment

In January 1862, **Brigadier General William Sherman** asked the federal government to send teachers to instruct the former slaves on the Sea Islands of South Carolina. This request eventually evolved into the **Port Royal Experiment**, which became a model for educating black people and organizing black communities. Later that year, Lincoln officially emancipated black Sea Islanders, and the U.S. Army began redistributing abandoned plantation lands to the freedmen. In exchange, many blacks on the Sea Islands produced cotton for Union factories and enlisted in the military.

Black and white missionaries from the North also established a string of schools on the islands. These schools educated thousands of former slaves and inspired others to found schools for freed people throughout the South. Unfortunately, federal support for the schools waned after Lincoln's assassination.

### General David Hunter and General Order 11

The Union's **General David Hunter** twice defied Lincoln's decree regarding the status of blacks during the war. In March 1862, he ignored the ban on blacks in the military and recruited black men for a special combat unit. In May 1862, he issued **General Order 11** to emancipate slaves in Georgia, Florida, and South Carolina. Lincoln disbanded the combat unit and nullified the order.

### General William Sherman and Special Field Order 15

In January 1865, after his infamous **March to the Sea** through Georgia, **General William Sherman** met with twenty black leaders in Savannah to determine the needs of former slaves. The freedmen told Sherman and Secretary of War **Edwin M. Stanton** that black people wanted land. A few days later, Sherman issued **Field Order 15** to redistribute confiscated land in forty-acre parcels to blacks in Florida and on the Sea Islands off Georgia and South Carolina. Only blacks were allowed to settle these lands.

In less than a month, more than 40,000 freed people received land from the government. The new landowners also received surplus government mules. After the war ended, President Andrew Johnson allowed white planters to reclaim these lands. As a result, thousands of blacks became destitute.

> *Sherman's generosity led freed blacks throughout the South to believe that they would all receive "forty acres and a mule" as repayment for centuries of servitude. However, most freed blacks never received this. Consequently, this phrase has come to signify an empty promise.*

### The Freedmen's Bureau

General Oliver O. Howard ran the **Bureau of Freedmen, Refugees, and Abandoned Lands**. More commonly known as the **Freedmen's Bureau**, this agency was created a month before the war ended to provide food, clothing, and medicine to freed people and poor whites. The Bureau also founded the **Freedmen's Bank** and established more schools. Although the Bureau provided freed people some protection against aggressive whites who tried to take their land and exploit their labor, the organization ultimately undermined blacks.

Essentially, the agency steered freed people into the abusive free-labor systems that replaced slavery. southern state and local governments supported these systems in order to meet the region's demand for food and jumpstart the agrarian economy. The Freedmen's Bureau was perpetually underfunded by Congress and thus never had the manpower or resources equal to the huge task facing it.

# Presidential Reconstruction

When the Civil War ended in April 1865, President Lincoln asserted that the former Confederate states merely had been "out of their proper practical relation with the Union." In fact, Lincoln firmly believed that these states "had never really left the Union." A few days after Lincoln made this statement, on April 14, 1865, Confederate sympathizer **John Wilkes Booth** assassinated Lincoln. Lincoln's vice president, **Andrew Johnson**, immediately became president. Surprisingly, Johnson pardoned thousands of Confederate leaders and championed the restoration of white supremacy in the South.

An outraged Congress quickly established the **Committee of Fifteen** to devise progressive new plans for Reconstruction. Republicans fought Johnson's repeated attempts to block constitutional amendments and congressional acts meant to protect freed people and punish ex-Confederates. In the end, Republicans' triumph over the president paved the way for Radical Reconstruction.

### JOHNSON'S PLAN

A former Tennessee slaveholder, President Johnson did everything in his power to reinstate southern elites. He implemented a three-pronged strategy to stymie congressional attempts to reform the South:

1. **The Amnesty Proclamation** to pardon former Confederate leaders. This proclamation allowed these elites to reclaim land given to freed people and returned white supremacists to power in the state governments.
2. The vetoing of all legislation designed to grant and protect African Americans' civil liberties.
3. The rallying of conservatives and reactionaries to halt all attempts to change the social order of the South.

### Johnson's Amnesty Proclamation

Johnson shrewdly issued and implemented his Amnesty Proclamation during the congressional recess from May to early December 1865. The proclamation resembled Lincoln's Ten-Percent Plan. For example, it required that southern states approve the **Thirteenth Amendment** to abolish slavery before they could rejoin the Union. But Johnson added a couple of stipulations of his own. He denied amnesty to rich Confederates (i.e., those worth more than $20,000) and required the repudiation of all debts that were owed by the Union to Confederates.

Most important, he firmly believed that he should reconstruct the Union without the help of Congress.

President Johnson also accepted Reconstruction governments in Arkansas, Louisiana, and Tennessee created in 1862 during Lincoln's presidency. Moreover, he made governors out of **native Unionists** who had remained loyal during the war. Despite his professed hatred for Confederate leaders, Johnson pardoned 13,000 people, including former Confederate military and civilian officials and allowed the secessionist states to write new constitutions, even if 10 percent of voters had not taken the loyalty oath. As a result, Johnson readmitted all eleven Confederate states into the Union by December 1865 and prematurely declared Reconstruction over.

### Johnson's Presidential Vetoes

Johnson repeatedly exercised his right to veto legislation of the Republican Congress. Most of this legislation was passed to elevate the social and political status of black people. Congress overrode the following of Johnson's vetoes:

- **The Civil Rights Act of 1866**, which granted citizenship to blacks and safeguarded their civil liberties

- **The Fourteenth Amendment**, which safeguarded blacks' citizenship rights and reduced congressional representation of states that denied black males voting rights

- **The Freedmen's Bureau Bill**, which extended the life of the agency and increased its authority to help freed people and poor whites

### Race Riots and "Swing Around the Circle"

Many whites in the South responded furiously to the Civil Rights Act of 1866 and the Fourteenth Amendment. Riots erupted in Memphis, Tennessee, and New Orleans, and hundreds of blacks were murdered. The rampant racism and violence shocked Americans in the North who turned an accusing eye toward Johnson for his leniency.

The president in turn blamed the radicals in Congress in his infamous **"Swing Around the Circle"** speeches. Traveling throughout the country, he often got carried away lambasting Republicans, prowar Democrats, blacks, and anyone else who challenged him. As a result, he blackened the Democratic Party's already tarnished reputation and inadvertently persuaded many northerners to vote Republican in the 1866 Congressional elections.

*"Swing Around the Circle" refers to the pattern in which Johnson toured the country in 1866 in a mostly futile attempt to gain support among northern voters. He visited Philadelphia, New York City, upstate New York, and Ohio, then finally returned to Washington, D.C. This tour was incredibly unsuccessful.*

# Radical Reconstruction

The race riots and murders combined with Johnson's "Swing Around the Circle" campaign convinced northerners that the president could no longer be trusted to reconstruct the Union. Instead, they turned to Republicans, who consequently swept the 1866 congressional elections. **Radical Republicans** and their moderate allies dominated both the House of Representatives and the Senate and therefore had the ability to override any presidential vetoes. As a result, their ascension to office in early 1867 marked the beginning of **Congressional Reconstruction**, sometimes known as **Radical Reconstruction**.

## MILITARY RECONSTRUCTION

Congress began the task of reorganizing the South with the **First Reconstruction Act** in March 1867. Also known as the **Military Reconstruction Act** or simply the **Reconstruction Act**, this bill reduced the secessionist states' claim to conquered territories. Congress carved the South into five military districts, which were each governed by a Union general in charge of the Reconstruction process.

Congress also declared martial law and dispatched troops to keep the peace and protect persecuted blacks. All former secessionist states had to once again draft a new constitution, ratify the **Fourteenth Amendment**, and provide suffrage to blacks. To safeguard black voting rights, Republicans passed the **Second Reconstruction Act,** placing Union troops in charge of voter registration. Congress overrode two presidential vetoes to pass these bills.

## THE FIFTEENTH AMENDMENT

Radicals believed that giving blacks the right to vote was the only way to prevent southern elites from seizing power again. Even though Congress demanded that the southern states enfranchise blacks, Republicans still feared that whites might one day revoke this right. To prevent this, they decided to incorporate black suffrage into the Constitution itself: in 1869 they passed the **Fifteenth Amendment** to guarantee that all black males had the right to vote. Furthermore, Republicans made ratification a prerequisite for all southern states still awaiting readmission. Three-fourths of the states finally ratified the amendment in 1870.

### Enfranchising Blacks in the South and North

The Fifteenth Amendment enfranchised not only blacks but also poor southern white males. Prior to the Civil War, all southern states had restricted the vote to landowners. This restriction excluded most white males—as well as blacks and women—from political participation. The amendment also forced reluctant northern states to enfranchise blacks. Even when most state constitutions in the South gave blacks the right to vote, most northern states still refused to do so. The Fifteenth Amendment changed the political status of blacks throughout the entire United States.

### The Quest for Women's Suffrage

The passage of the Fifteenth Amendment in 1869 had an enormous effect on the women's suffrage movement as well. Prior to the Civil War, the quest for women's suffrage and abolition had been closely united, as both groups strove to achieve political and civil rights for those not represented in politics. After the Union victory, many women like **Elizabeth Cady Stanton** and **Susan B. Anthony** thought they had won suffrage for both blacks and women. But radicals in Congress feared that if they granted the right to vote to all men *and* women, they would lose support in both the South and North. Consequently, many women felt betrayed by their exclusion from the Fifteenth Amendment.

## REPUBLICANISM TAKES ROOT IN THE SOUTH

With their right to vote safeguarded, southern blacks flocked to register, and by the beginning of 1868, more than 700,000 freedmen had signed up. Not surprisingly, all declared themselves Republicans, as they identified the Democrats with secession and slavery. Almost the same number of landless white males registered.

### Black Political Power

African-American civic societies and grassroots political organizations sprouted up everywhere. Most of them were led by prominent blacks who had been freedmen before the war. Black voters quickly dominated the electorate in South Carolina, Alabama, Louisiana, Florida, and Mississippi, giving the Republican Party control over the Reconstruction process in those states. The new voters also elected many black politicians to state legislatures throughout the South. Fourteen black politicians served in the House of Representatives, and Mississippians elected two blacks to the Senate.

## JOHNSON TRIED AND ACQUITTED

Congress passed several bills in 1867 to limit President Johnson's power. The **Tenure of Office Act** sought to protect prominent Republicans within the Johnson administration by forbidding their dismissal without congressional authorization. Although the act applied to all office holders approved by Congress, radicals specifically wanted to keep Secretary of War Edwin M. Stanton in office to check Johnson's control over the military. In defiance, Johnson ignored the act, fired Stanton in the summer of 1867 during a congressional recess, and replaced him with Union General **Ulysses S. Grant**. Afraid that Johnson could effectively end military reconstruction in the South, Congress ordered the president to reinstate Stanton when it reconvened in 1868. Johnson refused, Grant subsequently resigned, and Congress put Stanton back in office over the president's objections.

Tired of presidential vetoes and obstruction to Congressional Reconstruction, House Republicans impeached Johnson by a vote of 126 to 47 for violating the Tenure of Office Act and slandering Congress. The Senate tried Johnson in May 1868 in front of a gallery of spectators. Radical Representatives **Thaddeus Stevens** and Benjamin Butler served as prosecutors but couldn't convince a majority of senators to convict the president. The final tally was one vote shy of a conviction.

*Even though President Johnson had stubbornly opposed Congress, he had not violated the Constitution. Several Republican senators realized that radicals wanted to remove Johnson simply because he had disagreed with them over Reconstruction, not because of a technical violation of the Tenure of Office Act. No other president was impeached until Bill Clinton in 1998.*

# Reconstruction in the South

As the Union Army advanced deeper into southern territory during the war's end, more and more slaves enjoyed the fruits of freedom. The army did free some slaves, but most freed themselves by refusing to work and walking away. Tens of thousands of blacks, for example, followed Sherman's troops on his **March to the Sea** in 1864. The end of the war brought jubilation and celebrations. Thousands of blacks left their homes in search of lost family members, while many black couples took the opportunity to marry, knowing no one could ever forcibly separate them again.

Most former slaves faced considerable challenges with their newly acquired freedom. Despite the Radical Republicans' best efforts to protect their civil liberties and voting rights, the freed men and women still faced persecution from racist whites. By the end of Reconstruction blacks had freedom—but not equality.

> Sherman's **March to the Sea** was a sign that the Union victory was imminent. On November 12, 1864, he led his troops out of Atlanta toward the Atlantic coast, and the Confederacy could present no obstacle great enough to stop him.

### CARPETBAGGERS AND SCALAWAGS

Many northerners jumped at opportunities in the South in the wake of Confederate General Lee's surrender in early April of 1865. These **"carpetbaggers"** (nicknamed for the large carpet bags many of them brought with them) came for a variety of reasons: to promote education, to modernize the South, and to seek their fortunes. White southern Unionists, or **"scalawags,"** also played roles in achieving the same aims. Both carpetbaggers and scalawags served in legislatures in every reconstructed state.

### THE BLACK CODES

White elitist regimes in the southern states did everything in their power to prevent blacks from gaining too much power. After Republicans in Congress passed the Civil Rights Act of 1866, every southern legislature passed laws to exert more control on African Americans. These **Black Codes** ranged in severity and outlawed everything from interracial marriage to loitering in public areas.

Southern whites passed these laws partly because they feared a free black population, especially in states where blacks outnumbered whites. Many also worried that freed slaves would terrorize their masters, rape white women, and ruin the economy. Most planter elites passed the codes simply to ensure that they would have a stable and reliable work force.

Black Codes often dictated that former slaves sign labor contracts for meager wages. Although Congress forced state legislatures to repeal the codes once the radicals took control of Reconstruction, whites still managed to subtly enforce them for years after Reconstruction had ended.

Black Codes differed from state to state but were all similar in the following ways:

- All blacks had to sign labor contracts.

- Blacks could not own land.

- Individuals accused of vagrancy who were unable to pay fines could be sentenced to hard labor on chain gangs.

- States could force orphaned children into apprenticeships that resembled slavery.

- Whites could physically abuse blacks without fear of punishment.

### BLACK CHURCHES AND EDUCATION

Most freed men and women had a burning desire to educate their children. They recognized that knowledge (especially the previously forbidden ability to read and write) was power and that their futures depended upon it. The Freedmen's Bureau and former abolitionist groups from the North succeeded in founding schools for thousands of blacks. Because white clergymen had often upheld slavery in their sermons prior to the Civil War, many blacks went on to establish their own congregations.

### THE SHARECROPPING SYSTEM

Blacks craved economic independence and resisted white efforts to consign them to chain gangs or wage labor on large plantations. Instead, they preferred the **sharecropping system**, in which former plantation owners divided their lands and rented each plot—or share—to a single black family. The family farmed its own crops in exchange for giving a percentage of the yield to the landowner. In fact, many families sharecropped on their former masters' lands. Landless whites also became sharecroppers for the elites, so that by 1880, almost all farmers in the South sharecropped.

### THE KU KLUX KLAN

Violence also posed a serious threat to African Americans in the South. A secret white-supremacist society called the **Ku Klux**

*Ironically, the new sharecropping system kept blacks tied to their small plots and indebted to white landowners in ways that closely resembled slavery. Cotton prices steadily declined in the postwar years, from roughly fifty cents per pound in 1864 to a little over ten cents a pound at the end of Reconstruction. With very little money, most black farmers could only purchase items on credit at the local shops. Consequently, blacks generally experienced very little real freedom.*

**Klan** formed in Tennessee in 1866 to terrorize blacks. White-robed Klansmen would harass, beat, and lynch both blacks and white Republicans. They ordered blacks to stay away from voting polls and punished those who didn't obey; in one extreme case, Klansmen butchered several hundred black voters in Louisiana in 1868. Congress eventually passed the **Ku Klux Klan Act** of 1871, which allowed it to act against terrorist organizations. Still, racist violence continued to be a serious problem.

# Grant's Presidency

As the presidential election of 1868 drew near, Republicans nominated Civil War hero **Ulysses S. Grant**. Grant had proven himself an effective leader in the army and served as a reminder that Republicans had won the war. Democrats nom-inated former governor of New York **Horatio Seymour**. Sey-mour hated emancipation, supported states' rights, and wanted to wrest control of Reconstruction out of Congress's hands. In the end, Grant received 214 electoral votes to Sey-mour's 80, but only 300,000 more popular votes. Republicans also maintained control of Congress. During the Grant years, Congress funded more projects and distributed more money than ever before in U.S. history.

## A MULTITUDE OF SCANDALS

Scandal and corruption characterized Grant's two terms in office. Although the president himself was never involved, his lack of polit-ical experience hampered his ability to control other politicians.

### The Fisk-Gould Gold Scandal

Scandal rocked Washington before Grant had even completed his first year in office. In 1869 the financial tycoons **Jim Fisk** and **Jay Gould** bribed many cabinet officials, including Grant's own brother-in-law, to overlook their attempt to corner the gold market. They even conned Grant himself into agreeing not to release any more of the precious metal into the economy. On September 24, 1869, they succeeded in inflating gold prices. The U.S. Treasury managed to prevent an economic catastrophe by releasing more gold into the economy, in spite of Grant's earlier promise.

### The Crédit Moblier Scandal

Corruption also infected the railroads. In 1872, Union Pacific Railroad executives created a dummy construction company called **Crédit Moblier**. They then hired Crédit Moblier at outrageous prices to lay track. To protect their huge profits, the executives bribed several congressmen and even Vice-President **Schuyler Colfax** to keep quiet. Colfax ultimately resigned after an exposé revealed his shady dealings. Even though Grant had no involvement in the scandal, it nevertheless damaged his reputation.

### The Whiskey Ring Scandal

Yet another scandal broke two years later in 1874, when investigators discovered that several Grant-appointed federal employees had skimmed millions of dollars from excise tax revenue. The president vowed to hunt down and punish all those involved in the **Whiskey Ring** but swallowed his harsh words upon discovering his own secretary's involvement.

### THE ELECTION OF 1872

Fed up with scandals in Grant's administration, a significant number of Republicans broke from the radicals and moderates in Congress just before the 1872 elections. Known as **Liberal Republicans**, these men wanted to end corruption, restore the Union as quickly as possible, and downsize the federal government. They nominated *New York Tribune* editor **Horace Greeley** for the presidency.

Strangely enough, Democrats also nominated Greeley, because he opposed the army's presence in the South and wanted to end Reconstruction. Despite the scandals, radicals and moderates again nominated their war hero Grant. On Election Day, Grant easily won with 286 electoral votes to Greeley's 66, and received more than 700,000 more popular votes.

### The Liberal Republicans

Led by businessmen, professionals, reformers, and intellectuals, Liberal Republicans helped shape politics in the postwar years. They disliked big government and preferred limited government involvement in the economy. Some historians have argued that the Liberal Republicans even opposed democracy because they detested universal manhood suffrage and didn't want to enfranchise blacks.

### THE DEPRESSION OF 1873

Although Grant faced as many problems in his second administration as he had during his first, none were so catastrophic as the **Depression of 1873**. Bad loans and overspeculation in railroads and factories burst the postwar economic boom and forced millions of Americans onto the streets over the next five years. The poor clamored for cheap paper and silver money for relief, but Republicans refused to give in to their demands out of fear that cheap money would exacerbate inflation. Instead, they passed the **Resumption Act of 1875** to remove all paper money from the economy. The act helped end the depression in the long run, but it made the interim years more difficult to bear.

### THE END OF RADICAL RECONSTRUCTION

The Resumption Act proved politically damaging for the Radical and moderate Republicans in Congress. Because they insisted on passing hard-money policies during a time when up to 15 percent of Americans had no work, many Republicans in the North voted with the Democrats in the 1874 congressional elections. Their votes, combined with white votes in the South, ousted many Republicans from Congress and gave the Democrats control of the House of Representatives for the first time since 1856. The remaining radicals in Congress suddenly found themselves commanding the weak minority party. In short, the elections of 1874 marked the end of Radical Reconstruction.

# The End of Reconstruction

As the economy plummeted, so too did northerners' willingness to pursue Radical Reconstruction. Americans had neither the time nor the energy to worry about helping former slaves, punishing Ku Klux Klan terrorism, or readmitting states when so many of them didn't even have jobs. In fact, many in the North had grown tired of Radical Republican zeal altogether.

### THE CIVIL RIGHTS ACT OF 1875

Despite their weakness, Republicans managed to pass one final piece of radical legislation through Congress. The **Civil Rights Act of 1875** aimed to eliminate social discrimination and facilitate true equality for black Americans by stipulating the following:

- Racial discrimination would be outlawed in all public places such as theaters, hotels, and restaurants.
- Blacks would have the same legal rights as whites.
- Blacks could sue violators in federal courts.

#### Toothless Legislation

The Civil Rights Act of 1875 proved highly ineffective, because Democrats in the House of Representatives made it virtually unenforceable. The law required individual blacks to file their own claims to defend their rights; the federal government wouldn't do it for them. Because lawsuits required money, time, and considerable effort, House Democrats knew that the law would have very little practical impact.

## REDEMPTION

The weak Republican foothold in the South had only gotten weaker as northerners lost interest in Reconstruction. By the mid-1870s, the depression and the Klan had driven off most white Unionists, carpetbaggers, and scalawags, which left African Americans to fend for themselves. Without any support from southern whites or Congress, Democrats easily seized power once again and "redeemed" the southern state legislatures one by one. Some Democrats even employed violence to secure power by killing Republicans or terrorizing blacks away from the polls. By 1877, Democrats once again controlled every southern state.

### COURT RULINGS AGAINST RADICAL RECONSTRUCTION

Several Supreme Court rulings in the 1870s and 1880s also heralded the death of Reconstruction. For example:

- **The *Slaughterhouse* cases of 1873:** the Fourteenth Amendment did not protect citizens from state infringements on their rights.

- ***United States v. Cruikshank* in 1876:** only states, not the federal government, could prosecute individuals in violation of the 1871 Ku Klux Klan Act.

- **The *Civil Rights* cases of 1883:** the Fourteenth Amendment only applied to discrimination by the government (not from individuals).

### THE ELECTION OF 1876

Democrats poured a lot of energy into the 1876 presidential election in order to oust Grant and redeem the White House. The party nominated New York prosecutor **Samuel J. Tilden**, who railed against the corrupt Grant administration. After briefly toying with the idea of choosing Grant again for an unprecedented third term, Republicans finally selected Ohio governor **Rutherford B. Hayes.**

Hayes had served in the war as a Union general, had no overly controversial opinions, and came from the politically important state of Ohio. On Election Day 1876, Hayes won only 165 electoral votes and lost the popular election by roughly 250,000 votes. Tilden, on the other hand, had won the popular vote and had 184 electoral votes, but he lacked the extra electoral vote necessary to become president.

### The Compromise of 1877

The election results in South Carolina, Louisiana, and Florida were still in dispute because of confusing ballots. Normally, the president of the Senate would recount the ballots in front of Congress. Because the president of the Senate was a Republican and the Speaker of the House was a Democrat, neither man could trust the other to count the votes honestly.

Instead, Congress passed the **Electoral Count Act** in 1877 to establish a special committee to recount the votes fairly. The committee consisted of fifteen men from the House, the Senate, and the Supreme Court—eight Republicans and seven Democrats. Not surprisingly, the committee concluded by a margin of one vote that Hayes had won the disputed states. Deadlock ensued once again, until both sides agreed to compromise.

In the **Compromise of 1877**, Democrats and Republicans agreed to let Hayes become president in exchange for the complete withdrawal of federal soldiers from the South. Shortly after Hayes took office, he ordered the last remaining troops out of South Carolina and Louisiana. Reconstruction had finally ended.

Some historians have suggested that had Lincoln not been assassinated, radicals in the House might have impeached him instead of Andrew Johnson. Defend or refute this argument using specific examples.

Had Lincoln not been assassinated in 1865, it is likely that he would have continued to clash with the Radical Republicans in Congress during his second term. It is unlikely, however, that he would have incensed them to the point of impeachment. After the Civil War, Lincoln and the Radical Republicans had very different visions for Reconstruction, but these differences might have been resolved through compromise and a process of give-and-take, as they had been during the war.

The Radical Republicans saw the war as part of the larger struggle to end slavery, whereas Lincoln hoped for a swift and final end to the war and restoration of the Union as soon as possible. Because of the enormous toll the war was taking on northern families and resources, Lincoln feared that strong public support for the war would wane if the fighting continued much longer. He was also growing pessimistic about the prospects for reconciliation between North and South once the fighting stopped. His fears were justified: by late 1863 and early 1864, more and more northern Democrats were clamoring for a truce and peaceful resolution. The forgiving stipulations for readmission in the Proclamation of Amnesty and Reconstruction of 1863 were an attempt to entice Unionists and those tired of fighting in the South to surrender.

Lincoln's Reconstruction policies, including the Ten-Percent plan, were lenient toward southern secessionists. Lincoln favored self-Reconstruction by the southern states without assistance from Washington. His offer to pardon all Confederates was designed to appeal to poorer whites who had done the fighting, and his pledge to protect private property attempted to appease the former plantation owners of the southern elites. Above all, Lincoln did not want Reconstruction to turn into an extension of the conflict between North and South.

# *Student Essay*

The Radical Republicans, on the other hand, wanted to punish the South for their rebellion. Furthermore, they believed that Congress—not the Executive Branch—should direct the process of Reconstruction. They sought to transform southern society and recast it in the image of the North. The Radicals' desire to change the South went beyond the desire for revenge, however. Many in Congress wanted to improve education and labor conditions to benefit the oppressed classes in southern society, both black and white. To accomplish these goals, they eventually passed the progressive Civil Rights Act of 1866, the First Reconstruction Act, the Second Reconstruction Act, the Ku Klux Klan Act of 1871, the Civil Rights Act of 1875, and the Thirteenth, Fourteenth, and Fifteenth Amendments.

President Andrew Johnson angered Radical Republicans because he repeatedly tried to scuttle legislation like the Civil Rights Act of 1866 and the Fourteenth Amendment. Lincoln very well might have pursued similar policies, but it may not have resulted in his impeachment. Like Johnson, he wanted reunification to be swift and painless, but unlike Johnson, he would have steered clear of the scandals that nearly brought his successor down. It is important to remember that although Johnson was impeached, the Senate fell short of the two-thirds majority required to throw him out of office because Democrats and Republicans outside the Radical circle did not want to see Benjamin Wade, the Radical Republican Senate leader, succeed him in the White House. (Johnson was without a vice president of his own, and Wade was next in line.) It is still less likely that Congress would have taken steps to push Lincoln out of the White House because the result would have been a Johnson Presidency, and history shows that Lincoln was more adept at the politics of compromise than Johnson.

# Test Questions and Answers

*1. Describe the purposes of Reconstruction in the post–Civil War era.*

- To reunite the Union and reform the South by emancipating blacks and protecting their civil rights
- To penalize those who had led the rebellion
- To redistribute land more equally
- To devise a new labor system in the South
- To help revive the South's economy

*2. What measures did President Lincoln take during Wartime Reconstruction to speed the end of the Civil War?*

- He issued the Emancipation Proclamation
- He outlined his Ten-Percent Plan in the Proclamation of Amnesty and Reconstruction

*3. How did Lincoln respond to congressional and military attempts to emancipate the slaves?*

- Lincoln wanted Congress and the military to compensate slave owners according to the Confiscation Act.
- He nullified the military's special field orders regarding emancipation.

*4. How did Congressional Reconstruction, Presidential Reconstruction, and Wartime Reconstruction under Lincoln differ? How were they similar?*

### Differences:

- Lincoln's Ten-Percent Plan required oaths of allegiance from only 10 percent of former Confederates.
- Congress required the majority of white men in Confederate states to take loyalty oaths.
- Congress wanted martial law declared in the South for the duration of Reconstruction.

- Congress wanted to punish ex-Confederates.
- Johnson excluded more categories from amnesty on paper, but in reality granted more pardons than Lincoln and Congress desired.

### Similarities:

- Lincoln and Johnson wanted to return land to pardoned ex-Confederates.
- Lincoln and Congress wanted to deny pardons to those who abused or killed captured black and white Union soldiers.

**5. How did blacks utilize their newly won freedom and rights during the Reconstruction years? What obstacles did they face?**

### Blacks:

- Tried to reunite with lost family members
- Wanted to own land and become self-sufficient
- Tried to become involved in state and national politics

### But they:

- Encountered racial terrorism
- Were barred in many states from owning land
- Had few job opportunities
- Became trapped in sharecropping or the wage-labor system

**6. How did southern whites respond to Reconstruction?**

- They terrorized free blacks.
- They boycotted elections.
- They supported conservative leaders.
- A few Unionists joined the Republican Party.

7. *In what ways can Reconstruction be described as a success? As a failure?*

**Success:**

- Radical Republicans passed the Thirteenth, Fourteenth, and Fifteenth Amendments.

- Blacks gained some political power for the first time.

- Congress passed laws to help improve the lives of former slaves.

**Failure:**

- Reconstruction did not end racial terrorism.

- It did not prevent racist whites from taking away blacks' voting rights and civil rights.

- It failed to revive or even significantly transform the southern economy.

# Timeline

| | |
|---|---|
| **1862** | First and Second Confiscation Acts passed. |
| **1863** | Abraham Lincoln issues the Proclamation on Amnesty and Reconstruction. |
| | Lincoln issues the Emancipation Proclamation. |
| **1864** | Lincoln is reelected. |
| **1865** | Sherman issues Special Field Order #15. |
| | Congress establishes the Freedmen's Bureau. |
| | Robert E. Lee surrenders to Grant. |
| | John Wilkes Booth assassinates Lincoln. |
| | Andrew Johnson becomes president. |
| | Johnson begins Presidential Reconstruction. |
| | The Thirteenth Amendment is ratified. |
| **1866** | Congress passes the Civil Rights Act of 1866. |
| | The Ku Klux Klan is founded in Tennessee. |
| | Race Riots erupt in Memphis and New Orleans. |
| | Johnson "Swings Around the Circle" in an attempt to gain support from northern voters. |
| **1867** | Radical Reconstruction begins. |
| | Congress passes the First and Second Reconstruction Acts. |
| | Congress passes the Tenure of Office Act. |
| **1868** | Johnson is impeached by the House of Representatives. |
| | The Senate acquits Johnson. |
| | The Fourteenth Amendment is ratified. |
| | Ulysses S. Grant is elected president. |
| **1869** | Jim Fisk and Jay Gould attempt to corner the gold market. |
| **1870** | The Fifteenth Amendment is ratified. |
| **1871** | Congress passes the Ku Klux Klan Act. |

| 1872 | The Republican Party splits. |
| | The Crédit Moblier scandal erupts. |
| | Samuel J. Tilden prosecutes Boss William Tweed. |
| | Grant is reelected president. |
| **1873** | Depression of 1873 begins. |
| | Supreme Court hears Slaughterhouse cases. |
| **1874** | Democrats retake control of the House. |
| | The Whiskey Ring scandal erupts, futher tarnishing President Grant's record. |
| **1875** | Congress passes the Civil Rights Act of 1875. |
| | Congress passes the Resumption Act. |
| **1876** | Democrats and Republicans dispute presidential-election results. |
| **1877** | Congress passes the Electoral Count Act. |
| | Democrats and Republicans strike the Compromise of 1877. |
| | Rutherford B. Hayes becomes president. |
| | Hayes withdraws all federal troops from the South. |

# Major Figures

**John Wilkes Booth**  A famous actor in his day and also a fanatical supporter of the South, Booth shot Abraham Lincoln in the back of the head in Ford's Theater in Washington, D.C., on April 14, 1865.

**Schuyler Colfax**  The vice president during Grant's first term, Colfax was passed over for a second term because of his role in the Crédit Mobilier scandal of 1872.

**Henry Winter Davis**  A Radical Republican Congressman during the Civil War, Davis cosponsored the Wade-Davis Bill with Senator Benjamin Wade.

**James "Jim" Fisk**  A self-made stockbroker and corporate executive, Fisk joined Jay Gould and others in an attempt to corner the American gold market in 1869.

**Jay Gould**  A corrupt Erie Railroad executive and speculator, Gould attempted to corner the American gold market. He failed, instead causing a stock-market crisis in September 1869.

**Ulysses S. Grant**  A politician during the Reconstruction years, Grant was nicknamed "Unconditional Surrender" Grant after his successes as the Union's top general in the Civil War. He briefly served as secretary of war after Andrew Johnson fired Edwin M. Stanton, but resigned when Stanton was reinstated. In 1868 he defeated Horatio Seymour to become the eighteenth president of the United States. Although he was an honest man, Grant's cabinet was filled with corruption, and his presidency was marred by scandals such as the Fisk-Gould gold scheme, Crédit Moblier, and the Whiskey Ring. He retired after his second term.

**Horace Greeley**  The nominee by both the Democratic Party and the Liberal Republicans for the presidency in 1972, Greeley was the choice because both parties wanted a swift end to Reconstruction, limited government, and reform. This political alliance only weakened the Liberal Republicans' cause in the North, where most Americans still did not trust the Democrats. As a result, Ulysses S. Grant easily defeated Greeley.

**Rutherford B. Hayes**  A nominee for the 1876 presidency, Hayes ran against Democrat Tilden. In the wake of the corruption scandals associated with Ulysses S. Grant, Republicans chose Hayes because he was relatively unknown, had no controversial opinions, and came from the politically important state of Ohio. Even though Hayes received fewer popular and electoral votes than Tilden, he still became president after the Compromise of 1877, when Democrats traded the White House for an end to Reconstruction.

**General David Hunter**  A Union general during the Civil War, Hunter ignored the ban on blacks in the military and recruited black men for a special combat unit.

**Andrew Johnson**  A former tailor, governor, and senator from Tennessee, Johnson, a Democrat, was chosen to be Abraham Lincoln's vice-presidential running mate in the 1864 election to persuade middle states to remain in the Union. He became the seventeenth president after John Wilkes Booth assassinated Lincoln. Although he hated the southern aristocracy, he also had no love for blacks and fought Congress over the Fourteenth Amendment and the Civil Rights Bill of 1866. Johnson believed that only he (not Congress) should be responsible for Reconstruction, and recognized new state governments established according to the Ten-Percent Plan. He was impeached by the House of Representatives in 1868, but was acquitted by the Senate.

**Abraham Lincoln**  A former lawyer from Illinois, Lincoln became the sixteenth president of the United States in the election of 1860. Because he was a Republican and associated with the abolitionist cause, his election prompted South Carolina to become the first state to secede from the Union. Lincoln believed that the states had never truly left the Union, but fought the war until the South surrendered unconditionally. He proposed the Ten-Percent Plan for Reconstruction in 1863, but was assassinated by John Wilkes Booth before he could see it through.

**Horatio Seymour**  A former governor of New York, Seymour ran on the Democratic ticket against Republican Ulysses S. Grant in the presidential election of 1868. Seymour campaigned for an end to Reconstruction in the South and repudiation of black civil rights. He lost both the popular vote and the electoral vote.

**William Sherman**  A brigadier general, Sherman served as the commander of the Union troops in the South Carolina Sea Islands in 1862. During his tenure, Sherman requested that teachers be sent to the islands to educate black refugees. Not to be confused with General William T. Sherman, who was one of the principal union military commanders.

**Edwin M. Stanton**  No relation to Elizabeth Cady Stanton, Edwin Stanton served as Secretary of War during the Civil War and Reconstruction years under both Abraham Lincoln and Andrew Johnson. Even though he was formerly a Democrat, he supported Radical Reconstruction of the South. Radical Republicans in Congress tried to protect Stanton from Johnson's wrath with the 1867 Tenure of Office Act. This act required Johnson to seek permission from Congress before removing any congressionally appointed administrators. Johnson ignored the law, and fired Stanton anyway. Republicans in the House used this violation as an excuse to impeach Johnson.

**Elizabeth Cady Stanton**  No relation to Edward M. Stanton, Elizabeth Cady Stanton was one of the first American feminists. She worked for social and political equality for women, helped to organize the Seneca Falls Convention in 1848, and drafted the *Declaration of Sentiments*.

**Thaddeus Stevens**  A staunch Radical Republican, Stevens fought for harsher punishments of former Confederates and for protection of African-American rights after the war. He helped draft the Fourteenth Amendment to the Constitution and the Reconstruction Acts of 1867. He also prosecuted Andrew Johnson in the president's 1867 Senate trial.

**Samuel J. Tilden**  A New York prosecutor, Tilden first became famous in 1871 and 1872 when he brought down the mighty Boss William Tweed on corruption charges. He then ran for president on the Democratic ticket against Rutherford B. Hayes in 1876. Even though he received more popular votes, he fell just one electoral vote shy of becoming president. After much debate, Democrats and Republicans struck the Compromise of 1877, in which Hayes became president in exchange for a complete withdrawal of federal troops from the southern states.

**Harriet Tubman**  Nicknamed the "Moses of Her People" for her success and bravery as an Underground Railroad conductor, Tubman served the Union as a spy, a scout, and a nurse during the Civil War. After the war, she continued to fight for African-American and women's rights.

**Benjamin Wade**  A Radical Republican senator both during and after the Civil War, Wade opposed Lincoln's Ten-Percent Plan for Reconstruction. Instead, he cosponsored the harsher 1864 Wade-Davis Bill along with Congressman Henry Winter Davis.

# Suggested Reading

• Foner, Eric. *Reconstruction: America's Unfinished Revolution, 1863-1877*. New York: Perennial, 2002.

This book details Reconstruction beyond the basic events and provides a context-rich look at this historical period.

• Smith, Jean Edward. *Grant*. New York: Simon & Schuster, 2001.

This is an in-depth look at the life of President Ulysses S. Grant. Though he served two terms, his presidency is generally regarded as a failure. Still, recent history has been a bit kinder to Grant, in light of his success as a military general. This book presents both sides of Grant.

• Trefousse, Hans Louis. *Impeachment of a President: Andrew Johnson, the Blacks, and Reconstruction*. New York: Fordham University Press, 1999.

Trefousse sheds new light on Johnson's impeachment and the events surrounding it. He demonstrates how Johnson's impeachment has been used as a precedent for turning Congress against the president. Professor Trefousse reexamines some of the common beliefs about Johnson in a profound way.

• Trelease, Allen W. *White Terror: The Ku Klux Klan Conspiracy and Southern Reconstruction*. Baton Rouge: Louisiana State University Press, 1995.

Trelease argues he point that the Ku Klux Klan was a reaction by white supremacists against the growing power of blacks. It gives a particularly detailed report of the southern side of Reconstruction.

# The Growing Nation:
## 1877–1901

- Gilded Age Politics
- Industrialization
- The Labor Movement
- Gilded Age Society
- The West
- The Rise and Fall of Populism
- The Spanish–American War

2

As Reconstruction ended and Americans approached a new century, dramatic contradictions emerged in the United States. Though North and South had reunited, sharp divisions and stark contrasts emerged in the North, South, and West. Although America beckoned to people from all over the world, immigrants often found hardship and prejudice in both growing cities and the frontier.

While pioneers staked their claims in the West, the government displaced and destroyed Native American populations. African Americans claimed their citizenship but suffered indignities and physical intimidation when they tried to exercise their rights. Booming industries and technological innovations spawned great cities and economic security for a new middle class. Yet ruthless entrepreneurs and corrupt politicians exploited a growing underclass of women, children, and men who became the working poor.

# Gilded Age Politics

The corruption and scandals that plagued President Ulysses S. Grant's administration worsened during the course of the **Gilded Age**, an era of tremendous growth in business and industry. Networks of powerful men and loyal underlings composed political machines in which bribes and pay-offs fueled politicians' quests for power. **Political bosses** embroiled in this **spoils system** (the process by which these bosses paid money to control votes, candidates, and other aspects of the voting system) obtained and maintained control over the political system for many years.

> *Powerful political "bosses" in different cities coerced residents to vote for their candidate of choice. Those candidates would then turn over kickbacks and bribes to the boss in appreciation for getting them elected. The most notorious party boss of his time was Boss* **William Tweed***, who ran the Tammany Hall Democratic machine in New York City. Most politicians elected in the post–Civil War era were the products of machine party politics.*

## THE STALWARTS, HALF BREEDS, AND MUGWUMPS

**Rutherford B. Hayes** squeaked into the White House by only one electoral vote after the **Compromise of 1877** (see page 27), and he remained virtually powerless during his four years in office. The real winners in the election were Republican spoils-seekers who flooded Washington, D.C., in search of civil service jobs. Unfortunately, disputes over the spoils split the Republican party (also known as the Grand Old Party) into three factions:

- **The Stalwarts**—led by New York Senator **Roscoe Conkling**—composed the conservative faction of the Republican party.

- **The Half-Breeds**—led by Maine Senator **James G. Blaine**—the moderate faction of the Republican party. The Stalwarts gave them their disparaging name.

- **The Mugwups**, a group of liberal Republicans who opposed the spoils system.

None of these groups trusted any of the others, and so the Republican party had trouble passing any significant legislation while in office.

### THE "FORGOTTEN PRESIDENTS"

Many historians have dubbed the Gilded Age presidents—Grant, Hayes, Garfield, Arthur, Cleveland, and Harrison—the **"Forgotten Presidents."** Some historians have even suggested that Gilded Age presidents lacked personality precisely because Americans didn't want any bold politicians who might ruin the peace established after the Civil War. Essentially, Americans wanted to focus on other matters like their own prosperity rather than face any more potentially divisive issues.

### Garfield and Arthur

Hayes had fallen out of favor with Republicans by the election of 1880, and he only planned to seek one term as president. They nominated the relatively unknown **James A. Garfield** and his Stalwart running mate, **Chester A. Arthur**. Democrats nominated Civil War veteran Winfield Scott Hancock, and the pro-labor **Greenback Party** nominated **James. B. Weaver**. Garfield received a sizeable majority of electoral votes on Election Day but won only slightly more popular votes than Hancock. Bickering for the spoils dominated Garfield's brief stay in the White House, which ended unexpectedly in 1881 when an insane Stalwart named Charles Guiteau shot and killed him. Guiteau hoped Arthur would become president and give more federal jobs to his loyal Stalwarts.

Although Arthur did replace Garfield, the assassination only convinced policymakers to reform the spoils system by passing the **Pendleton Act** in 1883. The act created the **Civil Service Commission** to hire federal employees based on examinations and merit rather than political patronage. Over time, these examinations gradually reformed the system.

### Grover Cleveland

Despite the Pendleton Act, political spoils continued to dominate politics and the next presidential election in 1884. Republicans nominated the Half-Breed James Blaine while Democrats nominated New York governor **Grover Cleveland**. Democrats accused Blaine of conspiring with wealthy plutocrats to win the White House, and Republicans attacked Cleveland for having fathered an illegitimate son. In the end, Cleveland barely defeated Blaine with forty more electoral votes and 29,685 more popular votes. Cleveland's four years in office between 1885 and 1889 were uneventful.

### Benjamin Harrison

Afraid that Democrats would succeed in lowering their precious protective tariffs, Republicans rallied big business in the North and nominated **Benjamin Harrison** for the presidency in 1888. A grandson of former president William Henry Harrison, Benjamin Harrison campaigned for an even higher tariff. Democrats nominated Cleveland again but couldn't garner enough electoral votes to keep the presidency. Harrison slid into office. He worked the Republican majority in Congress and passed the following acts:

- **The Sherman Silver Purchase Act** to purchase more silver for currency

- **The Dependent Pension Act** to distribute more money to aging Civil War veterans and their families

- **The McKinley Tariff**, a controversial tariff that set duties on foreign goods to about 50 percent

# Industrialization

The North emerged from the Civil War as an industrial powerhouse ready to take on the world. Rich with seemingly unlimited natural resources and millions of immigrants ready to work, the United States experienced a flurry of unprecedented growth and industrialization during the Gilded Age. As a result, some historians have referred to this era as America's **second industrial revolution** because it completely transformed American society, politics, and the economy. Mechanization and marketing were the keys to success in this age: companies that could mass-produce goods and convince people to buy them amassed enormous riches, while those that could not ultimately collapsed.

### TRANSCONTINENTAL RAILROADS

The mass industrialization of the economy during the Gilded Age had its roots in the Civil War. Besides creating a huge demand for a variety of manufactured goods, the war also spurred Congress and the northern states to build more railroads. The rather progressive Congress of 1862 also authorized construction of the first railroad to run from the Pacific to the Atlantic. Because laying track cost so much money, the federal government initially provided subsidies by the mile to the railroad companies in exchange for discounted rates.

Congress also provided federal grants for land on which companies could lay the track. With free land and tens of thousands of free dollars per mile, railroading quickly became a highly profitable business venture. The **Union Pacific Railroad** began construction on the transcontinental line in Nebraska during the Civil War and pushed westward while Leland Stanford's **Central Pacific Railroad** pushed eastward from Sacramento. Tens of thousands of Irish and Chinese laborers laid most of the track. The two lines met near Ogden, Utah, in 1869.

*Railroads formed the cornerstone of the new industrialized economy. They ferried raw materials, finished products, food, and people across the entire country in a matter of days instead of the months or years it had taken before the Civil War. By the end of the war, the United States had 35,000 miles of track, mostly in the industrialized North. By the end of the century, that number had jumped to almost 200,000 miles of track connecting the North, South, and West.*

### Vanderbilt: Railroad Tycoon

Soon, other railroads—including the Southern Pacific Railroad, the Santa Fe Railroad, and James J. Hill's Great Northern Railway—spanned the Western expanse. Federal subsidies and land grants made railroading such a huge business that it bred a new class of "new money" millionaires like Stanford and Hill. **Cornelius Vanderbilt** and his son William H. Vanderbilt were perhaps the most infamous of these railroad tycoons during this era. They bought out and consolidated many of the rail companies in the East and streamlined operations to lower costs. The Vanderbilts also established a standard track gauge and replaced the iron rails with lighter but more durable steel. Their innovation and cutthroat business practices earned them over $100 million.

> *Vanderbilt's use of the steel rail in the 1870s and 1880s helped give birth to the American steel industry. Prior to the mid-nineteenth century, railroaders had shied away from steel because of its high cost. But William Kelly's discovery of the **Bessemer process** for making steel revolutionized the industry: blowing cold air on hot iron would make high-quality steel for a fraction of the cost.*

### Railroad Corruption

Not all railroading profits were earned in a legitimate manner. The industry was filled with dozens of scams and embezzlement schemes to make insiders rich. Besides the infamous **Crédit Moblier scandal** (see page 23), railroads also inflated the prices of their own stocks and doled out uncompetitive rebates to favored companies. These practices hurt common people. Some of the states passed new laws to clamp down on the unruly railroads, but the Supreme Court shot all of them down when it ruled that only the federal government could regulate interstate commerce in the 1886 **Wabash Case.**

### CAPTAINS OF INDUSTRY

Whereas past generations had sent their best men into public service, young men during the Gilded Age sought their fortunes in the private sector, where a little persistence and ruthlessness could reap enormous profits almost overnight. Unregulated by the government, these so-called **captains of industry** did whatever they pleased to make as much money as possible. In fact, their business practices were quite often so unscrupulous that the term *industrialist* soon became synonymous with the nickname *robber baron*.

### Carnegie, Morgan, and U.S. Steel

By the end of the 1900s, **Andrew Carnegie** was the wealthiest and most famous steel magnate in the United States. Carnegie created a veritable steel empire through a business tactic called **"vertical integration."** Instead of relying on expensive middlemen, Carnegie bought out all of the companies needed to produce his steel. He made it, shipped it, and sold it himself. Eventually he sold his company to Wall Street banker **J. P. Morgan**, who in turn used the company as the foundation for the new **U.S. Steel Corporation** in 1901. By the end of his life, Carnegie had become one of the richest men in America with a fortune of nearly $500 million.

### Rockefeller's Standard Oil

Oil also became big business during the Gilded Age. Although Americans needed very little oil before the Civil War, demand surged during the machine age in the 1880s, 1890s, and early 1900s. Everything required oil during this era, from factory machines to ships; this demand continued with cars in the 1920s. The oil industry also popularized the use of bright kerosene lamps.

**John D. Rockefeller** and his **Standard Oil Company** became the biggest names in the oil industry. Whereas Carnegie had employed vertical integration to create his empire, the ruthless Rockefeller used a method called **"horizontal integration"** to make sure he monopolized the industry. He bought out all the other oil companies to make sure he had no competition, and in doing so, created one of America's first monopolies, or **trusts,** to corner the market on a single commodity.

## THE PLUTOCRACY

This period in American history witness a marked divide between the upper and lower classes. In time, the majority of plutocrats developed the belief that their riches had come not from their good fortune and circumstance but from their own superiority over the poorer classes.

### Social Darwinism

In line with Charles Darwin's sensational new theory of natural selection, many of the new rich applied the mantra of "survival of the fittest" to society. In the words of one **Social Darwinist**, "The millionaires are the product of natural selection." Many of the wealthy believed they had become so fabulously rich because they were smarter and had worked harder than everyone else.

### The Gospel of Wealth

On the other hand, more religious plutocrats preached the **"Gospel of Wealth,"** believing that God had given them riches for their genius and tenacity. The flip side to Social Darwinism and the Gospel of Wealth was that the poor were in turn considered ungodly and/or biologically inferior.

### Philanthropists

Fortunately, not all of the new rich believed the poor should be left to fend for themselves. Many of the new rich demonstrated a keen interest in helping the less fortunate. Andrew Carnegie was by far the most generous of these Gilded Age philanthropists. Having come from a poor family himself, Carnegie firmly believed he would be disgraced if he died wealthy without having helped others. As a result, he donated more than $350 million to dozens of organizations by the time he died.

## REGULATING BIG BUSINESS

To rein in the growing number of unwieldy trusts, Congress passed the **Interstate Commerce Act** in 1887, which outlawed railroad rebates and kickbacks. In addition, the act established the **Interstate Commerce Commission** to monitor the railroad companies' compliance with the new laws. To protect consumers by outlawing big trusts, Congress also passed the **Sherman Anti-Trust Act** in 1890.

### Toothless Legislation

Although designed to regulate the corrupt railroad companies, the Interstate Commerce Commission had so many exploitable loopholes that it had almost no effect. Railroads still continued to issue rebates, demand outrageous fares, and charge different customers different prices for the same journey. The act did, however, establish an arena in which the competing railroad corporations could settle disputes without fighting disastrous rate wars. In this sense, the Interstate Commerce Commission helped stabilize the industry rather than control it. The similarly weak Sherman Anti-Trust Act also had very little effect at reining in the trusts.

CHAPTER 2
1877–1901

# The Labor Movement

The workforce changed drastically as the economy became more industrialized and mechanized. Competition for jobs grew stiffer as millions of women, immigrants, blacks, and farmers moved to the cities to find work. A mechanized economy also meant that companies required new and different sets of job skills. Unfortunately, organized labor generally floundered without any government regulation.

*Many Americans regarded labor unions as socialists, anarchists, and rabble-rousers. The federal government even prosecuted a number of labor unions as trusts under the Sherman Anti-Trust Act of 1890. Nevertheless, so many skilled and unskilled workers joined labor unions between 1860 and 1900, that by the turn of the century, many Americans and the government had begun to reconsider employees' right to strike.*

### THE NATIONAL LABOR UNION

Founded in 1866, the first national labor union was simply called the **National Labor Union (NLU)**. The NLU sought to represent both skilled and unskilled laborers in one large organization. Though it had no ties to either political party, the union generally supported any candidate who would fight for shorter working days, higher wages, and better working conditions. The NLU only existed for six short years, thanks to the Depression of 1873. Union members found it difficult to bargain collectively when companies could easily hire thousands of new immigrant "scabs," or strike breakers, to replace them.

### THE KNIGHTS OF LABOR

Another union called the **Knights of Labor** survived the depression. Originally begun as a secret society in 1869, the Knights picked up where the NLU had left off. It too united all skilled and unskilled laborers, but unlike the NLU, it allowed blacks and women to join. The Knights won a series of strikes in their fight against long hours and low wages. The Knights of Labor also died prematurely after Americans falsely associated them with the anarchists responsible for the **Haymarket Square Bombing** in Chicago in 1886. Additionally, the Knights found it difficult to successfully bargain collectively because they represented such a diverse group of workers.

### LABOR STRIKES

Many of the fledgling unions that went on strike during the latter half of the nineteenth century did so to protest poor working conditions, long workdays, and inadequate pay. But most Americans at the time frowned on collective bargaining, which made it difficult for the unions to make any significant gains.

### The Railroad Strike of 1877

In 1877, when the railroad companies announced a second 10 percent pay cut in four years, workers met to organize a National Trainmen's Union and plan a general strike. After the railroads fired union organizers, numerous strikes erupted on July 16 throughout the country. President Hayes eventually authorized state governors to use federal troops to suppress the ensuing riots.

### The Coeur d'Alene Strike

The **Coeur d'Alene Strike** occurred in Coeur d'Alene, Idaho, in 1892, when several silver-mine owners collectively slashed miners' wages. The silver miners' union protested the wage cuts but had little effect, as eager immigrant scabs quickly replaced the organized laborers. Frustrated, a number of union protestors destroyed one of the mines in the city of Coeur d'Alene with dynamite. President Benjamin Harrison sent over 1,000 federal troops to end the violence.

### The Homestead Strike

Meanwhile, employees of Andrew Carnegie's Homestead Steel Works near Pittsburgh, Pennsylvania, had launched a strike of their own to protest wage cuts. Pittsburgh police refused to end the strike, so Carnegie hired 300 detectives from the renowned Pinkerton Detective Agency to subdue the protestors. Still, the laborers won a surprising victory after a rather bloody standoff. Harrison once again sent troops to break the **Homestead Strike**.

### The Pullman Strike

Grover Cleveland made a similar decision in 1894 to end the **Pullman Strike** at the Pullman Palace Car Company in Chicago. When the company cut employees' wages by 30 percent in the wake of the depression, labor organizer **Eugene V. Debs** organized a massive strike. Over 150,000 American Railroad Union Members refused to work. Some even destroyed Pullman's famed Palace cars and delayed trains as far away as California. Cleveland sent federal troops to break up the strike and had Debs arrested.

## THE AMERICAN FEDERATION OF LABOR

A new labor union called the **American Federation of Labor (AFL)** grew to form an umbrella organization that coordinated the efforts of several dozen smaller, independent unions.

Founded by **Samuel Gompers** in 1886, the AFL sought better wages, shorter working days, better working conditions, and the creation of all-union workplaces. Unlike its predecessors, the National Labor Union and the Knights of Labor, the AFL only represented skilled white male craftsmen in the cities and exluded farmers, blacks, women, and unskilled immigrants. The AFL survived the rocky Gilded Age and eventually became one of the most powerful labor unions in the twentieth century.

# Gilded Age Society

The Gilded Age also heralded the dawn of a new American society as the nation's base shifted from agriculture to industry. Millions of Americans flocked to the cities in the post–Civil War era. By 1900, nearly 40 percent of Americans lived in urbanized areas, as opposed to the 20 percent in 1860. Many young people left their farms in search of the new wonders cities had to offer: skyscrapers, electric trolleys, and department stores, among others. Industrialization and the population swell in urban areas also spawned consumerism and a middle class.

## INCREASED IMMIGRATION

A new wave of immigration contributed to a population explosion. Coming mostly from war-torn regions of southern and eastern Europe like Italy, Greece, Poland, Russia, Croatia, and Czechoslovakia, the majority of these new immigrants had less money and education than the Irish and Germans who had preceded them. By the early twentieth century, a wave of immigrants over a million strong flooded eastern cities every year. Most barely managed to eke out a living in the New World through low-paying, undesirable, and unskilled jobs in factories or in packinghouses.

### Nativist Resurgence

Nativist Americans often despised the new wave of immigrants, claiming they would never assimilate into American society because of their illiteracy, poverty, languages, and inexperience with democracy. Some Protestants also disliked the fact that new immigrants were primarily Catholic, Eastern Orthodox, or Jewish.

Moreover, there was a fear among some Anglo-Saxon Americans that the eastern and southern Europeans would either dilute the race or eventually "outbreed" American whites. In response, the **American Protection Association** formed and lobbied for immigration restriction. Congress eventually conceded and, in 1882, barred criminals and the extremely destitute from entry.

> *Interestingly, many Americans despised the Chinese, who had proven themselves in the West to be inexpensive yet excellent workers. Afraid that Chinese laborers would replace American laborers, workers' organizations pressed Congress to pass the* **Chinese Exclusion Act** *in 1882 to ban Chinese immigration. The act remained in place until 1943.*

## SLUMS

The sudden influx of nearly a million poor people a year gave rise to slums in the cities. Much of this population inhabited the new **dumbbell tenement** buildings, so named because they resembled giant dumbbells. Entire families usually lived together in tiny, one-room apartments, sharing a single bathroom with other families on the floor. As dumbbell tenements were filthy, poorly ventilated, and poorly lit, they were conducive to disease.

### Jane Addams and Hull House

Several reformers tried to fight the increasing poverty and social injustices that were rampant in the cities, including the college-educated **Jane Addams**, who founded **Hull House** in Chicago. Located in one of the city's poorest neighborhoods, Hull House provided counseling, daycare services, and adult education classes to help local immigrants survive in the United States. The success of Hull House soon prompted **Lillian Wald** to open the **Henry Street Settlement House** in New York.

The successes of Jane Addams and Lillian Wald led other reformers to open similar settlement houses in other eastern cities with large immigrant populations. In time, women like Addams and

Wald used their positions to fight for temperance, women's suffrage, civil rights, and improved labor laws.

### FAITH-BASED REFORM

Religious communities were another antipoverty force in the slums. Catholic churches and Jewish synagogues led the fight by offering services to the newly arrived immigrants, helping them find their way in the cities. Protestant speeches and lectures became very popular events, as did faith-based social organizations like the Young Men's Christian Association, or YMCA, and the Young Women's Christian Association, or YWCA.

### Christian Science

The post–Civil War period witnessed the birth of several new religions, such as **Christian Science**, which was founded by **Mary Baker Eddy,** who believed that faith could cure all disease. Hundreds of thousands of people converted, as the church spread throughout America.

### THE WOMEN'S MOVEMENT

Women achieved significant gains during the latter half of the nineteenth century. Many urban women found jobs, married later, had fewer children, and used various methods of birth control. Feminist **Charlotte Perkins Gilman**'s 1898 book *Women and Economics* demanded that women shirk their traditional roles as homemakers to find independence in the new America. She and other feminists like **Elizabeth Cady Stanton** also demanded the right to vote. Another leading figure, **Victoria Woodhull**, shocked Americans by advocating the use of contraceptives in spite of the **Comstock Law** of 1873, which outlawed the use of the U.S. mail to distribute contraceptives and information about contraceptives.

### PLESSY V. FERGUSON *AND CIVIL RIGHTS*

African Americans did not fare as well as women in the struggle for equality. In 1896, the Supreme Court even upheld the policy of segregation by legalizing "separate but equal" facilities for blacks and whites in the landmark decision ***Plessy v. Ferguson***. In doing so, the court condemned African Americans to more than another half century of second-class citizenship.

### Washington v. Du Bois

Black leaders continued to press for equal rights. For example, **Booker T. Washington**, president of the all-black **Tuskegee Institute** in Alabama, encouraged African Americans to become economically self-sufficient so that they could then challenge whites on social issues. The Harvard-educated black historian and sociologist, **W.E.B. Du Bois**, however, ridiculed Washington's beliefs and argued that African Americans should fight for social and economic equality at the same time. Their dispute highlighted the rupture in the Civil Rights movement during the end of the nineteenth century.

# *The West*

Railroads not only transformed industrial cities in the East but also in the West. This transformation happened primarily because travel had become easier, cheaper, and safer. The transcontinental lines moved people, grain, cattle, ore, and equipment across the vast expanses of the Midwest, over the Rocky Mountains and Sierra Nevada and to the fertile valleys of California and Oregon.

## THE HOMESTEAD ACT

Although Americans had continued to move in a steady stream westward, even during the Civil War, this phenomenon picked up steam once the war had ended. Several million Americans surged into the great unknown regions beyond eastern Kansas and Nebraska. Settlers particularly wanted cheap federal land offered by Congress in the **Homestead Act** of 1862. For a small fee, any settler could stake out a 160-acre western claim so long as he and his family improved the land by farming it and living on it.

## THE NATIVE AMERICAN WARS

In 1881 author **Helen Hunt Jackson** published her book, *A Century of Dishonor*, a book that described the federal government's history of cruelty toward Native Americans over the previous hundred years. The book launched a new debate about whites' relationship with Native Americans and prompted many people to conclude that assimilation would be the only solution to the problem.

### The Sioux Wars

As white settlers pushed farther and farther westward, they repeatedly shoved Native Americans off their lands. Not surprisingly, the two groups frequently clashed. In 1864, for example, Union troops slaughtered several hundred Native American women and children at the **Sand Creek Massacre** in Colorado.

The U.S. Army also fought the Sioux tribes in the Black Hills of Dakota Territory during the 1860s and 1870s. These battles were dubbed the **Sioux Wars.** Lieutenant Colonel **George Armstrong Custer** made his infamous Last Stand during this war at the **Battle of Little Bighorn**, when more than 250 of his troops fell under the hands of Chief **Sitting Bull** and his warriors. The Sioux's victory was short-lived, and they were defeated a year later.

### Chief Joseph, Geronimo, and Wounded Knee

The army also fought the Nez Percé tribe in the Pacific Northwest. United under **Chief Joseph**, the Nez Percé refused to relinquish their lands to white settlers without a fight. They fled all across the Northwest before the army finally defeated them and relocated the tribe to Kansas.

The Apaches in New Mexico Territory led by **Geronimo** also fought bravely to protect their homes until their eventual defeat. Hundreds of Native Americans also died at the **Massacre at Wounded Knee** in 1890 during the army's attempt to stamp out the **Ghost Dance Movement**, which called for a return to traditional Native American ways of life and challenged white supremacy.

### The Dawes Severalty Act

In order to make room for more whites, the federal government first tried to herd natives onto tribal-owned reservations on the poorest land in the Dakotas, New Mexico, and Oklahoma. Under pressure from reformers who wanted to "acclimatize" Native Americans to white culture, Congress eventually passed the **Dawes Severalty Act** in 1887. The Dawes Act outlawed tribal ownership of land and instead forced 160-acre homesteads into the hands of Indians and their families with the promise of future citizenship. The act tried to forcibly assimilate Native Americans into white culture as quickly as possible.

In 1893, American historian **Frederick Jackson Turner** argued in his now famous essay, The Significance of the Frontier in American History, that the closure of the West presented the United States with a serious problem. He claimed that the western frontier had been one of the nation's defining characteristics, and he worried about what would happen to American culture, society, and government now that the West had been won. The West had always represented a sense of infinite possibility for Americans; for Turner, the settling of the West left a void in the American identity.

## TRANSFORMATIONS IN AGRICULTURE

Investors and land speculators followed close behind the rugged homesteaders who had staked their claims in the great unknown and also had a share in transforming the West. Agricultural prices remained relatively high during the good times between the Depression of 1873 and the **Depression of 1893**, so many farmers with a little capital switched from subsistence farming to growing single cash crops. In the Midwest, growing only wheat or corn or raising cattle to maximize profits in the cities was common for farmers.

### The Plight of Small Farmers

The incorporation of farming, high protective tariffs, and the Depression of 1893 ruined subsistence farmers in the Midwest and South. Many of the cash crop farmers found themselves deep in debt and couldn't afford the unregulated railroad fares to ship their products to cities. Over a million impoverished farmers eventually organized under a social organization called the **National Grange** to fight for their livelihood. They managed to win some key victories in several Midwestern legislatures, supported the Greenback Party in the 1870s, and eventually by the **Populist Party** in the 1890s.

# The Rise and Fall of Populism

Benjamin Harrison's **McKinley Tariff** was one of the highest tariffs in U.S. history—even higher than the 1828 Tariff of Abominations that had nearly split the Union. The tariff particularly hurt farmers in the West and South, who sold their harvests on unprotected markets and bought expensive manufactured goods.

### THE POPULISTS

In seeking revenge for the McKinley Tariff, the farmers voted Republicans out of the House of Representatives in the 1890 congressional elections. Some of them even formed a pseudo-political party in the late 1880s called the **Farmers' Alliance**. By the time the 1892 elections rolled around, the Alliance had merged with other liberal Democrats to form the **Populist Party**. Populists nominated former Greenback Party candidate **James B. Weaver** and campaigned for the following:

- Unlimited cheap silver money (they wanted a rate of sixteen ounces of silver to one ounce of gold)
- Government ownership of all railroads and telephone companies
- A graduated income tax
- Direct election of U.S. senators
- Single-term limits for presidents
- Immigration restriction
- Shorter workdays

## GROVER CLEVELAND ELECTED AGAIN

The Republicans and Democrats again nominated Benjamin Harrison and Grover Cleveland, respectively, for the presidency in 1892. Weaver and the Populists also entered the race, as did John Bidwell on behalf of the fledgling Prohibition Party. The Populists did surprisingly well and managed to receive over a million popular votes and twenty-two electoral votes. The McKinley Tariff had ruined Harrison's chance for reelection, so the presidency reverted to Cleveland, who became the only president to serve two inconsecutive terms.

Cleveland's second round in the White House was a lot rockier than his first. The Depression of 1893—the worst depression the country had ever seen—hit just months after he took the oath of office. Additionally, Congress passed the **Wilson-Gorman Tariff** in 1894 in spite of Cleveland's promise to significantly reduce the tariff. This certainly affected his popularity.

### Silver, Gold, and J. P. Morgan

Even worse, the federal government had nearly gone bankrupt. Wily investors had traded their silver for gold in a convoluted scheme that ultimately depleted the nation's gold reserves below the $100 million mark. Had this trend continued, the government would not have had enough gold to back the paper currency in circulation or prevent the economic collapse that would have resulted.

Cleveland addressed this situation by repealing the 1890 Sherman Silver Purchase Act to prevent the loss of any more gold. This had no effect, and by the following year, the government had only $41 million in the Treasury. Cleveland and Congress ultimately appealed to Wall Street financier J. P. Morgan to bail them out. For a hefty price, Morgan agreed to loan the government $62 million to put it back on its feet.

### Coxey's Army

The Depression of 1893 and Cleveland's repeal of the Sherman Silver Purchase Act only made the Populist movement stronger. More and more disillusioned Democrats flocked to the Populist Party in the hopes of winning free silver and more power for the people. The Depression also encouraged other would-be reformers to cry out for change. The wealthy Ohioan Jacob S. Coxey petitioned the government for cheap money and debt-relief programs. When **"Coxey's Army"** reached the capital in 1894, however, city officials arrested them for marching on the grass.

## ISLANDS IN THE PACIFIC

After the U.S. Census Bureau declared the continental frontier closed in 1890, Americans began looking overseas to expand. A number of islands in the Pacific Ocean became the first to fall under colonization and the American flag. Hawaii was the plum of the Pacific for its pleasant climate, which was perfect for growing sugar cane. Americans had actually been settling Hawaii and living with the native islanders for over a hundred years. The white American minority had repeatedly petitioned Congress for annexation and had even overthrown the peaceful Hawaiian **Queen Liliuokalani** to seize control of the government in 1893. Outraged, the anti-expansionist Grover Cleveland rejected annexation and condemned the revolt against the queen.

## CLEVELAND UPHOLDS THE MONROE DOCTRINE

Cleveland also threatened war with Great Britain over a territorial dispute in South America—one that didn't even involve U.S. territory. Both Venezuela and the British colony of Guiana claimed a huge tract of land rich with gold ore along the border. Invoking the Monroe Doctrine (i.e., the principle that mandated that the Americas were no longer open for European colonization), Cleveland threatened the British with war if they didn't back off.

Eventually, Britain acquiesced. They sought arbitration to settle the dispute, not so much because they feared the United States (Britain still had the largest navy in the world) but because they didn't want to alienate a potential ally as European relations grew increasingly chillier. Cleveland's bold stance impressed many Latin American nations, who began to see the United States as a friendly protector.

## THE ELECTION OF 1896

Cleveland had no chance for reelection to a third term. He had failed to correct the Depression of 1893, barely managed to keep the U.S. Treasury full, angered many middle-class constituents by using federal troops to end the Pullman Strike, and neglected to keep his promise to significantly reduce the Wilson-Gorman tariff. These problems proved insurmountable for him.

As the election of 1896 approached, Democrats instead nominated the so-called "Boy Orator" from Nebraska, **William Jennings Bryan**, on a Populist-inspired platform for free silver after he had delivered his rousing **"Cross of Gold Speech,"** condemning the gold standard. The Populists threw their support to Bryan and the Democrats to keep the Republicans out of office.

*Bryan's Cross of Gold Speech electrified Populists and Democrats. A passionate and dynamic speaker, Bryan compared Americans to the New Testament story of Jesus' final moments before crucifixion when proclaimed, "We will answer their [Republicans']demands for a gold standard by saying to them: 'You shall not press down upon the brow of labor this crown of thorns, you shall not crucify mankind upon a cross of gold!"*

### McKinley Kills Free Silver

The Republicans nominated Congressman **William McKinley**, sponsor of the controversial McKinley Tariff, on a pro-business platform. Wealthy Ohioan businessman **Marcus Hanna** financed most of the campaign and convinced his colleagues in the East to support McKinley. Despite Bryan's whirlwind speaking tour through the South and Midwest, it was Hanna's politicking that won McKinley the presidency that year.

McKinley appealed to a wide range of Americans. Conservative Americans feared cheap money and inflation so much that they flocked to McKinley and the Republican camp. Wealthy businessmen in the East dumped about $6–12 million into McKinley's campaign, making it the fattest campaign fund of any American candidate ever. Some Democrats quite reasonably claimed that McKinley had purchased the White House. McKinley ultimately killed the Populists' dream of free silver in 1900 when he signed the **Gold Standard Act** to peg the value of the dollar to an ounce of gold. He also signed the **Dingley Tariff** in 1897 to set overall tariff rates at about 45 percent.

*Free silver became an important issue in the late nineteenth centruy. The Depression of 1873 caused the market price of silver to drop dramatically. Inflationists turned to silver and hoped its free coinage would stabilize the economy. President McKinley killed this possibility in 1900.*

### A Key Election

Historians regard the election of 1896 as one of the most important elections of the nineteenth century, and certainly the most significant election since the Civil War. First, it represented a victory of urban middle-class Americans over agrarian interests in the West and South. Populism had never really spread into the cities, and Bryan's appeal for free silver and inflation had alienated even the poorest Americans in the cities who depended on a stable dollar for survival. The Bryan campaign thus marked the last attempt to win the presidency through appeals to rural voters. It also marked the death of the Populist movement, which lost steam when it supported the Bryan campaign, essentially merging with the Democratic Party.

*McKinley's victory also ushered in a new age in American politics that was dominated by conservatives and called the **Fourth Party System**. Republicans would control the White House for most of the next thirty-six years until the election of Franklin Delano Roosevelt in 1932. This period was marked by an enormous expansion of the middle class, continued migration to the cities, weaker political parties, the growth of industry, and more government concern for consumers and laborers.*

# The Spanish–American War

William McKinley entered the White House just as the nation was gearing up to its biggest foreign flare-up yet: the Cuban crisis. Spain still controlled the island just ninety miles south of Florida despite repeated American attempts to wrest it away. Depressed sugar prices in the 1890s led Cuban farmers to rebel against their Spanish overlords in a bloody revolution. Spanish forces under General "Butcher" Weyler tried to crack down on the insurrection by herding all suspected revolutionaries—including children—into concentration camps. Americans learned about the situation from the lurid **"yellow press"** of the day as newspaper titans **William Randolph Hearst** and **Joseph Pulitzer** printed sensationalistic stories to outdo each other in a competition for readers.

*Hoping to boost sales with exclusive coverage on the war with Spain, Hearst sent the renowned painter Frederick Remington to Cuba to cover the war. To Remington's dismay, he allegedly issued the order, "You furnish the pictures and I'll furnish the war!"*

### REMEMBER THE MAINE!

The controversial **de Lôme letter** outraged Americans. Published in newspapers in 1898, the letter from Spanish minister to the United States Dupuy de Lôme derided McKinley as a dimwitted politician. Shortly thereafter, more than 250 American seamen serving aboard the **U.S.S. *Maine*** died when the ship mysteriously exploded while anchored in Havana Harbor. Although Spanish officials and historians have concluded that a boiler-room accident caused the explosion, Americans at home quickly concluded that Spanish agents had sabotaged the ship. Millions cried, "Remember the *Maine*!" and pressured Congress and McKinley for war.

### WAR ERUPTS

McKinley didn't want war; however, he eventually requested a war declaration from Congress in April 1898 out of fear that William Jennings Bryan and "free silver" would win the election of 1900. Congress consented on the grounds that the Cuban people needed to be liberated. To justify the cause, Congress passed the

**Teller Amendment**, which promised Cuban independence once they had defeated the Spaniards. Americans won the war quickly and easily, thus causing the Spanish Empire to collapse.

### Dewey in the Philippines

Acting outside his orders, assistant secretary of the Navy **Theodore Roosevelt** ordered Commodore **George Dewey** to seize the Spanish-controlled Philippine Islands in Asia. Dewey defeated the Spanish fleet in a surprise attack on Manila Bay without losing a single man. Congress then annexed Hawaii on the pretext that the Navy needed a refueling station between San Francisco and Asia. While Dewey fought the Spanish on the sea, insurgent **Louis Aguinaldo** led a Filipino revolt on land. Although Britain didn't participate in the fighting, it did help prevent other European powers from defending Spain.

### The Rough Riders in Cuba

The U.S. Army, meanwhile, invaded Cuba with over 20,000 regular and volunteer troops. The most famous of the volunteers were the **Rough Riders**, commanded by the recently commissioned Lt. Colonel Roosevelt, who had left his civilian job to join the "splendid little war." As its name implied, this volunteer company consisted of a sordid lot of ex-convicts and cowboys mixed with some of Roosevelt's adventurous upper-class acquaintances. Roosevelt and the Rough Riders helped lead the charge to take the famous San Juan Hill outside the city of Santiago. Cuba eventually fell, and Spain retreated.

### POSTWAR LEGISLATION

The United States honored the **Teller Amendment of 1898** (which declared that the United States did not have an interest in controlling Cuba after the war) and withdrew from Cuba in 1902, but not before including the **Platt Amendment** in the Cuban constitution to give the United States a permanent military base at Guantanamo Bay. The war gave McKinley more headaches than it cured. First, McKinley had to fight an insurrection led by Filipino rebel Louis Aguinaldo against American forces in the annexed Philippines. It took several years of bloody jungle warfare before U.S. forces defeated him, but even then, Filipinos resisted assimilation into white American culture.

The Supreme Court ruled in the 1901 **Insular Cases** that people in newly acquired foreign lands did not have the same constitutional rights as Americans at home. Congress still upheld the 1900 **Foraker Act** that granted Puerto Ricans limited self-government and eventually full U.S. citizenship in 1917. Finally, McKinley had to contend with the vocal new **Anti-Imperialist League** and its prominent membership, which challenged his expansionist policies and the incorporation of new "unassimilable" peoples into America.

During the last third of the nineteenth century, America became involved with territorial expansion outside the continental United States. What impact did the acquisition of territory or increased influence in a region have on U.S. foreign policy from 1865–1910?

The spirit of expansion that characterized the manifest destiny movement resumed after the Civil War, only in more global terms. The acquisition of Alaska in 1867 paved the way for American expansion beyond the continental borders, and many in the United States seemed ready to participate in the international trend of imperialism. The arguments for expansion were justified on political, economic, military, and moral grounds, each of which played varying roles in the development of American foreign policy at the turn of the century. American involvement in Hawaii, Cuba, and the Philippines revealed an eagerness to redefine foreign policy along imperialistic principles, as well as an uncertainty about occupation and the other consequences of expansion.

Hawaii was a natural target for American expansion. Its strategic location and plentiful harbors appealed to commercial and military interests. Hawaii also had a historical trading connection for the United States and a large number of American sugar plantations. As interest increased, the American government negotiated terms with the Hawaiian government in 1887 and began to construct a naval base at Pearl Harbor. Some Hawaiians began to resent the growing American presence, including Queen Liliuokalani, who inherited the Hawaiian throne in the early 1890s. Tensions escalated after the Hawaiian economy collapsed because the United States reinstated an import tax on Hawaiian sugar. A group of American plantation owners, led by Sanford Dole, staged a revolt and overthrew the Queen. They immediately applied for annexation to the United States. The bill was stalled by Democrats in Congress until Grover Cleveland took office in 1893. Cleveland ordered an investigation of the Hawaiian situation, and rescinded his support after it became

# *Student Essay*

clear that Hawaiians did not universally desire annexation.
Cleveland's caution was harshly criticized by Republican
expansionists. They were forced to wait until Cleveland was
succeeded by William McKinley. Under the new administration,
Hawaii was annexed as an American territory in 1898, thus
beginning a quick period of rampant international expansion.

Having secured a stronghold in the Pacific, America turned its
attention to the Caribbean. Cuba had been in a state of revolt
against Spain since 1895. Cuban independence did not arouse
much support from the American government at first, but it was
becoming a popular cause among the American people. Americans
responded to the sensational headlines published by the yellow
journalists and were increasingly convinced that American
intervention was a moral imperative. The outcry peaked in 1898
when an explosion devastated the U.S.S *Maine*, which had been
ordered to Havana Harbor. Although the Spanish government had
indicated an initial willingness to negotiate peace in Cuba,
President McKinley could not ignore the public outrage. He asked
Congress for a declaration of war and set extreme demands for
Spain. Spain responded with its own declaration of war, and the
Spanish–American War ensued. America quickly prevailed, and
Cuba was granted its independence. With respect to foreign policy,
two important amendments revealed the haziness of American
objectives. The Teller Amendment of 1898 declared that the United
States did not have an interest in controlling Cuba after the war.
Three years later, however, the Platt Amendment stipulated the
right to intervene at any time deemed necessary and the right to
construct a naval base. According to those terms, the United States
did reoccupy Cuba for three years, and also established a naval
base at Guantanamo Bay in 1912.

On the eve of the Spanish–American War, Theodore Roosevelt, then the assistant secretary of the navy, ordered Commodore Dewey's Pacific Fleet to prepare for action in the Philippines. His request, which was unauthorized, serves as further evidence of the expansionist agenda. After the Philippines were ceded to the United States by Spain, a debate about annexation followed, and the various motivations for expansion became increasingly clear. Business interests were intrigued by the Philippines, as they saw them as an access point to the profitable markets of China. Others worried about the political and military consequences of relinquishing control, namely that the Philippines would quickly fall to another foreign power. Finally, the moral argument, embraced by McKinley himself, was that America needed to educate and Christianize the Filipino population (apparently not accomplished by centuries of Spanish colonization). The Philippines desired their own independence prior to the Spanish–American War, and they continued to wage a guerilla war against America for three more years. Finally in 1902, Congress passed an act that promised the Philippines eventual self-government, which did not come about until 1946.

During his time in office, McKinley was often criticized for lacking political convictions. His concern for public approval was particularly apparent in the area of foreign policy. Without clear objectives regarding expansion, America rushed into Hawaii and the Spanish–American War generally unprepared for the consequences. Despite the various challenges of occupation, the United States was able to extend its military and commercial interests internationally between the years of 1865–1910.

# Test Questions and Answers

1. *Examine the motivations for Americans and immigrants moving west in the late nineteenth century. What consequences did this westward movement have?*

- Availability of land through the Homestead Act

- Potential wealth through mines

- Railroads were built to transport people across the newly expanded country.

- Indians were removed from their land to make room for white Americans.

- Indian wars ensued.

2. *Explain the causes of the Spanish–American War.*

- Americans had begun expanding overseas after spanning the North American continent

- Americans sympathized with the Cubans under harsh Spanish rule.

- The Yellow Press sensationalized Cuban miseries.

- The de Lôme letter criticizing McKinley angered many Americans.

- Americans believed Spanish agents had sabotaged the U.S.S. *Maine.*

- McKinley feared that the free-silverite William Jennings Bryan would become president in the next election if he didn't bow to public demand and ask Congress for war.

3. *Trace the rise and fall of the Populist Movement.*

- Impoverished southern and midwestern farmers joined together in agricultural organizations like the National Grange (and later the Farmers' Alliance) to protest the McKinley Tariff.

- Agricultural organizations and former Greenback Party members later formed the backbone of the new Populist Party.

- Populists championed inflationary money policies (free silver), nationalized business and transportation, term limits for presidents, and a federal income tax, among other things.

- Populists backed Democrat William Jennings Bryan after he'd incorporated much of their platform into his own in 1896, thus ruining their chances to field their own candidate.

- McKinley's victory in 1896 and the Gold Standard Act of 1900 destroyed Populists' chances of ever winning "free silver."

### 4. How were the National Labor Union, the Knights of Labor, and the American Federation of Labor similar? How were they different?

- The National Labor Union represented both skilled and unskilled workers in the countryside and in the cities, but excluded blacks and women. The Union collapsed in the wake of the Depression of 1873.

- The Knights of Labor also represented both rural and urban skilled and unskilled, as well as blacks and women. It too collapsed after being falsely associated with the Haymarket Square Bombing in 1886.

- The American Federation of Labor represented only skilled urban laborers and excluded the unskilled, rural workers, blacks, and women. The AFL has survived to this day.

### 5. Describe some of the social trends during the Gilded Age.

- Millions of Americans moved to the cities and lived with modern conveniences such as indoor plumbing, electricity, telephones, skyscrapers, and cable cars.

- More and more Americans entered the middle class.

- Immigrants from southern and eastern Europe also poured into the cities by the millions.

- Many urban reformers (like Jane Addams) tried to help the urban poor by providing social services.

- Other reformers (like Mary Baker Eddy) founded new religious denominations to tackle urban poverty.

# *Timeline*

| | |
|---|---|
| *1862* | Congress passes the Homestead Act. |
| *1866* | National Labor Union forms. |
| *1867* | The National Grange forms. |
| *1869* | The Transcontinental Railroad is completed. |
| | The Knights of Labor forms. |
| | Wyoming grants women the right to vote. |
| *1870* | Standard Oil Company forms. |
| *1873* | Congress passes the Comstock Law. |
| | Depression of 1873 begins. |
| *1874* | Woman's Christian Temperance Union forms. |
| *1875* | Sioux Wars occur in Black Hills, Dakota Territory. |
| *1876* | Alexander Graham Bell invents the telephone. |
| | Custer's Last Stand takes place at the Battle of Little Bighorn. |
| *1877* | Railroad workers strike across the United States. |
| | The Nez Percé War occurs. |
| | Rutherford B. Hayes is elected president. |
| *1879* | Thomas Edison invents the light bulb. |
| | Mary Baker Eddy founds Christian Science. |
| *1880* | James A. Garfield is elected president. |
| *1881* | Garfield is assassinated. |
| | Chester A. Arthur becomes president. |
| | Booker T. Washington becomes president of the Tuskegee Institute. |
| | Helen Hunt Jackson publishes *A Century of Dishonor.* |
| *1882* | Congress passes the Chinese Exclusion Act. |
| *1883* | Congress passes the Pendleton Act. |
| *1884* | Grover Cleveland is elected president. |
| | Mark Twain publishes *Huckleberry Finn.* |
| *1885* | The Farmers' Alliance forms. |

| 1886 | The Haymarket Square Bombing occurs in Chicago. |
|------|--------|
| | The Supreme Court rules that only the federal government can regulate interstate commerce in the *Wabash* case. |
| | The American Federation of Labor (AFL) forms. |
| **1887** | Congress passes the Interstate Commerce Act. |
| | Congress passes the Dawes Severalty Act. |
| **1888** | Benjamin Harrison is elected president. |
| | Edward Bellamy publishes *Looking Backward*. |
| **1889** | Jane Addams founds Hull House in Chicago. |
| **1890** | Congress passes the Sherman Silver Purchase Act. |
| | Congress passes the Sherman Anti-Trust Act. |
| | Jacob Riis publishes *How the Other Half Lives*. |
| | Congress passes the McKinley Tariff. |
| | U.S. Census Bureau declares the continental frontier closed. |
| | The Sioux Ghost Dance Movement challenges white supremacy. |
| | The U.S. army challenges Native American ways of life in the Massacre at Wounded Knee. |
| | Alfred Thayer Mahan publishes *The Influence of Sea Power upon History*. |
| **1891** | The Populist Party forms. |
| **1892** | Miners strike in Coeur d'Alene, Idaho. |
| | Laborers win victory in the Homestead Steel Strike. |
| | Cleveland is reelected president. |
| **1893** | The Depression of 1893 ruins subsistence farming in the Midwest and South. |
| | Lillian Wald founds the Henry Street Settlement in New York. |
| | The Anti-Saloon League forms. |
| | Frederick Jackson Turner publishes *The Significance of the Frontier in American History*. |

| | |
|---|---|
| *1894* | "Coxey's Army" marches on Washington, D.C. |
| | Congress passes the Wilson-Gorman Tariff. |
| | The Pullman Strike occurs. |
| *1895* | J. P. Morgan bails out the U.S. government. |
| *1896* | The Supreme Court rules on *Plessy v. Ferguson*. |
| | William Jennings Bryan delivers his "Cross of Gold" speech. |
| | William McKinley is elected president. |
| *1897* | Congress passes the Dingley Tariff. |
| *1898* | Eugene V. Debs forms the Social Democratic Party. |
| | Charlotte Perkins Gilman publishes *Women and Economics*. |
| | The Anti-Imperialist League forms. |
| | The U.S.S. *Maine* explodes in Havana Harbor. |
| | The Spanish–American War begins. |
| | The United States annexes Hawaii. |
| | Congress passes the Teller Amendment. |
| | Admiral Dewey seizes the Philippines at Manila Bay. |
| *1899* | Aguinaldo leads the Filipino Insurrection against the United States. |
| *1900* | Congress passes the Gold Standard Act. |
| | Congress passes the Foraker Act. |
| | McKinley is reelected. |
| *1901* | U.S. Steel Corporation forms. |
| | The Supreme Court rules against equal constitutional rights for Americans on foreign soil in *Insular* Cases. |
| | Congress passes the Platt Amendment. |

**CHAPTER 2**
**1877–1901**

# Major Figures

**Jane Addams**  A Nobel Peace Prize–winner, Addams founded Hull House in 1889 to help immigrants make better lives for themselves in Chicago's slums. In doing so she raised awareness for the plight of the poor while simultaneously opening whole new opportunities for women.

**Chester A. Arthur**  Elected to the vice-presidency as James A. Garfield's running mate in 1880, Arthur became president in September 1881 after a crazed Stalwart assassinated Garfield. While he was president, Arthur refused to award Stalwarts any federal posts and helped legislate civil-service reform by signing the Pendleton Act in 1883.

**James G. Blaine**  A powerful congressman, senator, and secretary of state from Maine, Blaine was the leader of the Half-Breeds in the Republican Party during the Gilded Age. Like his archrival Roscoe Conkling of the Stalwarts, Blaine sought to exploit the spoils system by rewarding political supporters with federal civil-service jobs. He ran for president in the vicious campaign of 1884, but lost to Democrat Grover Cleveland.

**William Jennings Bryan**  A young Democratic congressman from Nebraska, Bryan was the greatest champion of inflationary "free silver" around the turn of the century. Deemed the "boy orator," Bryan opposed Grover Cleveland's repeal of the Sherman Silver Purchase Act, and won his party's nomination for the presidency in 1896 with his famous Cross of Gold Speech. Though he never left the Democratic Party, he was closely affiliated with the grassroots populist movement, and the Populist Party chose to back him in the election of 1900. Bryan ran for the presidency a total of three times (in 1896, 1900, and 1904), but lost every time. He died in 1925 after testifying in the infamous Scopes Monkey Trial.

**Andrew Carnegie**  A Scottish immigrant who came to the United States when he was thirteen, Carnegie built his Pittsburgh steel empire on a foundation of hard work and ruthless business tactics. He used a business method called vertical integration to control all aspects of making, selling, and shipping his steel. He was no friend of labor and sent in 300 Pinkerton Agents to end the 1892 Homestead Strike at one of his steel plants. Carnegie eventually sold his company to Wall Street financier J.P. Morgan, who used it to form the U.S. Steel Corporation trust in 1901. A firm believer that excessive wealth would shame him on his deathbed, Carnegie became one of the nation's first large-scale philanthropists by donating more than $300 million to charities, hospitals, libraries, and universities.

**Grover Cleveland**   A former Democratic governor of New York, Cleveland
   was elected president in 1884 after defeating James G. Blaine. His first
   term was mostly uneventful: his only battle came in his fourth year, when
   he tried to lower the protective tariff in order to reduce the Treasury surplus. He was defeated by Benjamin Harrison and the Republicans in 1888,
   but was reelected in 1892. His second term was much rockier: he unsuccessfully battled the Depression of 1893, sent federal troops to break up
   the Pullman Strike in 1894, and had to ask J. P. Morgan to loan the nearly
   bankrupt federal government over $60 million in 1895. He was the only
   president ever to serve two inconsecutive terms.

**Roscoe Conkling**   A powerful U.S. senator from New York, Conkling was the
   leader of the Stalwarts in the Republican Party during the Gilded Age. Like
   his bitter rival James G. Blaine of the Half-Breeds, Conkling sought to
   exploit the spoils system by rewarding political supporters with federal
   civil-service jobs.

**Eugene V. Debs**   The pro-labor founder of the Socialist Party, Debs helped
   organize the Pullman Strike at the Pullman Palace Car Company in
   1894. While serving time for instigating the strike, he began reading
   radical socialist literature. He ran unsuccessfully for the presidency in
   1908 against William Howard Taft and William Jennings Bryan and
   again in 1912, when he won roughly 6 percent of the vote. He was
   again sentenced to prison under the Espionage Act of 1917 after speaking out against America's role in World War I. Debs ran for president
   again on the Socialist Party ticket in 1920—from prison—and won
   almost a million popular votes.

**W.E.B. Du Bois**   A Harvard-educated black historian and sociologist, Du Bois
   pushed for both equal economic and social rights for African Americans.
   He disagreed with Booker T. Washington, among others, that economic
   success was the key to equality.

**Mary Baker Eddy**   Founder of the Christian Science Church in 1879, Eddy
   preached that disease could be healed by faith. The new church attracted
   hundreds of thousands of followers in the growing cities at the end of the
   nineteenth century and beginning of the twentieth century.

**James A. Garfield**   Elected president in 1880 on the Republican ticket,
   Garfield had spent less than a year in office when he was murdered by a
   crazed Stalwart who wanted Vice President Chester A. Arthur to be president. Garfield's assassination spurred Arthur and Congress to pass the

Pendleton Act in 1883 to enact civil-service reform and reduce exploitation of the spoils system.

**Geronimo**  An Apache leader, Geronimo led his people in a rebellion against white American settlement of the Southwest in the 1870s and 1880s. The Apaches were eventually defeated in 1886 and relocated to Oklahoma, Florida, and Alabama, where Geronimo died.

**Samuel Gompers**  A Jewish immigrant from Great Britain, Gompers founded the American Federation of Labor in 1886 to represent skilled urban craftsmen. He fought to win higher wages, better working conditions, shorter workdays, and all-union workplaces.

**Marcus Hanna**  A wealthy Ohio businessman, "Mark" Hanna served as William McKinley's campaign manager in the elections of 1896 and 1900. Despite protests from opponent William Jennings Bryan and the Democrats, Hanna convinced other plutocrats to contribute to McKinley's campaign in order to elect a pro-business president. McKinley's election proved that big business and wealth were necessary for twentieth-century politics.

**Benjamin Harrison**  The grandson of former president William Henry Harrison, the Republican Harrison entered the White House after defeating incumbent Grover Cleveland in 1888. His four years in office were unremarkable, although he did send federal troops to forcibly end the Coeur d'Alene Strike. He also signed the Sherman Silver Purchase Act, the Sherman Anti-Trust Act, and the McKinley Tariff in 1890. He was ousted from office in 1892 by returnee Grover Cleveland.

**Rutherford B. Hayes**  The Republican nominating convention chose Ohio governor Hayes to run against the Democrat Samuel J. Tilden for the presidency in the election of 1876. In the wake of the corruption scandals associated with Ulysses S. Grant, Republicans chose Hayes because he was relatively unknown, had no controversial opinions, and came from the politically important state of Ohio. Even though Hayes received fewer popular and electoral votes than Tilden, he nevertheless became president after the Compromise of 1877, when Democrats traded the White House for an end to Reconstruction.

**Chief Joseph**  Leader of the Nez Percé people of the Pacific Northwest, Chief Joseph opposed white expansion westward and relocation to reservations.

He led a band of nearly 1,000 warriors on a more than 1,000-mile journey across the Rocky Mountains to escape to Canada, but was captured by U.S. forces in 1887. His capture ended the Nez Percé War.

**William Kelly**  An American small businessman, Kelly discovered the Bessemer process to cheaply make high-quality steel by blowing cold air on hot iron in the 1850s. Unfortunately for him, the process he discovered was named after a British inventor who made the discovery on his own several years later. Kelly's and Bessemer's discovery allowed tycoons like Andrew Carnegie to make a killing in the steel business.

**William McKinley**  A powerful congressman from Ohio, McKinley pushed the McKinley Tariff through Congress in 1890, which raised the protective tariff rates on foreign goods to an all-time high. He later ran for president on a pro-Gold Standard platform against Democrat William Jennings Bryan in 1896. He won a resounding victory in the Electoral College, largely thanks to his campaign manager Marcus Hanna and donations from wealthy plutocrats. His election marked the beginning of the Fourth Party System, in which Republicans dominated the federal government. Although he was personally against the Spanish–American War and acquiring new territories, his administration has been remembered for its imperialist leanings. McKinley requested that Congress declare war against Spain in 1898, afraid that Democrats would oust him in the next presidential election if he did not. He also annexed the Philippines, though it was against his better judgment. He signed the Gold Standard Act in 1900; that year, he won reelection. In 1901, McKinley was assassinated by an anarchist.

**J.P. Morgan**  An incredibly wealthy Wall Street banker, Morgan saved the nearly bankrupt federal government in 1895 when he loaned the U.S. Treasury more than $60 million. He later purchased Andrew Carnegie's steel company for nearly $400 million and used it to form the U.S. Steel Corporation in 1901. U.S. Steel was the first $1 billion corporation when Morgan died.

**John D. Rockefeller**  A wealthy oil baron, Rockefeller dominated the blossoming oil industry when he formed the Standard Oil Company in 1867. Incredibly ruthless, he was the champion of horizontal integration and shaped Standard Oil into one of the nation's first monopolistic trusts by buying out his competition.

**Sitting Bull** Chief Sitting Bull, along with the Sioux of South Dakota, defeated General George Custer at the Battle of Little Bighorn in 1876. Sitting Bull eventually retreated to Canada after the U.S. army retaliated and nearly wiped out the Sioux. He was killed by the police in 1890.

**Elizabeth Cady Stanton** One of the first American feminists, Stanton worked for social and political equality for women. She helped organize the Seneca Falls Convention in 1848 and drafted the *Declaration of Sentiments*. Stanton pushed for racial and gender equality throughout the latter half of the nineteenth century.

**Frederick Jackson Turner** An historian, Turner published *The Significance of the Frontier in American History*, an 1893 essay that argued that western settlement had had an extraordinary impact on the social, political, and economic development of the United States. The essay is regarded as one of the most important works in America history.

**William Tweed** More commonly known as "Boss Tweed," this crooked Democrat controlled most of New York City and even much of the state. He preyed on immigrants and the poor, promising improved public works in exchange for votes. Tweed was eventually prosecuted by Samuel J. Tilden in 1872, and died in prison. The Tweed Ring exemplifies the widespread corruption and graft in machine politics in the North during this time.

**Cornelius Vanderbilt** A wealthy steamboat tycoon, Vanderbilt moved into the eastern railroad industry in the late nineteenth century. He was one of the first railroaders to replace his tracks' iron rails with steel. He also established a standard gauge for his railroads. Despite these improvements, Vanderbilt and his son were notorious robber barons who issued unfair rebates, hiked rates arbitrarily, and cared little for the American public.

**Booker T. Washington** President of the black industrial college Tuskegee Institute in Alabama, Washington pushed African Americans to achieve economic equality with whites. He did not advocate immediate social equality, because he believed that economic equality would eventually bring equal rights. Other black leaders like W.E.B. Du Bois sharply disagreed.

**James B. Weaver** A former Civil War officer, Weaver ran on the Greenback Party ticket in 1880 against James A. Garfield and Democrat Winfield

Scott Hancock. He ran again in 1892 as the Populist Party candidate against Grover Cleveland and Benjamin Harrison and won over a million popular votes and 22 electoral votes.

***Victoria Woodhull***  A leading figure of the women's movement, Woodhull shocked Americans when she and her sister began publishing a magazine advocating free love, contraception, and economic independence for women in 1870.

# Suggested Reading

• Cashman, Sean Dennis. *America in the Gilded Age: From the Death of Lincoln to the Rise of Theodore Roosevelt*. New York: New York University Press, 1993.

Cashman chronicles this crucial period in American history by explaining how America transforms itself from a new nation to a world power.

• Hine, Robert V. and John Mack Faragher. *The American West: A New Interpretive History*. New Haven, Connecticut: Yale University Press, 2000.

Yale history professor Faragher provides an extensive reexamination of the American West. Specifically, he illuminates the conflicting cultures that arose in the expansion of the West.

• McMath, Robert C. *American Populism: A Social History, 1877-1898*. New York: Hill and Wang, 1990.

This is a compact book that summarizes and explains populism. McMath emphasizes its social roots and its history in rural communities, illuminating this major American protest movement.

• Schlereth, Thomas J. *Victorian America: Transformations in Everyday Life, 1876-1915*. New York: Perennial, 1992.

Schlereth, an American Studies professor at Notre Dame, surveys numerous aspects of the Victorian period in America. His ability to provide a truly detailed account makes this period of American history come alive.

• Trachtenberg, Alan. *The Incorporation of America: Culture and Society in the Gilded Age*. New York: Hill and Wang, 1982.

Trachtenberg analyzes the expansion of capitalist power during the Gilded Age. His work provides insight into the origins of our corporate culture and its influence on American society, both in the past and the present.

# The Progressive Era and World War I: 1901–1920

- Big Stick Diplomacy
- Roosevelt and the Progressives
- The Taft Years
- Wilson's First Term
- World War I Erupts
- Mobilizing the United States for War
- The United States in World War I

As American society entered the twentieth century, it adapted to the ongoing processes of industrialization, as well as to demographic changes. Responding to these transformations, people interested in social welfare advocated reforms in business practices, government structure, and labor law, which formed the basis of a movement called progressivism. Progressivism was both a grassroots and an institutional phenomenon.

As the federal government sought to define the relationship between business and society, big business faced increasing legislation and regulation. Yet, a number of factors eventually pulled the United States away from progressivism and into World War I, the greatest war the world had ever known. Even though American forces only participated in the war during the final year, they gave Britain, France, and Italy a distinct advantage over their exhausted Austro–Hungarian, German, and Turkish enemies. Unfortunately, many conservatives at home would not allow Wilson to create the international governing body he desired to prevent future global conflicts. The United States and the rest of the world would regret this decision in the days leading up to the Second World War.

# Big Stick Diplomacy

An ardent imperialist, Theodore Roosevelt carried out much of William McKinley's foreign policies, as well as some aggressive policies of his own. His comfort with forcefully coercing other nations to comply with America's will on a number of occasions prompted anti-imperialists and other critics to dub his foreign policy **"Big Stick" Diplomacy**.

## CHINA AND THE FIRST OPEN DOOR NOTES

After losing the Sino–Japanese War of 1895, the Chinese could only watch as Japan, Russia, and the Europeans carved their ancient country into separate spheres of influence. Afraid that Americans would be unable to compete for lucrative Chinese markets, McKinley's policymakers scrambled to stop the feeding frenzy. In 1899 President **William McKinley**'s secretary of state, **John Hay**, boldly sent his **First Open Door "Notes"** to Japan and the European powers requesting that they respect Chinese rights and free trade. The British backed the agreement, but France, Germany, Russia, and Japan agreed only on the condition that other countries adhered to the note too.

### The Boxer Rebellion

Naturally, many Chinese deeply resented Japanese and European conquest, and as a result a new nationalistic movement called the **Boxer Movement** spread across China like wildfire. Hoping to cast out all foreigners, a highly deluded Boxer army invaded Beijing in 1900. The Boxer Army believed they would be divinely protected from enemy bullets. They took a number of foreign diplomats hostage and then barricaded themselves in the city. Nearly 20,000 French, British, German, Russian, Japanese, and American soldiers joined forces to rescue the diplomats. After the coalition had quelled the short-lived **Boxer Rebellion**, Hay then issued his **Second Open Door Note** in 1900 to request the other powers respect China's territorial status in spite of the rebellion.

## THE ELECTION OF 1900

Territorial gains overseas during the Spanish–American War and
events unfolding in China made foreign policy and imperialism
the dominant issue in the election of 1900.

Republicans nominated the popular McKinley for more prosperity and expansion and chose former Rough Rider Theodore
Roosevelt to be his new running mate. Democrats once again
selected the old favorite William Jennings Bryan on an anti-
imperialism platform.

To most of the Democrats' dismay, Bryan also insisted on pushing for free silver again, even though his free silver platform had
allowed McKinley to win in the previous election. Roosevelt and
Bryan traveled throughout the country and played to the crowds
on two whirlwind campaigns. In the end, free silver killed Bryan
once more, and McKinley won with almost a million more popular votes and twice as many electoral votes. McKinley's tragic
death by an anarchist's bullet, just months into his second term,
pushed Theodore Roosevelt into the White House.

> *President McKinley was assassinated by Leon Czolgosz on
> September 6, 1901. Czolgosz was quickly tried, found guilty, and
> executed. Some recent historians have speculated that he was
> clinically insane, but this was never proven.*

## THE PANAMA CANAL

Roosevelt was not one to shy from responsibility or action, and
the boisterous new president immediately went to work, particularly on his pet project to build a canal across Central America.
Territorial gains made during the war made it necessary to create
a canal in order to ferry merchant and military ships from the
American ports in the Atlantic to the Pacific.

### The Hay-Pauncefote Treaty

In a display of amity, Britain graciously annulled the 1850
Clayton-Bulwer Treaty that had previously prevented the United
States from building such a canal in the past. Instead, they signed

the new **Hay-Pauncefote Treaty** in 1901, giving Americans full ownership of any future canal. After purchasing land in the Colombian province of Panama from a French construction company, Roosevelt and Congress then petitioned the Colombian government to sell permanent rights to the land. The Colombians disagreed and demanded more money.

### Gunboat Diplomacy

Furious, Roosevelt struck a deal with Panamanian rebels, who were dissatisfied with Colombian rule. He offered independence and American protection in exchange for land to build a canal. The rebels quickly consented and captured the provincial capital in 1903 while U.S. Navy gunboats prevented Colombian troops from marching into Panama. Roosevelt immediately recognized Panama's independence and sent Hay to sign the **Hay–Bunau–Varilla Treaty**, which relinquished ownership of canal lands to the United States. Construction on the canal began the following year, despite Colombian protests. Contractors eventually completed the **Panama Canal** in 1914.

### ROOSEVELT'S COROLLARY TO THE MONROE DOCTRINE

Roosevelt further angered Latin Americans when he twisted the Monroe Doctrine by making policy according to his own interpretation. When several South American and Caribbean countries defaulted on their loans, Germany and Britain sent warships to forcibly collect the debts. Afraid that aggressive Europeans would use the debts as an excuse to permanently reinsert their feet into Latin America's doorway, Roosevelt simply slammed the door shut in their faces. In 1904, he announced his own **Roosevelt Corollary to the Monroe Doctrine** by declaring that the United States would collect the debts owed and then pass them on to the European powers. In other words, only the United States could intervene in Latin American affairs. He then sent troops to the Dominican Republic to enforce debt repayment and to Cuba to suppress revolutionary forces in 1906.

## TENSIONS WITH JAPAN

Relations between the United States and Japan during the Roosevelt years also soured. In 1905, Roosevelt mediated a dispute between Russia and Japan to end the Russo–Japanese War. Although Roosevelt's efforts won him the Nobel Peace Prize, both powers left the negotiating table unhappy and blamed the American president for their losses.

### The Gentlemen's Agreement

Tensions mounted when the San Francisco Board of Education caved into popular anti-Japanese sentiment and banned Japanese students from enrolling in the city's public schools. Japanese diplomats in Washington, D.C., protested loudly and even threatened war. Roosevelt resolved the situation in the 1906 **"Gentlemen's Agreement,"** in which San Francisco promised to retract the racist ban in exchange for Japanese pledges to reduce the number of yearly emigrants to the United States.

### The Great White Fleet

Roosevelt sent sixteen new battleships around the world, ostensibly on a good-will tour. In fact, they were sent to demonstrate American military might to the Japanese. When the **Great White Fleet** stopped in Tokyo in 1908, Japanese and American officials signed the **Root-Takahira Agreement**, in which both agreed to respect the Open Door policy in China and each other's territorial integrity in the Pacific.

CHAPTER 3
1901–1920

# Roosevelt and the Progressives

During his two terms as president, Roosevelt promoted his view of the federal government as an impartial force for the public good, rather than as an advocate for particular interests. For example, he used the power of the government to restrain corporations. In his second term, Roosevelt focused more on enacting social reforms. His progressive policies included engaging in anti-trust activities, supporting regulatory legislation, and championing environmental conservation. Roosevelt used his presidency as a **"bully pulpit,"** from which he gave speeches supporting his views on society and government.

### THE MUCKRAKERS

The term **muckrakers** referred to the investigative journalists and crusading writers who sought to expose injustice and corruption and spark social change. During Roosevelt's presidency, these writers helped spur the passage of progressive legislation with their works, including:

- *Wealth Against Commonwealth* (1894) by Henry Demarest Lloyd, investigating monopolies like the Standard Oil Company

- *History of the Standard Oil Company* (1904) by Ida Tarbell, also targeting Standard Oil

- *How the Other Half Lives* (1890) by Danish immigrant Jacob Riis, relying on photographs as well as text to describe the living conditions of the urban poor

- *The Shame of the Cities* (1904) by Lincoln Steffens, exposing municipal corruption

- *The Jungle* (1906) by Upton Sinclair, describing unsanitary conditions in the meatpacking plants

> *Roosevelt labeled exposé writers "muckrakers" after a character in the book* **Pilgrim's Progress** *who would search for stories about corruption (i.e., they would "rake" up "muck") where there was very little corruption in the first place. Roosevelt meant the name as an insult, but the muckrakers took up the name proudly.*

### ROOSEVELT'S SQUARE DEAL

Roosevelt's domestic progressive agenda came to be collectively known as the "Square Deal" and sought to regulate big business, protect consumers, and conserve the nation's natural resources.

### Trustbusting

As part of his strategy to regulate big business, Roosevelt revived the 1890 **Sherman Antitrust Act** and prosecuted the giant **Northern Securities Railroad Company** in 1902. The Supreme Court backed the president when it upheld the Sherman Antitrust Act and ordered Northern Securities to dissolve in 1904. Roosevelt then used the Sherman Antitrust Act to prosecute dozens of other trusts.

### The Anthracite Coal Strike

In 1902, the **United Mine Workers** went on strike in West Virginia and Pennsylvania to demand shorter workdays and better pay. Months passed with no resolution as mine managers refused to meet the workers' demands. In order to prevent a national coal shortage, Roosevelt finally intervened by threatening to seize the coalmines and use federal troops to run them, forcing management to seek arbitration. The strike eventually ended in October 1902. Soon after, the arbitration awarded miners both shorter workdays and higher wages.

### Regulatory Legislation

Roosevelt won the 1904 election with nearly 58 percent of the popular vote—the largest popular majority a presidential candidate had ever garnered. He therefore increased his push for progressive reforms in his second term with the following acts:

- **The Elkins Act** of 1903, which instituted penalties for giving and receiving railroad rebates. Railroads had given rebates to shippers in order to guarantee their continued business.

- **The Hepburn Railroad Regulation Act** of 1906, which gave the Interstate Commerce Commission the power to control railroad rates, inspect company books, and assign a uniform standard of bookkeeping.

- **The Meat Inspection Act** of 1906, which required federal inspectors to examine meat.

- **The Pure Food and Drug Act** of 1906, which allowed the federal government to regulate the sale of medicine and foods.

> **The Jungle** by Upton Sinclair provides gruesome detail on the meatpacking industry and caused profound ripples in society at the time of its publication. People were shocked about the filthy conditions in which their meat was manufactured; the public outcry at The Jungle led to the creation of the FDA. This book is still widely taught today.

### Conservation

Roosevelt supported environmental conservation policies as a major tenet of his domestic program. He added millions of acres to the national forest system to conserve forests for future use, and he also increased the size of the National Park System to protect some lands from development.

## PROGRESSIVISM ON THE STATE LEVEL

Many reformers sought legislative and electoral changes that would give more power to the voters. These progressives succeeded in achieving the following:

- **The direct primary**, to elect nominees for office instead of party bosses

- **The legislative initiative**, which allowed the electorate to vote directly for specific legislation, rather than going through the state legislature

- **The referendum**, which allowed the electorate to vote on whether to accept or reject government legislation

- **The recall**, which allowed the electorate to vote government officials out of office in special elections

### Robert M. La Follette

Governor Robert La Follette of Wisconsin incorporated many progressive policies into his government. Under his leadership, progressives in Wisconsin implemented a wide variety of measures, including:

- Workers' compensation and workplace regulation

- Environmental conservation legislation

- Higher taxes on railroads and other corporations

- The first modern state income tax in the nation

La Follette continued his push for progressive reform as a U.S. senator, representing Wisconsin from 1906 to 1925.

### AMERICAN SOCIALISM

The socialist movement in the United States also reached its height during the Progressive Era. The Socialist party contained diverse constituents, with its members extending beyond core urban immigrant areas to the rural Midwest and South. Different groups of socialists envisioned different solutions to society's problems, with some advocating radical action, such as the overthrow of capitalism. Other socialists advocated more moderate measures, which would include small private businesses as an alternative to large corporations.

*Founded in 1905, the* **Industrial Workers of the World (IWW)** *was considered one of the most radical socialist factions. Led by* **William Dudley Haywood**, *the IWW (also known as the Wobblies) advocated militant action such as sabotage to overthrow the government in favor of an all-inclusive union. The organization still exists today, though with considerably less influence.*

# The Taft Years

With the support of Theodore Roosevelt, **William Howard Taft** ran as the Republican candidate for president in the election of 1908. The Democrats again nominated **William Jennings Bryan**. Taft appealed to members of both parties and thus won the election with 321 electoral votes to Bryan's 162. However, Taft's popularity did not last long, and his presidency consequently lasted only one term. By the end of his presidency, he had alienated progressives and had fallen out of favor with his former friend and ally Roosevelt.

## TAFT'S DOLLAR DIPLOMACY

Whereas Roosevelt had employed big stick diplomacy to bend weaker nations to his will, Taft preferred to use the buck. He believed he could convince smaller developing nations to support the United States by investing American dollars into their economies. **"Dollar diplomacy,"** as pundits dubbed it, was intended to make allies as well as easy money for American investors.

### Dollar Diplomacy Fails

Taft put his new policy to the test in Manchuria. In 1909, he offered to purchase and develop the Manchurian Railway to prevent Russia and Japan from seizing control of it and colonizing north China. Unfortunately, both powers refused to hand over the railway to the United States, and the deal collapsed. The United States went on to dump millions into several unstable Latin American countries, such as Honduras, Nicaragua, Cuba, and the Dominican Republic. Eventually, occupation troops had to be sent to protect those investments. In short, Taft's dollar diplomacy failed miserably.

## MORE TRUST-BUSTING

After the failure of dollar diplomacy, Taft devoted himself instead to domestic matters and made trust-busting his top priority. Amazingly, he filed eighty lawsuits against monopolistic trusts in just four years, more than twice as many as Roosevelt had filed in almost eight years. In 1911, the Supreme Court used the previously neglected Sherman Anti-Trust Act when it dissolved John D. Rockefeller's **Standard Oil Company** for "unreasonably" stifling the competition. Taft also famously filed a suit against J. P. Morgan's **U.S. Steel Corporation** later that year, a move that infuriated Theodore Roosevelt, who had helped the company in the past.

## THE PAYNE-ALDRICH TARIFF

Many progressive Republicans hoped Taft would keep his campaign promise and reduce the protective tariff. Taft tried but didn't have enough political clout to prevent conservatives within the party from repeatedly amending the bill for a lower tariff. By the time the **Payne-Aldrich Tariff** reached the president, conservatives had made so many amendments to keep certain tariffs high that the overall tariff rate remained practically unchanged. Taft signed the bill in 1909 anyway and then strangely proclaimed it to be the best bill Republicans had ever passed. Outraged, progressives denounced both the tariff and the "traitor" Taft.

## THE BALLINGER-PINCHOT AFFAIR

Taft further alienated supporters when he fired **Gifford Pinchot** for insubordination. Pinchot was the head of the Forest Service. A progressive, popular conservationist, and personal friend of Roosevelt's, Pinchot had opposed Secretary of the Interior **Richard Ballinger**'s decision to sell public wilderness lands in Alaska and the Rocky Mountains to corporate developers. The president furthermore refused to reinstate Pinchot even after Roosevelt and several prominent Republicans appealed on his behalf. The 1910 **Ballinger-Pinchot Affair** thus blackened Taft's public image and made him many enemies within his own party.

## ROOSEVELT RETURNS WITH NEW NATIONALISM

Feeling betrayed by his one-time friend turned foe, Roosevelt left retirement in 1910 and dove back into politics to wrest back control of the Republican Party. During the following two years, he denounced Taft in scores of speeches delivered throughout the country. He also took the opportunity to promote his **New Nationalism** program, which entailed:

- Greater government regulation of business
- A graduated income tax
- Tariff reform
- A strong central government that acted in defense of the public interest

CHAPTER 3
1901–1920

The former Rough Rider took charge of the fledgling National Progressive Republican League within the Republican Party, trying to win the party's nomination for president in 1912. Divided, but still dominated by powerful pro-business conservatives, delegates at the nominating convention eventually chose to stick with Taft.

### The Election of 1912

Roosevelt thundered out of the convention still determined to win a third term. He took with him his Progressive allies and founded a new **Progressive Party**. Ultimately, four candidates ran for the White House in 1912:

- **William Howard Taft** for the Republicans
- **Theodore Roosevelt** for the Progressive Republicans
- **Woodrow Wilson** for the Democrats
- **Eugene V. Debs** for the Socialists

In the end, Roosevelt's Bull Moose Party split the Republican Party and allowed Wilson to win an easy victory. Wilson received 435 electoral votes to Roosevelt's eighty-eight and Taft's eight. Surprisingly, Debs managed to win nearly a million popular votes.

*The Progressive Republican Party quickly became known as the* ***Bull Moose Party*** *after Roosevelt claimed to be as politically strong "as a bull moose" to run against Taft and Wilson. Women's suffrage was an integral platform of the Bull Moose Party; in fact, the rules of the party stipulated that four women were to be members of the Progressive National Committee.*

# Wilson's First Term

Even though Woodrow Wilson had promised a new form of progressivism and foreign policy during his campaign in 1912, his policies ultimately resembled those of his predecessors. In other words, he continued to use federal power to regulate big business and protect consumers while exerting American power in Latin America.

## NEW FREEDOM PROGRESSIVISM

During the 1912 campaign, Roosevelt and Wilson offered different kinds of progressivism. Wilson countered Roosevelt's New Nationalism with his own **New Freedom** plan. New Freedom championed states rights, a limited federal government, and support for small businesses. During his two terms in office, however, Wilson compromised and incorporated many elements from New Nationalism into the New Freedom plan.

### Economic and Business Changes

Wilson and progressives passed a variety of economic and business reforms, including:

- **The Underwood-Simmons Tariff** in 1913, which lowered protective tariffs

- **The Glass-Owen Federal Reserve Act**, also in 1913, which established a system of 12 regional Federal Reserve Banks. Each of the Federal Reserve Banks came under the oversight of a **Federal Reserve Board.** This gave the federal government greater control over the U.S. banking system.

- **The Clayton Antitrust Act** in 1914, which outlawed unfair business practices

- **The Federal Trade Commission Act** in 1914, which created the **Federal Trade Commission (FTC)**, a federal regulatory agency with the power to investigate and prosecute businesses engaged in illegal practices. The FTC, with its broader powers, replaced the **Bureau of Corporations** instituted under Roosevelt and served as the foundation of Wilson's antitrust policies.

### Wilson's Other Reforms

Other progressive reforms included child labor legislation, aid to farmers, and the institution of an eight-hour workday for railroad employees. In addition, Wilson pleased progressives in 1916 by nominating Louis D. Brandeis to the Supreme Court. A committed progressive, Brandeis was also the Supreme Court's first Jewish member.

> Congress and the states ratified the **Sixteenth Amendment** in 1913 to establish the first federal income tax. The revenue generated from the tax offset the losses from the lower protective tariff. That same year Congress also ratified the **Seventeenth Amendment** to allow the electorate to elect their senators directly.

### WILSONIAN FOREIGN POLICY

Wilson envisioned the United States as a moral leader and force for democracy in the world and championed **"missionary diplomacy"** as opposed to Taft's "dollar diplomacy." Despite its strong idealistic underpinnings, Wilson's foreign policy differed very little from Taft's.

#### U.S. Intervention in Mexico

In 1913, Wilson denounced **Victoriano Huerta**'s revolutionary government in Mexico. This government had seized power and deposed the rightfully elected president. After a year of tense relations, Wilson finally decided to challenge Huerta's regime by sending U.S. troops to invade the Mexican port of **Veracruz**. Another revolutionary named **Venustiano Carranza** capitalized on the American invasion to overthrow Huerta and win the support of the United States. In retaliation, Mexican national hero **Pancho Villa** launched attacks on Americans in New Mexico and Arizona; the United States withdrew its forces from Mexico in 1917.

### U.S. Presence in the Caribbean

Wilson sent troops to the following locations:

- **Nicaragua** in 1914 to continue Taft's occupation to ensure political and economy stability

- **Haiti** in 1915 to suppress a revolution

- **Dominican Republic** in 1916 to prevent a revolution

- **Danish West Indies** in 1917 after the United States purchased the islands from Denmark and renamed them the U.S. Virgin Islands

# World War I Erupts

Although the United States willingly became involved in disputes and conflicts in the Western Hemisphere, Wilson hoped to avoid involving the United States in the Great War that engulfed Europe in 1914. Several events ultimately forced the United States to enter the war.

### THE ASSASSINATION OF ARCHDUKE FRANZ FERDINAND

On June 28, 1914, a Serbian nationalist assassinated **Archduke Franz Ferdinand,** heir to the Austro-Hungarian Empire, in Sarajevo. Austria-Hungary declared war on Serbia following the assassination, prompting every other major European power to choose sides in the largest-scale war the world had ever experienced. Great Britain, France, Russia, Italy, and Japan formed the **Allied Powers** on one side, and Germany, Austria-Hungary, and Turkey formed the Central Powers on the other.

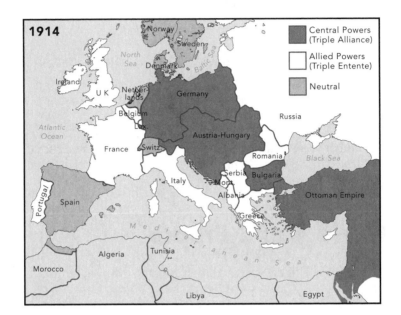

## AMERICAN NEUTRALITY

Wilson tried to keep the United States neutral during the initial years of the war. Even though geography provided a natural buffer, war propaganda eventually crossed the Atlantic and split American public opinion. Moreover, the traditional American policy of neutral trading ultimately collapsed as Britain's blockade of Germany forced the United States to trade mainly with the Allies.

## U-BOATS, THE LUSITANIA, AND THE SUSSEX

In response to the British blockade, Germany blockaded England with its deadly fleet of submarines, or **U-boats**. While the United States objected to this expansion of the war zone, the situation did not become a crisis until the Germans sank the British passenger ship *Lusitania* on May 7, 1915. 1,198 people died in the *Lusitania* attack, including 128 Americans. Wilson and the German government negotiated to maintain relations after this incident and again after a 1916 attack on the French passenger ship *Sussex*.

### The Zimmerman Note

Despite earlier pledges, the Germans began attacking both neutral and Allied ships in an unrestricted submarine warfare campaign in 1917 to strangle Britain economically. Wilson had no choice but to cut all diplomatic ties with Germany. Then, in February 1917, the British disclosed the contents of an intercepted German telegram promising to expand Mexican territory if Mexico invaded the United States. This **Zimmerman Note** outraged Americans, who put more pressure on Wilson to declare war on Germany.

### WILSON DECLARES WAR

Unrestricted submarine warfare combined with Germany's blatant disregard for American sovereignty and territorial integrity ultimately forced Wilson to ask Congress to declare war in April 1917. Congress overwhelmingly consented to join the Allies against Germany, Turkey, and Austria-Hungary.

CHAPTER 3
1901–1920

# Mobilizing the United States for War

After deciding to enter the war, the Wilson administration immediately took several steps to gather the resources necessary to fight. The U.S. government funded the war by selling **Liberty Bonds** and collecting billions of dollars in new taxes.

> Passed in 1917, the **Selective Service Act** established a nationwide draft and required all able-bodied men between the ages of twenty-one and thirty to register (the draft was later expanded to all men between eighteen and forty-five). The military drafted almost 3 million men to prepare for World War I.

## WAR BOARDS

In 1916, the **Army Appropriation Act** established the **Council of National Defense** to oversee production of food, fuel, and railroads during the war. The council, in turn, created the following:

- **The War Industries Board**, headed by **Bernard Baruch**, organized and coordinated military purchases beginning in 1917. The board had extensive powers over U.S. production.

- **The National War Labor Board** settled disputes between labor and industry starting in 1918. Under pressure from the labor-friendly board, industries granted concessions such as an eight-hour workday and the right to bargain collectively.

## COMMITTEE ON PUBLIC INFORMATION

Journalist George Creel headed the **Committee on Public Information** to produce propaganda in favor of the war effort. In addition to distributing films and printed material, the committee also had considerable control over information about the war that appeared in the popular press.

## ESPIONAGE AND SEDITION ACTS

The **Espionage Act** of 1917 and the **Sedition Act** of 1918 effectively banned public criticism of governmental policy during the war. More than 1,000 people received convictions under these acts, which the Supreme Court upheld in 1919. Many of those convicted had ties to the growing Socialist party, including antiwar labor leader and presidential candidate **Eugene V. Debs**.

*Significant public opposition to German culture intensified in the United States during the war. Even though many German-Americans supported the war against Germany, many Americans still looked upon them as potential traitors. As a result, many companies fired their German-American employees, especially those who worked in war-related industries.*

### DOMESTIC LABOR

The war also brought changes in the domestic labor force. The flow of millions of working men into the armed forces and a reduction in immigration resulted in a labor shortage. To fill that gap, white women, African Americans, and workers of other races and ethnicities took jobs formerly held by white men.

### Women in the Labor Force

During the war, women took jobs previously held by men, such as working on loading docks, operating heavy machinery, and working on the railroads. Some women even joined labor unions, although the American Federation of Labor (AFL) frequently opposed the entry of women into the work force. Most women only held their new jobs for the duration of the war.

### The Nineteenth Amendment

During the war, suffragists increased the intensity of their campaign for the right to vote. Leaders included **Alice Paul**, who led the militant **National Woman's Party** and **Carrie Chapman Catt**, who took over the more moderate **National American Woman Suffrage Association** in 1915. Women's roles in the labor force ultimately helped Congress and the states to ratify the **Nineteenth Amendment**, which granted women the right to vote in 1920.

### African Americans in the Labor Force

Many African Americans migrated from the South to urban areas in the North during the war years to take advantage of the labor shortage. This influx began the **Great African American Migration**, in which roughly 10 percent of all black southerners relocated to the North. Additionally, cotton-crop destruction by boll weevils and high unemployment rates in the South escalated the migration.

# The United States in World War I

World War I had devastating repercussions for many nations. Although the United States had entered the war late, the nation still suffered major casualties. Some 112,000 American soldiers died in World War I, half from influenza and half from the fighting itself. Among all nations involved, some 10 million soldiers died. New military technologies and the use of trench warfare contributed to the high casualty rates.

*In November 1917, **Vladimir Lenin** and the **Bolshevik Party** overthrew a months-old, provisional republican government in Russia. The new communist government quickly arranged a peace settlement with Germany and effectively dropped out of the war. This allowed Germany to shift all its resources in the East to the Western front to fight France, Britain, and the United States.*

### EFFECT OF U.S. FORCES

**General John J. Pershing** commanded the American Expeditionary Force sent to assist the British and French in Europe in 1917. U.S. forces, however, did not participate in any major fighting until 1918, when they helped achieve an Allied victory at the **Second Battle of the Marne**. Their defensive units defeated, German officials ultimately signed an armistice in November 1918.

### THE FOURTEEN POINTS

On January 8, 1918, Wilson delivered a speech to a joint session of Congress that set forth, in a series of **Fourteen Points,** the aims for which he considered the United States to be fighting. Five of the points called for:

- Freedom of the seas

- Armament reduction

- Open diplomacy

- Free trade

- Impartial negotiation regarding colonial claims

Eight other points set forth recommendations for the institution of new national boundaries in the conquered Ottoman and Austro-Hungarian empires. The last point advocated an association of nations, or **League of Nations**, to mediate future disputes and protect countries' "political independence and territorial integrity."

## THE PARIS PEACE CONFERENCE

In December 1918, the major combatants met at a peace conference in Paris. Wilson, Georges Clemenceau from France, David Lloyd George from Britain, and Vittorio Orlando from Italy made up the so-called **Big Four** that dominated the negotiations. On June 28, 1919, all sides signed the **Treaty of Versailles**, despite Germany's objection that the treaty would destroy its economy. The settlement required the following stipulations of Germany:

- Accept full responsibility for the war
- Pay $33 billion in reparations for the entire cost of the war
- Accept a foreign troop presence for fifteen years
- Cede some of its territory
- Abandon its colonies overseas

The Treaty of Versailles also divided the former Ottoman Empire in the Near and Middle East between Britain and France and established Wilson's League of Nations.

## U.S. CONTROVERSY OVER THE TREATY

Wilson presented the Treaty of Versailles to the Senate in the summer of 1919 but encountered intense opposition. Republican Senator **Henry Cabot Lodge** and his **"reservationist"** allies denounced the treaty primarily because he disliked the League of Nations. Another group of **"irreconcilables"** objected to any American participation in the League. To gather public support, Wilson began a cross-country speaking tour, which was cut short in September 1919 when he fell ill. He later suffered a serious stroke that ruined any chance of the Senate ratifying the treaty. Congress formally declared the war over simply by passing a joint resolution in 1920.

Theodore Roosevelt, Woodrow Wilson, and William Howard Taft all ran in the presidential election of 1912. Roosevelt and Wilson presented different kinds of progressivism to voters. Compare the two men's visions for the nation, focusing on their position regarding big business. In addition, describe Taft's relationship to progressives, and explain the effect of his rivalry with Roosevelt on the election.

The 1912 election coincided with a defining moment in the history of the federal government's relationship to big business. Theodore Roosevelt's presidency (1901–1909) witnessed the rise of a progressivism that placed big business in check, through both regulation or outright trustbusting. The candidates in the 1912 election presented different versions of this progressive impulse in their respective platforms. Roosevelt's "New Nationalism" stressed regulation of big business for the public good, while the New Freedom plan, as set forth by Democratic candidate Woodrow Wilson, presented a bolder, more intrusive plan to break up trusts and foster economic competition. Ironically, the victorious Wilson incorporated key aspects of New Nationalism during his presidency.

Despite the reputation he had earned as a trustbuster during his time in the White House, Roosevelt thought regulation was a better method for dealing with trusts. Though he carried out 40 antitrust suits while in office, his two-pronged "Square Deal" approach resulted in regulatory legislation, such as the Hepburn Railroad Regulation Act, which increased the powers of the Interstate Commerce Commission. Roosevelt began to think that trusts should be broken up only on a selective basis. For example, although he attacked Northern Securities for antitrust violations, he accepted an acquisition by U.S. Steel. When his chosen successor, President William Howard Taft (1909–1913) targeted that trust, Roosevelt was infuriated and remarked that Taft was incapable of distinguishing between a good trust and a bad one.

# *Student Essay*

Taft, the third major candidate in 1912, had lost the support of many progressives, (including Roosevelt) during his administration. He surpassed Roosevelt both in the amount of land he placed in the federal conservation system and in the number of antitrust suits he brought—Taft's base was mostly comprised of probusiness conservative Republicans. Taft's alienation of Progressives began early in his administration. Key actions eroding that support were his praise of the Payne-Aldrich Tariff, which had raised many rates instead of lowering them, and his treatment of the Ballinger-Pinchot dispute, which outraged many conservationists. In the election, he and Roosevelt, who ran under the banner of his own Progressive party, split the Republican vote, with Roosevelt finishing second, allowing the Democrat Wilson to gain the presidency.

During the 1912 campaign, Wilson attacked the very structure of big business, favoring an economy based around small companies in competition with one another. But when he finally won the presidency, his administration changed course, enacting regulatory policies like those advocated by Roosevelt. Wilson supported the 1914 creation of the Federal Trade Commission (FTC), a replacement for Roosevelt's Bureau of Corporations. The powers of the new federal regulatory agency surpassed those of the Bureau of Corporations, and the FTC echoed Roosevelt's approach to managing business. Wilson's administration did not entirely abandon trust-busting legislation. Outlawing specific corporate structures and actions, the Clayton Antitrust Act, passed in 1914, was a New Freedom approach to business. Its impact was diluted when Congress weakened the final version of the bill.

The fact that all three major candidates for the presidency in 1912 displayed progressive tendencies—to varying degrees—shows how strong the progressive movement in American politics had become. In part, government may have been forced to counter big business because trusts had at that moment assumed unprecedented power. The triumph of regulation, as opposed to the unbridled trustbusting initially advocated by Wilson, may speak to its long-term utility as a means for the federal government to keep big business in check.

# Test Questions and Answers

**1. In what ways did progressivism and concerns for social justice work as a force for change?**

- Progressive reforms changed state and city political structures.

- Corporate regulation increased during the era.

- Labor conditions improved.

- Legislators passed laws to promote environmental conservation.

- Legislators passed laws regarding food and drug safety.

**2. What were some of the measures enacted during the Progressive Era to control big business?**

- Creation of the Federal Trade Commission in 1914

- Expansion of the Interstate Commerce Commission through the Hepburn Railroad Regulation Act of 1906 and the Mann-Elkins Act of 1910

- The Clayton Antitrust Act of 1914, which outlawed practices like interlocking directorates in large corporations and price discrimination

**3. What role did muckrakers play in the progressive movement?**

- Muckrakers were a group of writers and journalists who published exposés about various aspects of society. They provided publicity for progressive causes, which helped mobilize public support for reform measures.

- Muckraking works included Ida Tarbell's *History of the Standard Oil Company* and Upton Sinclair's *The Jungle*.

- The muckrakers' influence led to the 1906 passages of the Pure Food and Drug Act and the Meat Inspection Act.

### 4. Explain Theodore Roosevelt's Square Deal.

- The term came to describe Roosevelt's agenda as president: his desire to act in the best interests of society as a whole by regulating business, enacting social reform, and instituting environmental conservation measures.

- A key aspect of the concept was Roosevelt's goal to provide both labor and business with a fair resolution to disputes.

### 5. In what ways did Taft alienate progressives?

- His administration incited distrust with the Ballinger-Pinchot controversy.

- Acceptance of, and, ultimately, praise for the Payne-Aldrich Tariff alienated progressives.

### 6. How did Roosevelt's New Nationalism treat business differently than Wilson's New Freedom?

- New Nationalism envisioned a strong central government to regulate big business.

- New Freedom envisioned a limited central government that would enact initial measures against big business, thereby breaking up monopolies and resulting in a self-regulating system of smaller businesses.

- The Wilson administration ultimately incorporated the regulatory policies of New Nationalism.

### 7. What events prompted the United States to enter World War I?

- The sinking of the *Lusitania* and controversy over neutral shipping rights

- Germany's decision to engage in unrestricted submarine warfare

- Propaganda about the war

- The Zimmerman Note

## 8. What effects did World War I have on the U.S. labor force?

- Many workers left the labor force to join the army.

- Many women, African Americans, and other racial and ethnic minorities joined the labor force.

- The government protected labor rights.

- Many of these changes in labor demographics and labor conditions reverted to a prewar state when WWI ended.

# Timeline

| 1900 | Republican president William McKinley is reelected. His vice president is Theodore Roosevelt. |
|------|-----------------------------------------------------------------------------------------------|
| 1901 | On September 6, an anarchist shoots McKinley during the Pan American Exposition. McKinley dies several days later, and Theodore Roosevelt becomes president. |
| 1902 | The Anthracite Coal Strike begins in May. It ends in October after the sides agree to submit to arbitration by a Roosevelt-appointed commission. The resolution of the strike results in Roosevelt's phrase "square deal." |
|      | Roosevelt prosecutes the Northern Securities Company, charging it with violation of antitrust legislation. Two years later, the Supreme Court upholds the Sherman Antitrust Act, ordering Northern Securities to dissolve. |
| 1903 | Congress creates the Department of Commerce and Labor, containing a Bureau of Corporations to investigate businesses conducting interstate commerce. |
|      | W.E.B. Du Bois publishes *The Souls of Black Folk*. |
| 1904 | Japan attacks the Russian fleet stationed at China's Port Arthur, beginning the Russo-Japanese War. |
|      | Roosevelt wins reelection. |
|      | Roosevelt announces his "Roosevelt Corollary" to the Monroe Doctrine, giving the United States leave to involve itself in the domestic affairs of countries in the Western Hemisphere. |
| 1906 | Upton Sinclair publishes *The Jungle*. |
|      | The Hepburn Railroad Regulation Act expands the mandate of the Interstate Commerce Commission. |
|      | The Meat Inspection Act requires federal inspectors to examine meat. |
|      | The Pure Food and Drug Act applies federal regulations to the sale of medicine and foods. |
| 1908 | Republican William Howard Taft wins the presidency. |
| 1909 | National Association for the Advancement of Colored People (NAACP) is founded. |
| 1910 | Congress passes the Mann-Elkins Act, expanding the powers of the Interstate Commerce Commission (ICC). |
|      | Jane Addams publishes *Twenty Years at Hull House*. |

| 1911 | A fire breaks out at the Triangle Shirtwaist Company in New York City. The blaze, which kills 146 workers, helps gain support for fire codes, labor laws, and workplace regulation. |
| --- | --- |
| | The Taft administration initiates an antitrust suit against U.S. Steel, angering Theodore Roosevelt. |
| 1912 | Roosevelt runs for president as head of the "Bull Moose" Party, splitting the Republican vote with Taft, the Republican party's nominee, and allowing for the victory of Democratic challenger Woodrow Wilson. |
| 1913 | The ratification of the Sixteenth Amendment to the Constitution allows for a federal income tax. |
| | The Seventeenth Amendment to the Constitution is ratified, which institutes popular election of U.S. senators. |
| | Wilson signs the Glass-Owen Federal Reserve Act, establishing a system of regional Federal Reserve Banks under the oversight of a Federal Reserve Board. |
| 1914 | A Serbian nationalist assassinates Archduke Franz Ferdinand, the heir to the Austro-Hungarian Empire, leading to the start of World War I in Europe. |
| | The Panama Canal opens, linking the Atlantic and Pacific Oceans across the Isthmus of Panama. |
| | The Federal Trade Commission (FTC) is created to regulate businesses practices. |
| | The Clayton Antitrust Act passes, outlawing practices like interlocking directorates in large corporations and price discrimination. |
| | U.S. troops invade the Mexican port of Veracruz. |
| 1915 | Germans sink the *Lusitania*, killing 1,198 people, including 128 Americans. |

| | |
|---|---|
| **1917** | Germany begins unrestricted submarine warfare. Following that development, Wilson breaks diplomatic relations with Germany. |
| | The British relate the Zimmerman Telegram to Wilson, soon sparking the United States' entry into World War I. |
| | The United States declares war on Germany. |
| | The Selective Service Act establishes a nationwide draft. |
| | The Espionage Act passes. The Sedition Act passes in 1918. Both acts target public criticism of government policy. |
| | In Houston, Texas, a deadly clash occurs between black soldiers and the police. The incident results in the execution of nineteen black soldiers. |
| | The Bolshevik Party overthrows a provisional republican government in Russia. The new government arranges a peace with Germany in March of the following year, and exits the war. |
| **1918** | Wilson delivers his Fourteen Points to Congress. The speech, which sets forth the aims Wilson considers the United States to be fighting for, includes a proposal for the League of Nations. |
| | The Sedition Act is passed. |
| | The Second Battle of the Marne marks a turning point in World War I. In November, German officials sign an armistice. |
| **1919– 1920** | In the "Red Scare," Attorney General A. Mitchell Palmer and his assistant John Edgar Hoover organize raids in which authorities arrest alleged radicals. |
| **1919** | The ratification of the Eighteenth Amendment orders prohibition. |
| | At the end of the peace conference in Paris, all remaining participants in World War I sign the Treaty of Versailles, despite Germany's objections about the extremely punitive nature of the pact. |
| | Wilson presents the Treaty of Versailles to the Senate, where the document encounters opposition. |
| | The "Red Summer" sees race riots in many U.S. cities, including Washington, D.C., and Chicago. |
| | Steel workers strike for union recognition and an eight-hour day. Workers return to their jobs four months later, without the concessions. |
| **1920** | The ratification of the Nineteenth Amendment gives women the right to vote. |

# Major Figures

**Bernard Baruch**  A Wall Street financier, Baruch headed the War Industries Board during World War I. The WIB had extensive powers to oversee all aspects of American war production.

**Carrie Chapman Catt**  A suffragette who led the National American Woman Suffrage Association in the early twentieth century, Catt helped secure the passage of the Nineteenth Amendment, which enfranchised women.

**Eugene V. Debs**  Leader of the Socialist Party, Debs ran for president on the Socialist ticket in 1908 and 1912. When Debs criticized the government during World War I, authorities arrested and convicted him under the Espionage and Sedition Acts. Debs ran for president again from prison in 1920.

**William Dudley Haywood**  As leader of the Industrial Workers of the World, Haywood sought to replace the government with a union comprising all American workers.

**Robert M. La Follette**  A progressive politician, La Follette served as the governor of Wisconsin from 1901 to 1905 and instituted a number of progressive reforms. He later served as Wisconsin's senator from 1906 to 1925 and ultimately tried to run for president.

**Vladimir Lenin**  Leader of Russia after the Bolshevik Revolution of November 1917, Lenin negotiated a separate peace settlement with Germany in 1918 to withdraw from World War I.

**Henry Cabot Lodge**  Republican senator and chair of the Senate Foreign Relations Committee, Lodge led the "reservationist" opposition to the Treaty of Versailles. Concerned that the League of Nations would hinder American foreign policy, Lodge attached numerous amendments to the treaty before passing it to the full Senate. Wilson refused to accept the changes, and therefore the United States never entered the League of Nations.

**Alice Paul**  A suffragette who led the National Woman's Party, Paul helped secure the ratification of the Nineteenth Amendment to enfranchise women.

**John J. Pershing** Commander of the American Expeditionary Force during World War I, Pershing refused to place American troops under Allied command when the United States entered the war, preferring instead to wait until he had enough troops to engage in different tactics. Pershing also pursued Poncho Villa into Mexico before the war but was unable to capture Villa.

**Gifford Pinchot** As head of the U.S. Forest Service under William Taft, Pinchot had opposed Secretary of the Interior Richard Ballinger's plans to sell public lands. Taft dismissed Pinchot for insubordination despite Republicans' appeals that he remain. The affair damaged Taft's reputation as a progressive and contributed to the growing rift in the Republican Party.

**Theodore Roosevelt** Republican president of the United States from 1901–1908, Roosevelt established a reputation for taking on corporate trusts, regulating industry to help consumers, and boldly exerting American dominance in Latin America. After splitting with his successor, William Howard Taft, Roosevelt unsuccessfully ran for president in 1912 on the Progressive Party ticket. Taft and Roosevelt's feud ultimately split the Republican vote and allowed Woodrow Wilson to win.

**Upton Sinclair** A muckraker, Sinclair wrote about the deplorable working conditions in the meatpacking industry in his novel *The Jungle* (1906). The book disgusted government officials and Roosevelt so much that Congress passed the Meat Inspection Act, requiring federal inspection of meat.

**William Howard Taft** Republican president of the United States from 1909–1912, Taft alienated himself from progressive Republicans after mishandling the Payne–Aldrich Tariff and the Ballinger–Pinchot Affair. His former ally and boss Theodore Roosevelt, ran for the presidency on the Progressive Party ticket in 1912, ultimately splitting the Republican vote.

**Poncho Villa** A Mexican rebel and national hero, Villa helped overthrow Victoriano Huerta's regime and then fought to oust his previous ally, Venustiano Carranza. President Wilson initially backed Villa but then recognized the Carranza government. Feeling betrayed, Villa attacked American interests and subsequently eluded the grasp of American forces in Mexico.

**Woodrow Wilson** Democratic president of the United States between 1913 and 1920, Wilson ran on a progressive platform he called the New Freedom to reduce the size of the federal government. Once in office, however, he carried out policies similar to Theodore Roosevelt's. After failing to keep the United States out of World War I, Wilson defined American war aims with his Fourteen Points. He was unable to implement them in full at the Paris Peace conference and failed to convince the Senate to ratify the Treaty of Versailles or enter the League of Nations.

# Suggested Reading

• Crunden, Robert M. *Ministers of Reform: The Progressives' Achievement in American Civilization, 1889–1920.* Chicago: University of Illinois Press, 1985.

Many of these thinkers shared a common background and platform, which Crunden describes in detail.


• Keegan, John. *The First World War.* New York: Vintage Books, 2000.

Keegan offers a very thorough account of the campaigns of the war from start to finish. Specifically, he expounds upon the three disasters at Gallipoli, the Somme, and Passchendaele. Keegan's is one of the premier books on the topic.


• Kennedy, David M. *Over Here: The First World War and American Society.* New York: Oxford University Press, 2003.

Kennedy's book uses World War I as a lens through which to view American society in the twentieth century. He believes that the way America conducted itself in this war reveals essential characteristics about America as a country.


• Macmillan, Margaret. *Paris 1919: Six Months that Changed the World.* New York: Random House, 2003.

After World War I, the "big three" (President Woodrow Wilson, British prime minister David Lloyd George, and French premier Georges Clemenceau) met in Paris to try and restore a sense of stability and peace in the world. Macmillan's book chronicles the numerous events that unfolded during that time.


• Morris, Edmund. *Theodore Rex.* New York: Modern Library Press, 2001.

This biography puts a lively spin on Theodore Roosevelt's two terms as president. Many of his achievements—such as a national conservation policy—are still alive and well in the American political system, which makes this book extremely relevant to modern America as well.

• Weinberg, Arthur, and Lila Shaffer Weinberg. *The Muckrackers*. Chicago: University of Illinois Press, 2001.

*The Muckrackers* explains the way in which muckrackers were able to change America from a passive country to one affected by social and political uprisings.

**CHAPTER 3**
**1901–1920**

# The Roaring Twenties: 1920–1929

4

- Political Conservatism and Prosperity
- Prohibition and the Rise of Organized Crime
- The Culture of Modernism
- Resistance to Modernity
- Impact of Black Culture on Mainstream America
- Emergence of the "New Woman"
- The Stock Market Crash of 1929

The popular images of the twenties—late-night jazz sessions, sequined flappers doing the Charleston, and dapper young men drinking bathtub gin in smoky speakeasies—gave rise to its various nicknames, such as the "Roaring Twenties," the "Jazz Age," and the "Era of Excess." Automobiles, airplanes, radio, movies, mass consumerism, advances for women, and new concepts of morality also pushed Americans into the modern era.

On the other hand, many Americans opposed the headlong rush into modernity and struggled to reassert older, more conservative Protestant values. Republicans, for example, dominated domestic and foreign policy issues and underscored the new American isolationism by refusing to join the League of Nations. They also succeeded in passing stricter immigration laws, as well as the Eighteenth Amendment prohibiting the sale and consumption of alcohol. Membership in the Ku Klux Klan and fundamentalist Christian organizations also skyrocketed to combat immigration, the rise of black nationalism, and new scientific theories that challenged established religious beliefs.

# Political Conservatism and Prosperity

Tired of war and the political squabbling that had characterized the final years of Woodrow Wilson's presidency, Americans craved stable leadership and economic prosperity in the 1920s. Weary voters elected three probusiness conservative Republican presidents in the 1920s: **Warren G. Harding, Calvin Coolidge**, and **Herbert Hoover**. As a result, continuity—rather than change—characterized the political climate of the 1920s.

## WARREN G. HARDING AND NORMALCY

Republican candidate **Warren G. Harding** promised voters a return to **"normalcy"** if elected president in 1920. Disillusioned by the upheaval of World War I, most Americans found Harding's cautious and conservative politics compelling. His popular image as a small-town newspaper editor from the Midwest combined with his consistently neutral policies contributed to his overwhelming victory over Democratic opponent James Cox.

During his three years in office, Harding supported big business, relaxed government control over industry, and promoted high tariffs on imports.

### Resistance to the League of Nations

In order to restore stability both at home and abroad, Harding adopted several measures to reduce the country's international commitments. He signed several peace treaties with Germany, Austria, and Hungary soon after taking office and proposed an arms-reduction plan for a new Europe. In doing so, Harding sidestepped the extremely controversial issue concerning American membership in the **League of Nations** that had plagued Woodrow Wilson. Harding's plan allowed the United States to focus more fully on domestic matters while taking a backstage role in the reconstruction of Europe.

### Scandal

President Harding gave many of the top cabinet positions and civil service jobs to his old chums from Ohio. Unfortunately for the president, the **"Ohio Gang"** quickly sullied Harding's name by accepting bribes, defrauding the government, and bootlegging. In fact, grand juries indicted several of Harding's appointees; a few even received prison sentences. The chain of unending scandals prompted many Americans to questions Harding's own integrity and ability to lead.

The **Teapot Dome scandal** shocked Americans most of all. In 1923, journalists discovered that Harding's secretary of the interior, **Albert B. Fall**, had illegally authorized private companies to drill for oil on public lands. Investigators later determined that these companies had bribed the nearly bankrupt Fall to ignore their actions while they drilled. The naïve Harding escaped implication in the scandal only when he died unexpectedly of a heart attack in 1923. Although the nation expressed grief over his death, more scandals continued to surface throughout the decade and continued to tarnish Harding's reputation.

**CHAPTER 4
1920–1929**

## CONSERVATIVE CALVIN COOLIDGE

The quiet vice president **Calvin Coolidge** entered the White House following Harding's death in 1923. His reserved demeanor, moral uprightness, and distance from the Harding scandals allowed him to win the presidency in his own right the following year in the election of 1924. Although "Silent Cal" Coolidge's personality and public persona differed greatly from Harding's, the two men thought along the same lines politically. Coolidge continued to support big business, propose higher tariffs, and push for deregulation of business and the economy. As a result, his victory in 1924 marked the demise of Progressivism.

## THE PRESIDENCY OF HERBERT HOOVER

Like Harding and Coolidge, **Herbert Hoover** won the presidency in 1928 on a platform for big business and against big government. Having grown accustomed to the prosperity associated with previous conservative presidents, Americans rejected Democratic candidate Alfred E. Smith and voted for Hoover.

*Ironically, Hoover's inflexible conservatism ultimately prevented him from facing the impending economic crisis. The European demand for American exports had dropped, farmers were more and more in debt, and Americans were continuing to live extravagant lifestyles, primarily on credit.*

# Prohibition and the Rise of Organized Crime

The **Eighteenth Amendment** took effect in January 1920, banning the manufacture, sale, and transport of all intoxicating liquors. Referred to by supporters as "the noble experiment," Prohibition succeeded at lowering the consumption of alcohol, at least in rural areas. At the same time, the amendment created a lucrative black market for alcohol sales. Illegal, or **bootlegged**, liquor became widely available in cities. Typically, smugglers brought this liquor into the United States from other countries, while other Americans produced it in small homemade stills. "**Speakeasies**," illegal bars where men and often women drank publicly, opened in most urban areas.

### GANGSTERS AND RACKETEERS

While Prohibition did not necessarily lead to criminal activity and the formation of gangs, both of which existed long before, it did provide criminals with a financially rewarding new business. "**Scarface**" **Al Capone** emerged as the best-known gangster of the era. He moved to Chicago in 1920 and soon became the city's leading bootlegger and gambling lord, protecting his empire with an army of gunmen. Capone's profits reached approximately $60 million annually by 1927. Although authorities generally tolerated bootleggers and speakeasies at first, they cracked down on the gangsters when a Chicago bootlegging gang disguised as police officers gunned down members of a rival gang in the **St. Valentine's Day Massacre**. Authorities eventually prosecuted Capone in 1931 for federal income tax evasion.

### PROHIBITION REPEALED

Because of the widespread availability of black-market liquor, federal authorities had trouble enforcing Prohibition. Still, President Herbert Hoover wanted to continue the morally worthy "experiment" in spite of growing opposition from the general public. Congress eventually passed the **Twenty-First Amendment** in 1933 to repeal Prohibition.

# The Culture of Modernism

The expansion of radio broadcasting, the boom of motion pictures, and the spread of consumerism united the nation culturally. At the same time, these changes contributed to the breakdown of America's traditional vision of itself. As a result, a new national identity began to form.

### THE IMPACT OF RADIO

The popularity of radio soared during the 1920s, bringing Americans together and softening regional differences. With the arrival of the first developed radio station in 1920, the format of radio programming changed dramatically, expanding to include news, music, talk shows, sports broadcasts, political speeches, and advertising. The American public eagerly welcomed radios into their homes, signaling their openness to a changing culture. By simply turning on the radio, they received standardized information transmitted through national broadcasts. They also encountered advertising campaigns designed to change their spending habits and lifestyles.

### THE RISE OF MOTION PICTURES

The American movie industry began in New York City, but when it moved to California in 1915, a true entertainment revolution began. By 1929, nearly every citizen attended the movies weekly, eager to see the latest comedy, thriller, and western. As movie attendance rose, so did the fame of the actors and actresses who performed in them. The "movie star" soon became a figure of glamour and fame.

## MASS PRODUCTION AND THE AUTOMOBILE

Mass production allowed **Henry Ford** and his **Ford Motor Company**—the industry leader during the 1920s—to sell cars at prices that the working class could afford. This vastly increased the automaker's market. Cars made on an assembly line could be produced approximately ten times faster than cars assembled using more traditional means. The rapid increase in the supply of new cars combined with dramatically lower prices led to a vast increase in the total number of cars sold. Throughout the course of the decade, the number of cars on American roads tripled to 23 million.

Car ownership changed the way many people experienced American life. Owning cars allowed Americans in rural areas to take advantage of the amenities of nearby cities. Many smaller towns simply disappeared as increased competition closed numerous small businesses.

*Americans loved cars so much that automobile manufacturing had become the most productive industry in U.S. history by 1930. Roughly one in five people owned cars when the Great Depression hit.*

### AVIATION

Other modes of transportation also progressed in the 1920s. On May 21, 1927, **Charles Lindbergh** completed the first successful solo flight across the Atlantic. The American public celebrated the flight as a triumph not only of individual heroism but also of technological advancement. This flight foreshadowed the emergence of the commercial airline industry, which would boom in the ensuing decades.

### MODERNIST LITERATURE

Intrigued by what they saw as the fast-paced, fractured, unmoored modern world around them, writers in the 1920s struggled to develop a new type of language for expressing a new type of reality. Poets and fiction writers used new techniques such as **free verse** and **stream of consciousness** to capture the national mood.

*Free verse is a form of poetry without a set scheme of rhyme or meter. Stream of consciousness is a literary style in which writers try to give a literary representation of characters' actual thought processes.*

### The Lost Generation

Some of the most prominent American writers of the 1920s actually lived in Europe. Known collectively as the **Lost Generation**, writers such as Ernest Hemingway, Gertrude Stein, Ezra Pound, and Harold Stearns penned bitter commentaries on postwar America. Cynical about the country's potential for progress and about what they perceived to be misappropriated values, these writers found community abroad and produced some of the most creative literature and poetry in American history.

### The Southern Renaissance

In the South, authors dealt with their regions' own transformation from a traditional society to one more influenced by changes in the wider American culture. Bible Belt authors, for example, found abundant material in the struggles of individuals who did not want to relinquish their agrarian lifestyles to modernism. Prominent writers of this movement included William Faulkner, Thomas Wolfe, Alan Tate, and Ellen Glasgow.

*Mississippi native William Faulkner received the Nobel Prize for Literature in 1949 for his modernist novels* The Sound and the Fury, Light in August, *and* As I Lay Dying. *Faulkner mined the emotional depths of the American South and succeeded in both humanizing and mythologizing the tragedy of southern history. Many literary scholars consider him the most important American writer of the twentieth century.*

# Resistance to Modernity

### THE RED SCARE

Americans feared communist and socialist ideas in the wake of the Russian Revolution of 1917. In late 1919, communist fears picked up steam, and in January 1920, police across the nation seized more than 6,000 suspects in a raid to find and expel suspected communists. The government deported many socialists, including several in the New York legislature. Fortunately, the worst of the **Red Scare** had passed by 1921.

### THE EMERGENCY IMMIGRATION ACT

Compelled by imagined threats of foreign influences on American values and the rapidly rising rates of postwar immigration in 1920 and 1921, Congress passed the **Emergency Quota Act of 1921**. The act restricted new arrivals of immigrants to 3 percent of foreign-born members of any given nationality. The **Immigration Act of 1924** reduced this number further to 2 percent.

> Both the Emergency Quota Act of 1921 and the Immigration Act of 1924 blatantly favored northern and western Europeans and limited the influx of darker-skinned Catholics from southern and eastern Europe. The act also banned immigrants from East Asia.

### THE SACCO AND VANZETTI TRIAL

The trial of two Italian anarchists, **Nicola Sacco** and **Bartolomeo Vanzetti,** illustrated Americans' intolerance for foreign ideas and individuals. Tried and convicted for robbery and murder in Massachusetts in 1920, Sacco and Vanzetti faced an openly bigoted judge who failed to give the defendants a fair trial. Although protesters rallied behind them for six years, Sacco and Vanzetti never received a retrial, and state authorities executed them in 1927.

### THE KU KLUX KLAN

The **Ku Klux Klan** reemerged in the 1920s as a misdirected effort to protect American values. Unlike the Klan of the nineteenth century, which had terrorized blacks in the South, the new KKK of the 1920s had a strong following among white Protestants throughout the country. It targeted blacks, immigrants, Jews, Catholics, and other minority groups that threatened the KKK's homogenous values and identity.

Through the course of the decade, the Klan gained a significant amount of political power, exerting both direct and indirect influence on state politics throughout the country. However, by the end of the 1920s, the Klan attracted considerable negative publicity, which, combined with the diminished threat of immigration, led to its downfall.

### THE SCOPES TRIAL

In 1925, a Tennessee court tried high school biology teacher **John Scopes** for teaching the theory of evolution in his classroom in spite of a prohibitory state law. Protestant leaders like **William Jennings Bryan** (a three-time Democratic candidate for president) spoke out against evolution, while Scopes's famed defense attorney **Clarence Darrow** tried to ridicule Christian fundamentalism. Clarence Darrow hounded and ridiculed William Jennings Bryan on the witness stand so extensively that some blame Darrow for Jenning's death from a stress-related illness several days after the trial concluded.

The so-called **Scopes "Monkey" Trial** captured the nation's interest. Although the court found Scopes guilty of violating the law, it only fined him $100. The high-profile trial illustrated the growing tension between tradition and progress.

# *Impact of Black Culture*

As Americans became interested in the new musical sounds coming from cities such as New Orleans, New York, St. Louis, and Chicago, jazz music became the rage of the decade, typifying the fluidity and energy of the era. African Americans also captured their culture in literature and art. Many whites became fascinated by the image of the black American that emerged during the 1920s.

## NEGRO NATIONALISM

**Marcus Garvey** led the "Negro Nationalism" movement, which celebrated the black experience and culture. As the leader of the **United Negro Improvement Association (UNIA)**, Garvey advocated for the establishment of a Negro republic in Africa for exiled Americans. He argued that racial prejudice ran too deep in white American attitudes to ever be satisfactorily fixed and that black Americans should flee to their ancestral lands. Garvey's influence lessened after he went to prison in 1925 for federal mail fraud. His deportation to Jamaica in 1927 effectively ended his power within the African-American community.

## THE NAACP

**The National Association for the Advancement of Colored People (NAACP)**, established in 1910, remained active in the 1920s. Unlike the UNIA, the NAACP sought to resolve the racial issues in American society. The organization focused specifically on the dissemination of information and the implementation of protective legislation. In 1922, for example, the NAACP succeeded in getting a bill passed that helped end lynching. Although the bill remained mired in the House of Representatives for three years, public attention surrounding the bill helped reduce the number of lynchings in the United States.

## THE HARLEM RENAISSANCE

The **Harlem Renaissance** was one of the major African-American cultural and artistic movements during the era. Black authors depicted experiences from urban Manhattan to rural Georgia and included Claude McKay, Langston Hughes, Zora Neale Hurston, and Alain Locke. Their poems and narratives not only captured the diversity of the African-American experience but also highlighted the rich culture of black America.

## JAZZ

The growth of **jazz** music in the 1920s coupled the cultural expression of black Americans with mainstream culture by tapping into the emerging spirit of youth, freedom, and openness. The jazz movement also dissolved many traditional racial barriers in music, allowing young musicians of all races to collaborate and forge individual avenues of expression.

# Emergence of the "New Woman"

Women's roles changed at an unprecedented rate. Oppressive taboos such as those against smoking, drinking, and sexually provocative behavior slackened during the decade as women sought more freedom and self-expression. Some women began experimenting with new styles of dress, danced more, and discussed sex openly and freely. However, historians note that most women in the 1920s still adhered to traditional gender roles and customs despite the new freedoms and morality.

CHAPTER 4
1920–1929

### SUFFRAGE AND THE NINETEENTH AMENDMENT

After the **Nineteenth Amendment** granted women the right to vote in 1920, former suffragettes formed the **League of Women Voters** to educate American women about candidates, issues, and the political process. Although some Americans feared the political leanings of the new electoral contingency, the addition of women voters had very little impact on voting trends because many women did not exercise their newly earned right to vote.

Many immigrant and southern women, for example, often chose not to vote because they didn't want to challenge the traditional authority of their husbands. On the other hand, those who did vote showed little solidarity in their commitment to the advancement of women in society. Activists like **Alice Paul** of the newly formed Woman's Party lobbied for feminist goals, such as equal rights and greater social justice. The majority of American women, however, still found such radical feminism distasteful and instead chose to fight for moderate and gradual reform through established parties.

Division within the women's movement ultimately led to the defeat of the **Equal Rights Amendment (ERA)**. Proposed in 1923, the ERA would have granted men and women equal legal rights. Female lobbyists did succeed in convincing Congress to pass other significant laws to help women. For example, the **Sheppard-Towner Act** passed in 1921 awarding federal funds for healthcare to women and infants. Unfortunately, such protective legislation and social welfare programs suffered without legislators' vigilant care, and Congress eventually abandoned the Sheppard-Towner program in 1929 to cut costs. Most other legislative efforts concerning women met similar fates.

*Although more and more women began working outside the home throughout the 1920s, they filled primarily service and clerical jobs. Women had few professional opportunities, because social norms still dictated that they should be homemakers above all else. Most working women kept their jobs only until marriage.*

### FLAPPERS

**Flapper** women became the icon of the 1920s with their short "bobbed" hair, makeup, dangling jewelry, short skirts, and zest for modernity. Unlike the women of previous generations, flappers drank, smoked, danced, flirted, and caroused with men freely and easily. Even though very few women actually became flappers, the image appealed widely to the filmmakers, novelists, and advertisers who made them famous. Thrust into the limelight, flappers helped transform Americans' conservative conceptions of propriety and morality.

# The Stock Market Crash of 1929

The prosperity of the 1920s finally ended when the **"bull market"** suddenly showed the strain of overvaluation in the fall of 1929. The value of the stock market had more than quadrupled during the 1920s primarily because Americans had purchased stock **"on margin"** by using the *future* earnings from their investments to buy even more stock. Even though buying stock on margin grossly distorted the real value of the investments, most people naively assumed the market would continue to climb. Therefore, they funded their lavish lifestyles on credit.

When the market buckled and stock prices began to slip, brokers made "**margin calls**" requesting investors to pay off the debts owed on stock purchased on margin. Unfortunately, most people didn't have the cash to pay back the brokers. Instead, they tried to sell all their investments quickly to come up with the extra money. The surge in stock dumping eventually caused the most catastrophic market crash in American history on **Black Tuesday**: October 29, 1929. In spite of attempts by major investors to bolster the rapidly declining market, Black Tuesday marked the beginning of the rapid economic collapse known as the **Great Depression**.

Identify a major work of literature that effectively deals with the tensions and struggles inherent in American life in the 1920s and describe how it accomplishes this aim.

The satirical novel *Babbitt* by Sinclair Lewis reveals the impact of the major economic and political upheavals of the 1920s on the average citizen. In this novel, Lewis identifies the rise of consumer culture, threats to traditional social institutions, and the implications of industrialization for workers. The character George Babbitt represents an everyman who is struggling to meet society's demands while maintaining his personal integrity.

During the 1920s, abundant production of goods led to the rise of mass-market consumer culture, which encouraged people to associate their personal identities with the material goods they purchased. George thinks constantly about what he buys and what he could buy. While he tries to remain practical and frugal, he secretly basks in the feeling of wealth his possessions invoke. Through exaggerated details and images, Lewis highlights the inflated significance that such possessions bore for his characters. The increasing accessibility of these goods gave the American people a hollow sense of success that was previously earned only through hard work and self-sacrifice.

Economic and cultural changes, including the rise of the middle class and the feminist movement, threatened the basic institutions of family, morality, and religion during the 1920s. It is obvious how bored George has grown with old conventions. He displays an increasing dissatisfaction with his marriage and his family and begins to crave interactions with the wild, independent women he has heard stories about. He loses interest in proper, traditional women like his wife and no longer wants to kiss an "unflushing cheek" with his "unmoving lips." He craves the unknown, and the previously forbidden joy of unchecked personal freedom.

Paradoxically, George presents himself to the world as a conservative person committed to traditional institutions. His reckless yearnings are confined to his inner life, which he conceals

# *Student Essay*

by maintaining the appearance of a more traditional person. George embodies the conflict of a society throttling into modernity—at once exhilarated and frightened by its potential—while also yearning nostalgically for the stability of tradition. He both loves technology and finds himself a slave to it. During his rebellion, "he felt that he had found something in life, and that he had made a terrifying, thrilling break with everything that was decent and normal." Yet every time George starts to lose direction, he immerses himself in his suburban lifestyle with newfound fervor.

As a result of tension between the modern and the traditional, mainstream individuals routinely found their personal integrity in compromise. Consequently, both traditional morals and new trends seemed equally hollow to sophisticated observers like Sinclair Lewis, as well as such writers as F. Scott Fitzgerald and T. S. Eliot. Hypocrisy is the norm in Lewis's worlds where people continuously uphold public standards that differ dramatically from private behavior; George constantly claims not to care about public opinion, but the demands of upholding moral standards torture him inside. By presenting words like "Marriage" and "Domestic Matters" in capital letters, Lewis not only mocks the importance people placed on traditional institutions but also effectively portrays the hollowness of these institutions' inflated ideas. Lewis's satire of middle-class life shows that dreams of material wealth, affluence, and status existed as empty illusions, which would ultimately only disappoint and mislead his characters and his readers.

# Test Questions and Answers

## 1. How were Harding's, Coolidge's, and Hoover's presidencies similar?

- All supported big business.

- All demonstrated a flagrant disregard for the Progressive ideals that had characterized Theodore Roosevelt's and Woodrow Wilson's presidencies.

- All opposed government intervention in the economy.

- All wanted to maintain a high degree of economic prosperity.

## 2. Discuss the ways in which conservative Americans challenged the new culture of modernity in the 1920s.

- Congress passed the Emergency Immigration Act to restrict the number of immigrants from eastern and southern Europe.

- The heavily biased Sacco-Vanzetti trial demonstrated many Americans' nativist feelings.

- The Red Scare highlighted Americans' fears concerning the spread of communism.

- A new Ku Klux Klan emerged to uphold conservative white Protestant ideals.

- The Scopes Trial illustrated the degree to which many Americans objected to scientific challenges to their traditional religious beliefs.

## 3. What effect did automobiles have on Americans?

- They improved transportation and prompted the government to lay better roads.

- They prompted the development of suburban communities.

- They encouraged millions of people to leave the countryside and move to the cities.

## 4. How did fundamentalist Christianity express itself in the 1920s?

- Fundamentalists served as the backbone of the temperance movement and later for Prohibition.

- Fundamentalists also protested the teaching of evolution, most famously in the 1925 Scopes Trial.

## 5. How did the roles of women change during the 1920s?

- Many women experimented with new styles of dress, featuring bobbed hair, short skirts, and dangling beads made popular by the "flappers."

- Women discovered new freedoms as Americans revised older Victorian concepts of morality and sexuality.

- Women joined the workforce in significant numbers.

- The Nineteenth Amendment granted women the right to vote.

## 6. In what ways did racial tensions surface during the 1920s?

- The Emergency Immigration Act banned "undesirable" immigrants from southern and eastern Europe.

- The Sacco-Vanzetti trial proved the prevalence of nativist sentiments in America at the time.

- Membership in the Ku Klux Klan surged.

- A new Black Nationalism emerged.

## 7. What new trends in American literature flourished during the 1920s?

- New writing devices like stream of consciousness and free verse defied conventional conceptions of style.

- Black American authors captured the uniqueness of the Black American experience.

- Southern writers highlighted the tensions between tradition and modernism as experienced by small-town Americans.

# Timeline

| | |
|---|---|
| **1919** | The Red Scare begins. |
| **1920** | Prohibition begins with the Eighteenth Amendment. |
| | Women earn equal suffrage in the Nineteenth Amendment. |
| | Former suffragettes form the League of Women Voters. |
| | Warren G. Harding is elected president. |
| **1921** | Congress passes the Emergency Immigration Act. |
| | Congress passes the Sheppard-Towner Act. |
| **1923** | The Teapot Dome scandal shocks Americans. |
| | Harding dies and Vice President Calvin Coolidge becomes president. |
| | The Equal Rights Amendment (ERA) is proposed. |
| **1924** | Coolidge is elected president. |
| | Congress passes the Immigration Act of 1924. |
| **1925** | Biology teacher John Scopes is tried for teaching evolution. |
| **1927** | Charles Lindbergh completes the first solo flight across the Atlantic. |
| | Nicola Sacco and Bartolomeo Vanzetti are executed. |
| **1928** | Herbert Hoover is elected president. |
| **1929** | Al Capone is prosecuted for tax evasion. |
| | The stock market crashes on Black Tuesday. |

# Major Figures

**William Jennings Bryan**  The former Populist Party poster boy, champion of free silver, and three-time presidential candidate, Bryan served as a key witness against biology teacher John Scopes in the 1925 Scopes Trial.

**Al Capone**  Perhaps the most infamous gangster in American history, "Scarface" Capone led a major bootlegging ring in Chicago during the 1920s. He managed to evade prosecution until a court convicted him of income tax evasion in 1929.

**Calvin Coolidge**  A superconservative from Massachusetts, Coolidge served as vice president under Warren G. Harding and became president in 1923 after Harding died in office. He then became president in his own right in 1924, but declined the offer to run again in 1928. Like both his predecessor and his successor Herbert Hoover, Coolidge struck down the remnants of Progressive-style legislation in favor of rewarding big business.

**Clarence Darrow**  Undoubtedly the most famous lawyer in his day, Darrow represented John Scopes during the 1925 Scopes "Monkey" Trial. Although he technically lost the case, his relentless badgering of William Jennings Bryan ridiculed Christian fundamentalism.

**Albert Fall**  Secretary of the Interior under Warren G. Harding, Fall accepted bribes from oil companies to look the other way while they illegally drilled for oil on public lands. The Teapot Dome scandal of 1923 rocked Washington and sullied the president's reputation.

**Henry Ford**  Inventor of the Model T Ford that launched the Ford automobile company, mechanical genius Ford transformed industrial America with his perfected method of assembly-line production that could produce several brand-new cars every minute.

**Marcus Garvey**  An early civil rights activist, Garvey urged descendants of former slaves to return to their ancestral homes in Africa and take pride in their own culture and achievements.

**Warren G. Harding**  Harding's election in 1920 not only killed Woodrow Wilson's hopes of joining the League of Nations, but inaugurated a decade of conservatism and benefits for big business. The Teapot Dome scandal erupted in 1923 shortly before his untimely death.

**Herbert Hoover** President of the United States from 1929–1933, Hoover supported big business and limited government regulation of industry or the economy.

**Alice Paul** An ardent suffragette and women's rights activist, Paul campaigned for social, economic, and political equality for women as the leader of the Women's Party.

**Nicola Sacco** A Massachusetts jury convicted Italian anarchist Sacco and his accomplice Bartolomeo Vanzetti for a bank robbery and murder in1920. Their speedy and rather unfair trial highlighted Americans' disdain for immigrants.

**John Scopes** A high school biology instructor, Scopes brought the debate between Christian fundamentalism and Darwin's theories of natural selection to the fore when he challenged a Tennessee state law forbidding the teaching of evolution. A court ultimately found him guilty in the infamous 1925 Scopes "Monkey" Trial and fined him $100.

**Bartolomeo Vanzetti** A Massachusetts jury convicted Italian anarchist Vanzetti and his accomplice, Nicola Sacco, for a bank robbery and murder in1920. Their speedy and rather unfair trial highlighted Americans' disdain for immigrants.

# Suggested Reading

- Galbraith, John Kenneth. *Great Crash 1929*. Boston: Mariner Books, 1997.

Galbraith uses wit to explain one of the most peculiar periods in American history and exposes the shady actions of investors, as well as the government's reticence to involve itself in the economy.

- Goldberg, David. *Discontented America: The United States in the 1920s*. Baltimore: Johns Hopkins University Press, 1999.

Historian Goldberg synthesizes social and political history to depict the 1920s in an unusual light. He emphasizes the fact that this decade was a postwar period and consequently presents the facts of the 1920s in a new way. In particular, he sheds light on the pervasive sense of discontent in America and the consequences of that discontent.

- Latham, Angela. *Posing a Threat: Flappers, Chorus Girls, and Other Brazen Performers of the American 1920s*. Middleton, Connecticut: Wesleyan University Press, 2000.

Latham presents a dual image of women during the 1920s. She admits that women were exploited by some of their endeavors during this time period, but she also points out that some women were able to take control of their own exploitation.

- Watson, Steve. *The Harlem Renaissance: Hub of African-American Culture, 1920-1930*. New York: Pantheon, 1995.

This "first self-conscious black literary constellation in American history" entails a mix of artwork and text. Watson explores the internal contradictions of the Harlem Renaissance with his illuminating narration.

# The Great Depression and the New Deal: 1929–1939

- The Depression Begins
- Hoover's Response
- FDR and the First New Deal
- Opposition to the New Deal
- The Second New Deal
- The End of the New Deal

The New Deal marked a major turning point in American history. Never before had the federal government become so involved in the daily lives of ordinary people. Unlike his Republican predecessor Herbert Hoover, Roosevelt and the New Dealers tried to directly help as many people as conservatives in Congress and the Supreme Court would permit. Much historical evidence suggests that had Roosevelt not been elected president, the Depression would have been much worse. The Canadian economy, for example, remained virtually unchanged during the entire ten-year period after the Crash of 1929 due to the relatively conservative government's policies of nonintervention.

The New Deal ultimately failed to end the Depression. Hunger, homelessness, and unemployment still affected millions of Americans even as late as December 1941, when the United States entered World War II. Many historians and economists have suggested that the New Deal would have been more successful had Roosevelt put even more money into the economy. Only after the surge in demand for war munitions, ships, tanks, and airplanes did the economy finally right itself and leap forward.

# The Depression Begins

The "Roaring Twenties" came to a crashing halt in 1929. By late October, more and more people had pulled their money out of Wall Street. Consequently, the Dow Jones Industrial Average fell steadily during a ten-day period until it finally crashed completely on October 29, 1929. This day came to be known as **"Black Tuesday."**

On Black Tuesday, investors panicked and dumped an unprecedented 16 million shares. The practice of buying on margin had destroyed Americans' credit and only made the effects of the **Crash of 1929** (or **Great Crash**) worse. Within only one month's time, American investors had lost tens of billions of dollars.

### CAUSES OF THE DEPRESSION

Although the 1929 stock-market crash had acted as the catalyst, a confluence of several factors actually caused the Great Depression.

### A Changing Economy

The foundation of the American economy slowly shifted from heavy industrial production to mass manufacturing. In other words, whereas most of America's wealth had come from producing iron, steel, coal, and oil at the end of the nineteenth century, manufacturing consumer goods like automobiles, radios, and other goods formed the basis of the economy in the twentieth century. As Americans jumped on the consumer bandwagon, more and more people began purchasing goods on credit, promising to pay for items later.

When the 1920s economic bubble burst, creditors had to absorb the cost of millions in bad loans that debtors couldn't repay. Moreover, policymakers found it difficult to end the Depression's vicious circle—Americans couldn't buy goods until they had jobs, but no factories wanted to give people jobs because they couldn't sell goods to a penniless population.

### Buying on Margin

Americans had also purchased millions of dollars in stock on credit. Investors could purchase a share of a company's stock, and then use the *projected* earnings of that stock to buy even more. Not surprisingly, many people abused the system to invest huge sums of imaginary money that existed only on paper.

### Overproduction in Factories

Overproduction in manufacturing also contributed to the economic collapse. Factories produced more and more popular consumer goods in an effort to match demand during the 1920s. Output soared as more companies utilized new machines to increase production, but workers' wages remained relatively stagnant throughout the decade. Eventually, the price of goods plummeted when factories began producing more goods than people demanded.

### Overproduction on Farms

Farmers faced a similar overproduction crisis. Increasing debt forced many of them to plant more and more profitable cash crops such as wheat every year. Unfortunately, wheat depletes the soil's nutrients and renders it unsuitable for planting over time, but impoverished farmers couldn't afford to plant any other crop. Harvesting more wheat only depressed prices and forced them to plant even more the next year, which perpetuated the cycle.

### Bad Banking Practices

Poor banking practices didn't help the situation. Many twentieth-century banks were little better than the fly-by-night variety of the previous century, especially in the rural areas of the West and South. The federal government didn't regulate the banks, and Americans had nowhere to turn to lodge complaints against bad banks. In fact, the majority of people had no idea what happened to their money after they handed it over to bankers.

Many bankers capitalized on the bull market to buy stocks on margin with customers' savings. This money simply vanished when the market collapsed, and thousands of families lost their entire savings in a matter of minutes. Hundreds of banks failed

CHAPTER 5
1929–1939

during the first months of the Depression, which produced an even greater panic and rush to withdraw private savings.

### Income Inequality

Income inequality—the greatest in American history—made the Depression extremely severe. At the end of the 1920s, the top 1 percent of Americans owned more than a third of all the nation's wealth, while the poorest 20 percent of people owned a meager 4 percent of the wealth. The middle class, meanwhile, had essentially shrunk into nonexistence. As a result, only a few Americans had vast amounts of wealth while the rest lived barely above the poverty level.

### Old War Debts

The aftermath of World War I in Europe played a significant role in the downward spiral of the global economy in the late 1920s. According to the Treaty of Versailles, Germany owed France and England impossible sums in war reparations. France and England in turn owed millions of dollars to the United States. Starting in Germany, a wave of Depression spread through Europe as each country became unable to pay off its debts. As a result, the Great Depression affected the rest of the industrialized world.

# Hoover's Response

President **Herbert Hoover** and other officials downplayed the crash at first. They claimed that the slump would be temporary, and that it would clean up corruption and bad business practices within the system. Wall Street might not boom again, but it would certainly be healthier. The Republican president also believed that the federal government shouldn't interfere with the economy. In fact, he argued, if American families steeled their determination, continued to work hard, and practiced self-reliance, the United States could quickly pull out of the "recession."

## THE RECONSTRUCTION FINANCE CORPORATION

Instead of tackling the problem pro-actively, Hoover took an indirect approach to jump-starting the economy. He created several committees in the early 1930s to assist American farm and industrial corporations. In 1932 he also approved Congress's **Reconstruction Finance Corporation** to provide loans to banks, insurance companies, railroads, and state governments. He hoped that federal dollars dropped into the top of the economic system would help all Americans as the money "trickled down" to the bottom. Individuals were not eligible for RFC loans. Hoover refused to lower the steep tariffs and shot down all "socialistic" relief proposals, such as the **Muscle Shoals Bill** drafted to harness energy from the Tennessee River.

*The Crash of 1929 caused a panic that rapidly developed into a depression the likes of which Americans had never experienced. Millions lost their jobs and their homes as most factories laid off workers in the cities to cut production and expenses. Shantytowns, or "**Hoovervilles**," filled with the homeless and unemployed, sprang up overnight in cities throughout America.*

**CHAPTER 5
1929–1939**

## THE DUST BOWL

The Depression also hit farmers hard, especially those in Colorado, Oklahoma, New Mexico, Kansas, and the Texas panhandle. Years of farming wheat without alternating crops to replenish the soil had turned the earth into a thick layer of barren dust. Depressed crop prices due to overproduction also forced many farmers off their fields. Unable to grow anything, thousands of families left this **Dust Bowl** region in search of work on the West Coast. Author John Steinbeck immortalized the plight of these farmers in his 1939 novel ***The Grapes of Wrath***.

## THE BONUS ARMY

Middle-aged World War I veterans were also among the hardest hit. In 1924, Congress had agreed to pay veterans a bonus stipend to be collected in 1945. As the Depression worsened, more and more of the veterans demanded their bonuses early. When Congress refused to pay up, more than 20,000 vets formed the

**"Bonus Army"** and marched on Washington, D.C., in the summer of 1932. They set up a giant, filthy Hooverville in front of the Capitol and were determined not to leave until the government paid them. Hoover eventually ordered General Douglas MacArthur (of World War II fame) to forcibly remove the Bonus Army. Federal troops used tear gas and fire to destroy the makeshift camp in what the press dubbed the **Battle of Anacostia Flats**.

> *President Hoover's inability to recognize the severity of the crisis or the potential for disaster only worsened the Depression. Many historians and economists believe that Hoover could have dampened the effects of the Depression had he only regulated the finance sector of the economy and provided direct relief to the unemployed and homeless.*

### THE ELECTION OF 1932

The brutal treatment of America's war heroes further convinced people that Hoover simply didn't have the gumption or knowledge to resolve the economic crisis. Instead, all eyes focused on the optimistic Democrat, Governor **Franklin Delano Roosevelt (FDR)** of New York. A distant cousin of former president Theodore Roosevelt, FDR promised more direct relief and assistance rather than benefits for big business. Republicans nominated Hoover for a second term in the election of 1932 but couldn't compete with the Democrats. In the end, Roosevelt soundly defeated Hoover, carrying all but six states.

# FDR and the First New Deal

Roosevelt's policies did much to get Americans back on their feet. The New Deal not only provided **relief**, **recovery**, and **reform**, but it also drastically changed the federal government's role in politics and society. His successful application of John Maynard Keynes's economic theories transformed Democrats into social-welfare advocates. Even decades after the Great Depression, these politicians would fight for more government intervention in the economy, redistribution of wealth, and aid for the neediest.

## THE FIRST HUNDRED DAYS

Americans had voted for Franklin Delano Roosevelt in the election of 1932 on the assumption that the Democrat would spur Washington to dole out more federal assistance. True to his word, the new president immediately set out to provide relief, recovery, and reform in his bundle of programs, collectively known as the **New Deal**.

Roosevelt drew much of his inspiration for the New Deal from the writings of British economist **John Maynard Keynes,** who believed that government deficit spending could prime the economic pump and jump-start the economy. With the support of a panicked Democratic Congress, Roosevelt created most of the **"alphabet agencies"** of the **First New Deal** within his **First Hundred Days** in office.

### Banking Relief and Reform

On March 6, 1933—just two days after becoming president—Roosevelt declared a five-day national **bank holiday** to temporarily close the banks. Roughly 9,000 banks had closed during each year of the Depression under Hoover, and the new president hoped that a short break would give the surviving banks time to reopen on more solid footing. Congress also passed Roosevelt's **Emergency Banking Relief Act**, which gave Roosevelt the power to regulate banking transactions and foreign exchange, and the **Glass-Steagall Banking Reform Act** of 1933, which protected savings deposits. The act created the **Federal Deposit Insurance Corporation (FDIC)** that insured individuals' savings of up to $5,000 (today, deposits of up to $100,000 are insured). The act also forbade banks from investing in the stock market and regulated lending policies.

> After resolving the banking crisis, Roosevelt broadcast the first of his radio **"fireside chats"** to over 50 million listeners to encourage Americans to redeposit their money in the new banks. The fireside chats were a large reason for Roosevelt's popularity; they allowed Americans to feel a real sense of connection with the president.

### The Civilian Conservation Corps (CCC)

Congress also created the **Civilian Conservation Corps (CCC)** in March 1933. Commonly known as the CCC, the corps hired unemployed young men to work on environmental conservation projects throughout the country. For thirty dollars a month, the men worked on flood control and reforestation projects, improved national parks, and built many public roads. Approximately 3 million men worked in CCC camps during the program's nine-year existence.

### The Federal Emergency Relief Administration (FERA, CWA)

The so-called "Hundred Days Congress" also created the **Federal Emergency Relief Administration (FERA)** in May 1933. During the course of the Depression, FERA doled out $500 million to the states. The administration assigned roughly half of this money to bail out bankrupt state and local governments. States matched the other half (three state dollars for every one federal dollar) and distributed it directly to the people. Over the years, FERA gave more than three billion dollars to the states. In addition, FERA created the **Civil Works Administration (CWA)** to create temporary labor jobs to those most in need.

### The Agricultural Adjustment Administration (AAA)

Roosevelt encouraged the creation of the **Agricultural Adjustment Administration (AAA)** to assist farmers. The AAA temporarily reset production quotas for farm commodities, including corn, wheat, rice, milk, cotton, and livestock. The AAA also subsidized farmers to reduce production so that prices would eventually rise again.

Congress also passed the **Farm Credit Act** to provide loans to farmers in danger of bankruptcy.

### The Tennessee Valley Authority (TVA)

May 1933 heralded the creation of the **Tennessee Valley Authority (TVA)** as well. Congress created the TVA to modernize and reduce unemployment in the Tennessee River Valley, one of the poorest regions in the country even before the Depression.

The TVA hired local workers to construct a series of dams and hydroelectric power plants that brought cheap electricity to thousands of people. The public corporation also created affordable employee housing, manufactured cheap fertilizer, and drained thousands of acres for farming.

### The National Industrial Recovery Act (NRA, PWA)

Roosevelt and Congress attempted to revive the economy as a whole with the **National Industrial Recovery Act** in 1933. The act created two administrations:

- **The National Recovery Administration (NRA)**, which stimulated industrial production and improved competition by drafting corporate codes of conduct. The administration also sought to limit production of consumer goods to drive prices up.

- **The Public Works Administration (PWA)**, which constructed public roads, bridges, and buildings. In accordance with Keynesian economic theories, Roosevelt believed that improving public infrastructure would prime the pump and put more money into the economy.

### RESTRUCTURING AMERICAN FINANCE

Roosevelt spurred Congress to establish new regulations on the financial sector of the economy. After taking office, Roosevelt took the country off the gold standard, which had previously allowed citizens and foreign countries to exchange paper money for gold anytime they wanted. He also ordered Americans to hand over their stockpiles of gold to the U.S. Treasury in exchange for paper dollars. Roosevelt also created the **Securities Exchange Commission (SEC)** to regulate trading on Wall Street and curb the wild speculation that had led to the Crash of 1929.

### THE INDIAN REORGANIZATION ACT

Native Americans also received federal assistance. In 1934, Congress passed the **Indian Reorganization Act** to promote tribal reorganization and give federal recognition to tribal governments. More important, nearly 100,000 young Native American men participated in relief programs, such as the Civilian Conservation Corps, PWA, and WPA.

The Indian Reorganization Act changed relations between the various tribes and federal government because it reversed the 1887 Dawes Severalty Act. The Dawes Act had weakened tribal affiliations by stipulating that only individual Native Americans—not tribal councils—could own land. Unfortunately, despite Roosevelt's efforts to alleviate Native American suffering, the Indian Reorganization Act accomplished very little. Some tribes had difficulty understanding the terms of the new treaty, for example, while tribes like the Navajo simply rejected it.

| | Legislation/Policy/Program | How It Helped |
|---|---|---|
| **First New Deal** | | |
| March 9, 1933 | Emergency Banking Relief Act | Relief |
| March 31, 1933 | Civilian Conservation Corps (CCC) | Relief and Recovery |
| April 19, 1933 | The United States goes off the Gold Standard | Recovery and Reform |
| May 12, 1933 | Federal Emergency Relief Administration (FERA) | Relief |
| May 12, 1933 | Agricultural Adjustment Association (AAA) | Relief and Recovery |
| May 18, 1933 | Tennessee Valley Authority (TVA) | Relief, Recovery, and Reform |
| June 16, 1933 | National Industrial Recovery Act (NIRA) | Relief, Recovery, and Reform |
| June 16, 1933 | Public Works Administration (PWA) | Relief and Recovery |
| June 16, 1933 | Glass-Steagall Banking Reform Act (w/FDIC) | Reform |
| November 9, 1933 | Civil Works Administration (CWA) | Relief |
| June 6, 1934 | Securities Exchange Commission (SEC) | Reform |
| June 18, 1934 | Indian Reorganization Act (IRA) | Reform |
| **Second New Deal** | | |
| May 6, 1935 | Works Progress Administration (WPA) | Relief and Recovery |
| July 5, 1935 | National Labor Relations Act (Wagner Act) | Reform |
| August 14, 1935 | Social Security Act | Reform |
| February 29, 1936 | Soil Conservation and Domestic Allotment Act | Relief and Recovery |
| September 1, 1937 | United States Housing Authority (USHA) | Relief, Recovery, and Reform |
| February 16, 1938 | Second Agricultural Adjustment Association (AAA) | Relief and Recovery |
| June 25, 1938 | Fair Labor Standards Act | Reform |

**CHAPTER 5**
**1929–1939**

# Opposition to the New Deal

Roosevelt and the New Deal faced opposition from critics on both ends of the political spectrum. Politicians on the right referred to the New Deal as "Creeping Socialism" because they believed it threatened to subvert American capitalism. Others on the far left claimed that Roosevelt and New Dealers had not done enough to help people or stabilize the economy. They regarded capitalism as a dying system and believed that FDR had made misguided and futile attempts to salvage the doomed enterprise.

### CRITICS FROM THE RIGHT

Conservative critics of the New Deal feared that FDR would open the gates to the leftist movements that had already gained footholds throughout the world. In 1934, the **American Liberty League**, led by former Democratic presidential hopeful **Al Smith** and funded by the Du Pont family, claimed that FDR wanted to destroy free-enterprise capitalism and pave the way for communism, fascism, or both in America. Big business generally opposed the New Deal, too, out of fears that the federal government would support organized labor.

### CRITICS FROM THE FAR LEFT

The New Deal faced nearly as much criticism from the progressive left as from the conservative right. Some ultraliberals, for example, thought that FDR's New Deal conceded too much to the wealthy and failed to resolve the problems in the financial sector.

#### Father Charles Coughlin

A Catholic priest named **Charles Coughlin** became one of the most recognizable opponents of the New Deal when he began broadcasting his criticisms on a weekly radio program. He became so popular that he amassed a following of 40 million listeners within just a few years. He blamed the Depression primarily on crooked Wall Street financiers and Jews and campaigned for the nationalization of the entire American banking system.

### *Huey P. Long*

Senator **Huey P. "Kingfish" Long** of Louisiana also condemned the New Deal. He believed that income inequality had caused the Depression, and he promoted his **"Share Our Wealth"** program, or **"Every Man a King"** program, to levy enormous taxes on the rich so that every American family could earn at least $5,000 a year. He enjoyed enormous popularity during the first few years of Roosevelt's first term but was assassinated in 1935.

### *Francis E. Townsend*

Radio personality **Dr. Francis E. Townsend** also believed he had the solution to drastically reduce poverty. Townsend proposed that the government pay senior citizens approximately $200 every month on the condition that recipients had to spend all their money in order to put money back into the economy. He and Father Caughlin created the **National Union for Social Justice** and even ran as a candidate for the presidency in 1936.

*Soviet Russian agents in the United States actually launched a "popular front" campaign to actively support FDR and the New Deal. An unprecedented number of people joined the American Communist Party during this decade as well. Yet, many socialist activists denounced the New Deal because they believed it was still too conservative.*

# The Second New Deal

FDR responded to many of these critiques with a second bundle of New Deal legislation. Known simply as the **Second New Deal**, Congress passed this follow-up wave of legislation between 1935 and 1938.

The Second New Deal differed drastically from the First New Deal in that its legislation relied more heavily on **Keynesian-style deficit spending**. Keynes strongly believed that the government needed to increase spending during times of economic crisis in order to stimulate the economy. The acceptance of his ideas was in part due to complaints from critics like Huey Long but also simply because it was clear by 1935 that more Americans still needed federal relief assistance. Approximately half of the Second New Deal programs and policies were aimed at long-term reform.

### THE WORKS PROGRESS ADMINISTRATION

Congress launched the Second New Deal with the **Works Progress Administration (WPA)** in 1935 in an effort to appease those like Senator Long who clamored for more direct assistance from the federal government. Similar to the Public Works Administration of the First New Deal, the WPA hired nearly 10 million Americans to construct new public buildings, roads, and bridges. Congress dumped over $10 billion into these projects in just under a decade.

### THE SOCIAL SECURITY ACT

Congress also passed the **Social Security Act** in 1935. This act created a federal retirement pension system for many workers that was funded by a double tax on every working American's paychecks. It also created an unemployment insurance plan to temporarily assist those out of work, and made funds available to the blind and physically disabled. Finally, it stipulated that Congress would match federal dollars for every state dollar allocated to workers' compensation funds.

*The 1935 Social Security Act was undoubtedly the most sweeping of the new laws. This was not only because it provided income to some of the most destitute but also because it forever changed the way Americans thought about work and retirement. People came to recognize retirement as something every working American should be able to enjoy. Still, the program was criticized for not extending pensions to enough people, particularly unskilled African Americans and women.*

## MORE HELP FOR FARMERS

Roosevelt provided more assistance to farmers. After the Supreme Court declared the Agricultural Adjustment Administration unconstitutional in 1936, Democrats immediately responded with the passage of the **Soil Conservation and Domestic Allotment Act** the same year. This act continued to subsidize farmers to curb overproduction and also paid them to plant soil-enriching crops (instead of wheat) or to not grow anything at all so that nutrients would return to the soil. In 1938, Congress created a **Second Agricultural Adjustment Administration** to reduce total crop acreage.

## LABOR REFORM

Much of the Second New Deal legislation promoted organized labor and included these important acts:

- **The National Labor Relations Act**, or **Wagner Act**, passed in 1935, which protected workers' right to organize and strike

- **The Fair Labor Standards Act**, passed in 1938, which established a national minimum wage and a forty-hour work week in some sectors of the economy and the outlawing of child labor

Like the Social Security Act, these labor reforms also had a lasting effect. The 1935 Wagner Act paved the way for collective bargaining and striking. Within a year, fledgling labor unions had made great headway fighting for better hours and higher wages. For example, assembly-line workers in the General

Motors automobile factory used the Wagner Act to initiate a series of sit-down strikes (workers would sit at their stations and refuse to leave, preventing the company from hiring new "scab" workers). By 1937, the company had recognized their right to organize. The Fair Labor and Standards Act also helped promote concepts of minimum wages and child-labor laws.

> New federal protection for organized labor prompted many unskilled workers to unionize under the leadership of **John L. Lewis**, a ranking member of the American Federation of Labor. Lewis organized the **Committee of Industrial Organization** within the larger AFL framework, but tensions between the mostly skilled workers in the AFL and the unskilled workers in the CIO eventually split the two groups in 1937. The Committee of Industrial Organization then became the **Congress of Industrial Organizations** and remained independent until it rejoined with the AFL in 1955.

## THE ELECTION OF 1936

By the time the 1936 elections came around, Republicans barely stood a chance against FDR and the Democrats. The Democratic effort to provide relief, recovery, and reform had by this time become highly visible and had won the support of blacks (who voted Democrat for the first time in large numbers), unskilled laborers, and those in the West and South. Republicans nevertheless nominated moderate Kansas Governor **Alfred M. Landon** on an anti-New Deal platform. Not surprisingly, Roosevelt won a landslide victory—523 electoral votes to Landon's eight—and proved that Americans widely supported the New Deal.

# The End of the New Deal

In 1938, the New Deal steamroller came to an end. A conservative Supreme Court put the brakes on federal control of the economy and Keynesian-style deficit spending. Roosevelt's own political greed, as well as the recession in 1937, also turned many Americans against the New Dealers.

## LEGAL BATTLES

The Republican-dominated Supreme Court had begun to strike down several key pieces of First New Deal legislation in the mid 1930s. For example:

- **Schecter v. United States** in 1935 declared that the National Industrial Recovery Act violated the Constitution because it gave too many powers to the president and attempted to control *intra*state commerce rather than *inter*state trade.

- **Butler v. United States** in 1936 declared that the Agricultural Adjustment Administration also violated the Constitution because it unconstitutionally tried to exert federal control over agricultural production.

### Roosevelt's Court-Packing Scheme

Roosevelt believed the NRA and AAA were crucial to reviving the American economy and feared that any more conservative rulings would cripple or even kill the New Deal entirely. Consequently, he petitioned Congress in 1937 to alter the makeup of the Court; he believed that the justices' old age might affect their ability to concentrate on their work. He also asked for the power to appoint as many as six new justices (to bring the total to fifteen) and for the authority to replace justices over the age of seventy.

FDR's **"court-packing scheme"** backfired. Instead of winning over Democrats and New Dealers in Congress, it had the opposite effect. Even Roosevelt's most ardent fans were shocked by the president's blatant disregard for the cherished tradition of separation of powers. Roosevelt repeatedly denied charges that he wanted to bend the entire federal government to his will and defended his proposal by arguing that aging justices sometimes couldn't perform their duties. The court-packing debate dragged on for several months before Congress and Roosevelt compromised on making minor reforms in the lower courts, while keeping the Supreme Court untouched and intact. Still, the political damage had been done. Roosevelt's plan to "pack" the Supreme Court with pro–New Dealers did more than anything else to turn Americans and other Democrats away from him and the New Deal.

### THE ROOSEVELT RECESSION

Pressured by conservatives in Congress and even by ardent New Dealers in the cabinet, Roosevelt began to scale back deficit spending in 1937, believing that the worst of the Depression had passed. He drastically reduced the size of the Works Progress Administration, for example, and halted paying farmers federal subsidies.

The early retreat came too soon, and the economy buckled again in the resulting **"Roosevelt Recession."** The stock market crashed again in 1937, and the price of consumer goods dropped significantly. Contrary to conservative beliefs, the economy had not pulled far enough out of the Depression to survive on its own. Roosevelt tried to place the blame on spendthrift business leaders, but Americans didn't believe him. As a result, Democrats lost a significant number of seats in the House and the Senate in the 1938 congressional elections.

### THE HATCH ACT

Republicans in Congress further weakened Roosevelt's power with the **Hatch Act** of 1939, which forbade most civil servants from participating in political campaigns. The act also forbade public office holders (i.e., Roosevelt and New Dealers) from using federal dollars to fund their reelection campaigns. Finally the act made it illegal for Americans who received federal assistance to donate money to politicians.

Conservatives hoped these measures would completely divorce the functions of government from the campaign frenzy and ultimately dislodge entrenched New Dealers who preyed on a desperate public for votes. Blamed for the Roosevelt Recession, for the president's plan to dominate the federal courts, and with their political base kicked out from under them, Democrats and the New Deal met their end in 1938.

Roosevelt's decision to scale back deficit spending in order to appease Republicans and conservative Democrats was a huge mistake. Even though the New Deal had significantly reduced poverty, hunger, and the unemployment rate, the economy was still not ready to stand on its own. This was the last straw for many voters. The Republicans' return in the midterm congressional elections of 1938 was the final blow that effectively killed the New Deal.

Which had the greater effect on the American economy, the First New Deal or the Second New Deal? Which had greater significance after the Depression?

Both the First New Deal (1933–1934) and the Second New Deal (1935–1938) were part of President Franklin D. Roosevelt's plan to stimulate the U.S. economy through deficit spending, but the two bundles of legislation were quite different. The legislation of the First New Deal focused on providing immediate relief directly to the people and bankrupt states. The Second New Deal sought to reform the economy and prevent future depressions. The First New Deal had the more immediate effect on the U.S. economy, while the Second New Deal had much greater significance in securing the nation's finances after the Great Depression.

Most legislation passed during Roosevelt's First Hundred Days was intended to help the poorest Americans, whom his predecessor, Herbert Hoover, had refused to help. For example, the Federal Emergency Relief Administration (FERA), distributed over half a billion dollars in grants to the individual state governments and directly to the citizenry. The Civilian Conservation Corps (CCC), the Civil Works Administration (CWA), and the Public Works Administration (PWA) were also established to create jobs for the unemployed while improving the national infrastructure. The first Agricultural Adjustment Administration (AAA) provided subsidies to farmers as incentives to cut crop production and artificially raise the price of agricultural goods. These programs had an enormous impact on contemporary Americans who were then better able to survive the Depression.

The benefits of these bailout programs were short-term solutions that did not alter the structural flaws in the U.S. economy that had led to the Depression. These agencies funneled money to those who needed it but provided no guarantee that the Depression would not recur. Much of the legislation passed in the Second New Deal, however, tried to reform the system to prevent another catastrophic collapse in the future. The Wagner and Fair Labor Standards Acts altered the power imbalance between big

# *Student Essay*

business and labor by recognizing workers' right to bargain collectively and by establishing a minimum wage and forty-hour work week in select industries. These new laws provided a boost to rising labor organizations that have since become a powerful force in American politics and business. Additionally, the Social Security Act of 1935 started a federal pension system funded by employers and taxpayers to keep the disabled and elderly out of destitution.

Of course, some Second New Deal legislation was dedicated to reenforcing the relief provided by the First New Deal. Roosevelt and Congress formed several new relief organizations, such as the Works Progress Administration and the United States Housing Authority in response to criticisms that the First New Deal had not helped Americans enough. Likewise, there had been some reform-oriented agencies created in 1933 and 1934, such as the Federal Deposit Insurance Corporation, the Tennessee Valley Authority, and the Securities Exchange Commission. But for the most part Roosevelt and his fellow Democrats legislated the First New Deal to provide immediate relief, and the Second New Deal to initiate long-term reform.

The lasting legacy of both programs may be that they established a formula for dealing with economic crises: combining bailout with reform by using federal deficit spending—i.e., money borrowed by the government—to jumpstart the economy. Although the U.S. economy has suffered no disaster as great as the Depression since, in hard times it has relied on these same principles to alleviate recessions.

# Test Questions and Answers

### 1. What caused the Great Depression?

- Drastic income inequality
- The shifting base of the American economy from heavy industry to the production of consumer goods
- Overproduction on farms and in factories
- Bad banking practices
- Buying stock on margin
- Defaulted loans in Britain and France

### 2. How did the New Deal tackle the Depression?

- It provided immediate relief to the neediest Americans via programs like the Federal Emergency Relief Administration (FERA), the Civil Works Administration (CWA), the Public Works Administration (PWA), and the Works Progress Administration (WPA).
- It provided long-term recovery via programs like the Tennessee Valley Authority (TVA) and the National Industrial Recovery Administration (NIRA).
- It made long-term reforms to prevent another depression from occurring in the future with the Glass-Steagall Act, the Indian Reorganization Act, and the Fair Labor Standards Act.

### 3. How did the New Deal affect the banking and financial sectors of the economy?

- The national bank holiday temporarily closed all banks to slow the bank crisis and give banks a chance to reopen on solid footing.
- The Emergency Banking Relief Act gave Roosevelt the power to regulate banking transactions and foreign exchange.
- The Glass-Steagall Banking Reform Act of 1933 protected individuals' savings deposits by creating the Federal Deposit Insurance Corporation (FDIC).

- Roosevelt took the nation off the Gold Standard.

- Roosevelt also created the Securities Exchange Commission to monitor trading on the stock markets.

## 4. Why did some Americans attack the New Deal?

- Conservatives like Al Smith claimed that the New Deal subverted American capitalism.

- Socialists like Huey P. Long, Charles Coughlin, and Francis E. Townsend argued that the New Deal didn't do enough to change Wall Street, address income inequality, or help the poorest Americans.

## 5. Why did the New Deal end?

- The Supreme Court began to strike down several key pieces of the First New Deal like the Agricultural Adjustment Administration (AAA) and the National Industrial Recovery Act (NIRA).

- Roosevelt tried to "pack" the Supreme Court with pro-New Deal justices.

- The "Roosevelt Recession" caused by prematurely cutting back deficit spending.

- Republicans gained seats in the House and Senate in the 1938 midterm elections.

- Congress passed the Hatch Act in 1939 to severely restrict Roosevelt's power.

CHAPTER 5
1929–1939

# Timeline

| | |
|---|---|
| **1929** | The stock market crashes. |
| **1930** | Congress passes the Hawley-Smoot Tariff. |
| **1932** | The Reconstruction Finance Corporation is created. |
| | The Bonus Army camps in Washington, D.C. |
| | Franklin D. Roosevelt is elected president. |
| **1933** | **First Hundred Days** |

> • Emergency Banking Relief Act
>
> • Civilian Conservation Corps
>
> • Federal Emergency Relief Administration
>
> • Agricultural Adjustment Administration
>
> • Tennessee Valley Authority
>
> • National Industrial Recovery Act
>
> • Public Works Administration

The Twenty-First Amendment is ratified (repealing the Eighteenth Amendment).

| | |
|---|---|
| **1934** | Congress passes the Indian Reorganization Act. |
| | Roosevelt creates the Security Exchange Commission. |
| **1935** | **Second New Deal** |

> • Emergency Relief Appropriations Act
>
> • W. P. A.
>
> • Social Security Act
>
> • National Labor Relations Act
>
> • Resettlement Administration
>
> • National Housing Act

The Committee for Industrial Organization (CIO) is created.

The Supreme Court ruled on *Schecter v. United States*.

| | |
|---|---|
| **1936** | Roosevelt is reelected. |
| | The Supreme Court ruled on *Butler v. United States*. |

| | |
|---|---|
| *1937* | Roosevelt tries to "pack" the Supreme Court. |
| | The Roosevelt Recession begins. |
| *1938* | The CIO becomes the independent Congress of Industrial Organization. |
| *1939* | Congress passes the Hatch Act. |

CHAPTER 5
1929-1939

# Major Figures

**Father Charles Coughlin**  A Catholic priest in Michigan, Coughlin was also an outspoken critic of the New Deal. He blamed the Crash of 1929 on wealthy financiers and Jews and wanted the federal government to take over the entire banking system. The Catholic Church eventually cancelled his weekly radio show, but not before he had attracted millions of sympathetic listeners.

**Herbert Hoover**  A former engineer and millionaire, Hoover was elected to the presidency in 1928. Even though he had a reputation as a humanitarian for his relief efforts in World War I, Hoover was completely unprepared for the task of guiding the nation out of the Great Depression. After the Crash of 1929, he encouraged Americans not to panic, and promised there would be no recession. Even when millions began losing their jobs and homes, he still refused to act, instead believing that it was not the government's job to interfere in the economy. Many historians believe that he could have curbed the suffering in the Great Depression if only he had chosen to act.

**John Maynard Keynes**  A British economist in the early twentieth century, Keynes believed that deficit spending during recessions and depressions could revive national economies. His theories went untested until Franklin Delano Roosevelt applied them in the New Deal to bring the United States out of the Great Depression. The success of the New Deal converted Democrats to Keynesian disciples for the next several decades.

**Alfred M. Landon**  A Kansas governor, Landon ran against FDR on the anti-New Deal Republican ticket in the presidential election of 1936. Roosevelt beat him in a landslide victory that clearly demonstrated the American people wanted more relief, recovery, and reform.

**Huey P. Long**  A senator from Louisiana, Long criticized Franklin Delano Roosevelt and the New Deal for not doing enough to help the American people. He believed that the wealthy should be heavily taxed in order to redistribute income more evenly. He attracted the attention of millions, but was assassinated before he could seriously challenge the president. His criticisms played a role in shaping the Second New Deal.

***Franklin Delano Roosevelt***  A distant cousin of former president Theodore
Roosevelt, FDR had served as governor of New York before being elected
president in 1932. Roosevelt's New Deal programs and policies to end the
Depression focused on immediate relief, long-term recovery, and reform to
revive the economy. Despite the fact that he was usually wheelchair bound
(he had suffered from polio as a child), his optimism and charm did much
to convince Americans they had "nothing to fear but fear itself." He successfully led the United States through World War II, but died while still in
office on April 12, 1945.

# Suggested Reading

- Galbraith, John Kenneth. *The Great Crash 1929*. Boston: Mariner Books, 1997.

Galbraith compares the stock market crash in 1929 to the bull market in the 1990s. His telling parallels have made this book a bestseller.

- Kennedy, David M. *Freedom from Fear: The American People in Depression and War, 1929–1945*. New York: Oxford University Press, 2001.

Stanford History Professor David Kennedy explains the ways that Americans coped with the Depression and World War II. His masterful writing displays a firm grasp of the issues at hand.

- Kindleberger, Charles P. *The World in Depression, 1929–1939*. Berkeley: University of California Press, 1986.

Kindleberger analyzes the reasons for the Depression's persistence in the 1930s. An informative read, it provides extensive detail about the flaws in the economic system.

- Worster, Donald. *Dust Bowl: The Southern Plains in the 1930s*. New York: Oxford University Press, 1982.

Worster chronicles the dust-bowl devastation of the 1930s, which was some of the worst environmental trauma that the United States has experienced. In a recently written afterward, Worster draws a connection between the Dust Bowl and current problems in America.

# World War II:
## 1939–1945

- Precursors to War
- War Erupts Abroad
- The United States Enters the War
- War on the Home Front
- Victory in Europe
- Victory in the Pacific

World War II transformed the United States in nearly every way imaginable. After a decade of economic depression, the nation ventured across two oceans to take a lead role in defending the world for democracy. In the process, the United States converted its sickly economy into an industrial war machine. These tasks demanded a lot from the American people, who made tremendous sacrifices.

During the war, women and ethnic minorities also found new opportunities in the previously closed labor market. As a result, labor unions began to represent more and more of these new workers. At home and abroad, these unprecedented opportunities also presented a new set of challenges that would preoccupy political leaders throughout the rest of the twentieth century.

# Precursors to War

World War I planted many of the seeds for World War II. Outstanding war debts in Great Britain and France—combined with the heavy reparations payments forced upon Germany—facilitated the rise of **fascism**. Meanwhile, the strong desire for **isolationism** in the United States prevented the American government from participating in international efforts to check the increasingly aggressive Germany, Italy, and Japan.

## WAR DEBTS AND REPARATIONS

Outstanding debts created lasting problems for the major European powers because the British and French had borrowed heavily from the United States in the final two years of World War I. Under the terms of the Treaty of Versailles, both countries relied on war reparations from Germany to pay off their debts to the United States. During the 1920s, Germany could no longer keep up its payments, so the United States provided loans to the struggling nation according to the **Dawes Plan**. But the American economic crash in the early 1930s destabilized the already weak **Weimar Republic** in Germany. These adverse economic conditions encouraged the rise of fascism in Germany.

## AMERICAN ISOLATIONISM

The European default on war debts only reinforced American isolationism. By the end of World War I, Americans had grown tired of war and had turned their attention away from international affairs. Despite the urgings of President Woodrow Wilson, Congress refused to join the League of Nations. Although American leaders managed to enter a number of international agreements, isolationist sentiments prevailed in the face of a growing international crisis.

### 1920s Diplomacy

The United States collaborated with the international community on disarmament. Alarmed by the rapid growth of the Japanese navy, the United States government held the Washington Armaments Conference in 1921 and cosigned the following treaties:

- **The Five-Power Naval Treaty**, which restricted the size of the American, Japanese, British, French, and Italian navies.

- **The Four-Power Treaty**, which required the United States, Japan, Great Britain, and France to maintain the territorial status quo in the Pacific.

- **The Nine-Power Treaty**, which bound the United States, Japan, Britain, France, Italy, Belgium, China, the Netherlands, and Portugal to respect the territorial integrity of China and abide by the Open Door Policy.

### Roosevelt's Foreign Policy

**Franklin Delano Roosevelt** served as President Woodrow Wilson's secretary of the navy and endorsed an internationalist foreign policy in the late 1920s. Roosevelt supported the League of Nations and wanted to cancel European debts in order to stabilize the European economy. After becoming president in 1932, he promoted international cooperation (through trade) rather than military coercion. In order to accomplish this, he announced the **"Good Neighbor" Policy** in 1933 to reassure Latin American countries that the United States would not intervene in their internal affairs. He also formally recognized the Soviet regime in Russia in 1933.

> The **Nye Committee** in the Senate concluded that bankers and munitions-makers had convinced President Wilson to go to war and had profited as a result. The committee warned that the United States had to find ways to avoid making these mistakes again, prompting Congress to pass the Neutrality Act of 1935.

**CHAPTER 6**
**1939–1945**

### The Neutrality Acts

Congress also passed several laws designed to prevent American involvement in another European war. The **Johnson Debt Default Act** of 1934 prohibited private loans to all governments that defaulted on their war debts. Congress then passed the **Neutrality Act of 1935** to prohibit the sale of arms and munitions to nations at war.

The following year, Congress renewed these provisions and also forbade American corporations from loaning money to belligerent nations. Congress enforced the **cash-and-carry** policy when it passed the **Neutrality Act of 1937**, which required nations at war to purchase American goods with cash and to use their own ships to transport them back to Europe.

## THE RISE OF MILITARISM AND FASCISM OVERSEAS

Events overseas reinforced the American desire to maintain neutrality. By the early 1930s, militaristic and expansionist governments controlled Japan, Italy, and Germany. The League of Nations proved ineffective at stopping these countries as the world inched closer to war.

### The Japanese Invasion of Manchuria and China

The first stirrings of war occurred when militarists seized political power in Japan in 1931. Almost immediately, the Japanese invaded Manchuria, an area of China in which Japan had economic interests. Neither the United States nor the League of Nations attempted to intervene. Over the next several years, Japan sought to assert its military power in East Asia with these actions:

- Bombing the Chinese city of Shanghai in 1932
- Withdrawing from the League of Nations in 1933
- Renouncing the Five-Power Naval Treaty in 1934
- Invading China's northern provinces in 1937

### Italy and Ethiopia

Meanwhile, the nationalistic **Fascist Party** had maintained control over Italy under the leaders of **Benito Mussolini** since the 1920s. Beginning in the mid-1930s, Mussolini also flexed Italy's military might through these actions:

- Invading Ethiopia in northeastern Africa in 1935

- Withdrawing from the League of Nations in 1937

- Conquering the Kingdom of Albania in 1939

### The Rise of Nazism in Germany

Transformations in Germany alarmed European leaders even more. The economic problems facing the country in the aftermath of World War I helped fascist **Adolf Hitler** rise to power as leader of the National Socialists, or **Nazi Party**. The Nazis appealed to many Germans by pointing out the injustices of the Treaty of Versailles and blaming the country's troubles on Jews and other "inferior" races.

After becoming Chancellor of Germany in 1933, Hitler recalled the country's representatives to the League of Nations and began to rearm the German military in violation of the Treaty of Versailles. Within a few years, Hitler had used his military power to expand German territory. In March 1936, for example, German troops had invaded the Rhineland, an area placed under French control at the end of World War I. The French offered no resistance. Two years later, Hitler announced the annexation, or **Anschluss**, of Germany and his native country of Austria.

### The Munich Accords

In September 1938, Hitler demanded that Czechoslovakia grant Germany control of the **Sudetenland**, an area where many ethnic Germans lived but later agreed to meet with French and British envoys in Munich, Germany, to negotiate a peaceful settlement. Adopting a policy of **appeasement**, the British and French agreed to allow the annexation of the Sudetenland in exchange for Hitler's guarantee to halt territorial expansion.

Based on his accomplishments, British Prime Minister **Neville Chamberlain** triumphantly claimed he had secured "peace in our time." But the following March, Hitler broke the **Munich Accords** when he seized control of all of Czechoslovakia. Still, the British and French did nothing in the hope of avoiding another catastrophic war.

### The Invasion of Poland

Emboldened by the inaction of France and England, Hitler then looked toward Polish land that had once belonged to Germany before World War I, even though the British and French had promised to assist Poland against German aggression. In August, Hitler signed a nonaggression agreement with the Soviet dictator **Joseph Stalin** to ensure that Russia would not assist Poland and then ordered the invasion of Poland on September 1, 1939. France and Great Britain honored their promise to Poland and immediately declared war on Germany.

> Many historians consider the **Spanish Civil War** a "dress rehearsal" for World War II, because it involved many of the same countries. In 1936, the fascist General Francisco Franco began a rebellion against the Republican government of Spain. Germany and Italy supplied troops to the fascists, while the Soviet Union aided the pro-communist Loyalists. The United States, Britain, and France all declared their unwillingness to intervene. Some Americans went to fight anyway as part of the **Abraham Lincoln Brigade**, which joined citizens of several other countries to fight beside the Loyalists. Spain ultimately fell to the fascists on March 28, 1939.

**CHAPTER 6**
**1939–1945**

# War Erupts Abroad

The first two years of the war went well for Germany, Italy, and Japan. By the end of 1941, Germany and Italy had conquered much of Europe and planned to attack Great Britain and Russia. Japan continued to expand its influence in the Pacific and China, although to a lesser extent. The United States responded to these developments by increasing its aid to the Allies and by arming itself for the possibility of war.

## THE ESCALATION OF THE WAR

The war in Europe began with Germany's invasion and conquest of Poland, but very little happened the following winter. This **"phony war"** ended in the spring of 1940, when Hitler began his European military campaign in earnest.

### The Blitzkrieg

In the spring and summer of 1940, Hitler launched the **Blitzkrieg,** or "lightning war." This rapid series of successful invasions gave him control over much of Western Europe, including Denmark and Norway (in April), Belgium and the Netherlands (in May), and France (in June).

The Nazis established a pro-German regime in Vichy called **Vichy France** soon after the invasion. Meanwhile, the British gathered all their ships at **Dunkirk** and used them to return their troops to England.

*The Nazi-Soviet Pact of 1939 gave Stalin a brief opportunity to expand his reach in Eastern Europe without interference from Hitler. In fall 1940, the Soviets invaded the Baltic republics of Estonia, Latvia, and Lithuania, and then asserted control in Finland. In response, the United States established an embargo on arms shipments to Russia.*

**CHAPTER 6 1939–1945**

### The Battle of Britain

Hitler next turned his attention to the British Isles. During the summer and fall of 1940, the Germans regularly bombed English cities in preparation for a possible invasion. Inspired by the speeches of their new Prime Minister **Winston Churchill,** Britons deepened their resolve to resist Nazi aggression. The British Royal Air Force took to the skies to counter the German attack and helped win the **Battle of Britain**. Hitler's defeat forced him to put off another invasion until a later date.

### German Invasion of Russia

In the summer of 1941, Hitler broke the Nazi-Soviet pact and invaded the Soviet Union. Within four months, Hitler's armies had penetrated deep into Russia. But intense Russian resistance and bitter cold weather stopped the German advance in the winter.

The invasion of Russia proved to be Hitler's greatest blunder during the war. Opening a second front in Russia required the Nazis to divert considerable resources from the fighting in Western Europe for the remainder of the war. Moreover, Germany's invasion of Russia prompted Russia to form an alliance with Britain and later with the United States.

## INCREASING AMERICAN INVOLVEMENT

Despite an official policy of neutrality, the United States became increasingly involved in the war overseas. The American people expressed a strong preference for the Allies, a preference derived partly from the United States' affinity with Great Britain. President Roosevelt also supported the Allies and undertook policies to aid their cause, but stopped short of entering the war. In doing so, he slowly unraveled the constraints established by the earlier Neutrality Acts.

### Neutrality Act of 1939

After the invasion of Poland, President Roosevelt called a special session of Congress. He asked members to revise the previous neutrality acts that he had come to regard as mistakes. Congress obliged the president and authorized the sale of war goods to belligerent nations on a cash-and-carry basis in the **Neutrality Act of 1939**, though American ships still could not enter war zones or the ports of belligerents. Soon after, Roosevelt secretly circumvented the cash-and-carry policy when he provided the British with fifty destroyers in exchange for long-term leases on bases in British colonies in the Western Hemisphere.

## War Preparedness

Concerned that the United States would be unprepared if it had to go to war, Roosevelt and Congress bolstered American defenses by increasing military spending almost tenfold in 1940. Additionally, they passed the **Burke-Wadsworth Conscription Act**, the first peacetime draft in United States history. All men aged 21 to 35 had to register for a year's worth of military service.

## The Election of 1940

Roosevelt ran for an unprecedented third term against Republican challenger **Wendell Willkie** in 1940. When Willkie fell behind in the race, he accused Roosevelt of leading the country into war. Roosevelt responded by telling the American people, "Your boys are not going to be sent into any foreign wars." Roosevelt won the election by a landslide.

## Lend-Lease

In March 1941, Congress enacted the **Lend-Lease** policy, which permitted the president to loan or lease arms to any nation considered vital to American defense. Britain and China received arms first, followed by the Soviet Union after Hitler's invasion.

> Roosevelt justified Lend-Lease to the American people in a **fireside chat** radio broadcast. He argued that supplying weapons to Great Britain was the same as loaning a garden hose to a neighbor whose house was on fire to prevent the fire from spreading.

**CHAPTER 6**
**1939–1945**

## Shipping in the Atlantic

The United States also increased its shipping activities in the Atlantic Ocean, where German **U-Boat** submarines had proven adept at sinking British ships. In order to help deliver aid to the Allies, President Roosevelt claimed the western Atlantic neutral territory, and then extended American patrols as far as Iceland in July 1941.

In September, a German U-Boat fired on an American destroyer, prompting Roosevelt to order American ships encountering German submarines to "shoot on sight." When another U-Boat sunk an American destroyer the following month, Congress quickly authorized the arming of all merchant vessels and began permitting American ships to enter combat zones and the ports of nations at war.

### The Atlantic Charter

In August 1941, Roosevelt met with Churchill off the coast of Newfoundland, where the pair signed a set of "common principles" known as the **Atlantic Charter**. In addition to calling for the "final destruction of Nazi tyranny," the charter sought to establish the following:

- Self-rule for all peoples

- International economic cooperation

- Disarmament and a system of collective international security

- Freedom of the seas

### GROWING TENSIONS BETWEEN THE UNITED STATES AND JAPAN

The United States also inched away from strict neutrality in Asia. When Japan invaded China in 1937, Roosevelt responded by calling for a "quarantine" of aggressor nations. In 1940, Japan began working with its allies to secure a foothold in Southeast Asia and the Pacific in order to secure important war materials such as rubber and oil. Japan widened the scope of its war through measures such as:

- Securing the right to build airfields in Indochina from the Vichy government

- Occupying French Indochina

- Signing the **Tripartite Pact** with Germany and Italy to form the **Axis** alliance

- Signing a nonaggression pact with the Russians in order to ensure the safety of its northern front in China

### The American Response to Japanese Expansion

The United States responded to these actions by voicing its disapproval and pursuing economic policies meant to discourage Japan from further aggression. Congress and Roosevelt:

- Granted loans to China

- Refused to export arms to Japan

- Froze all Japanese assets in the United States

- Stopped exporting oil to Japan—a significant punishment, considering 80 percent of Japanese oil came from the United States

Roosevelt refused to lift the embargo until Japanese troops withdrew from China and Indochina. In Japan, Prime Minister Fumimaro Konoye sought a compromise, but militants led by War Minister **Hideki Tojo** pushed Konoye out of office. Japanese diplomats continued to negotiate with the United States while the military planned a strike on Allied bases in the Pacific. American intelligence learned of a forthcoming attack but did not know the target.

### Pearl Harbor

On the morning of **December 7, 1941**, Japanese planes took off from aircraft carriers and attacked the American naval base at **Pearl Harbor**. Within two hours, the Japanese had sunk or damaged nineteen ships, destroyed scores of planes, and killed over 2,400 service members and civilians. The next day, President Roosevelt and Congress condemned the attack and declared war on Japan. Because of the Tripartite Pact, Italy and Germany then declared war on the United States on December 11, 1941. This prompted Congress to respond in kind.

*Just after the attack on Pearl Harbor, Japanese Admiral Isoroku Yamamoto remarked, "I fear we have awakened a sleeping giant and filled him with a terrible resolve." Yamamoto's words proved true, as the atomic bombs that the United States dropped in retaliation wreaked massive devastation on their country.*

# The United States Enters the War

The Japanese had coordinated a campaign to cripple the Allied presence in the Pacific, so U.S. forces immediately went on the defensive upon entering the war. Within months, however, the Japanese had nevertheless succeeded in capturing several important Allied territories.

By the end of 1942, U.S. forces stopped the Japanese advance at several decisive battles and then went on the offensive. In battles on the Atlantic and in North Africa, the Americans helped the Allies stop the Germans as well, making Atlantic and Mediterranean waters safe for Allied ships. By early 1943, the tide had finally begun to turn in the Allies' favor.

### WAR IN THE PACIFIC

Following the attack on Pearl Harbor, the Japanese quickly conquered Allied territory in the Pacific and East Asia. Japanese **Admiral Isoruku Yamamoto** believed that only quick victories would allow Japan to beat the Allies. The attack on Pearl Harbor had damaged—but not crippled—the American navy. This was because all of the American aircraft carriers in the Pacific Fleet had left Hawaii several days before the attack.

### The Japanese Offensive

Japan followed up its attack on Pearl Harbor by capturing a succession of Allied outposts in the Pacific and in Asia. The Japanese quickly conquered:

- Guam, Wake Island, the Gilbert Islands

- Hong Kong and Singapore

- The Dutch East Indies (Indonesia)

- Burma

**Pacific Naval Battles**

1. Attack on Pearl Harbor
2. Sinking of the Prince of Wales and Repulse
3. **Java Campaign**

4. Raids into the Indian Ocean
5. Battle of the Coral Sea
6. Battle of Midway
7. **Guadalcanal Naval Battles**
8. **Solomon Islands Naval Battles**
9. Battle of the Komandorski Islands

10. Destruction of Truk
11. Battle of the Philippine Sea
12. **Leyte Naval Battles**
13. Sinking of the *Yamato*
14. **Final destruction**

### The Philippines

Within hours of the attack on Pearl Harbor, Japanese planes also bombed U.S. airfields in the Philippines. Later that month, American forces under the command of **General Douglas A. MacArthur** abandoned Manila and retreated to the Bataan Peninsula. In March 1942, MacArthur escaped to Australia under orders from his superiors. The following month, American troops retreated to the island of **Corregidor.** The remaining American forces at Corregidor surrendered on May 6.

### The Battle of the Coral Sea

The United States finally managed to halt Japanese advances at the **Battle of the Coral Sea** in early May 1942. The battle began when American forces encountered Japanese ships bound for New Guinea. The United States successfully turned the ships back. This victory prevented the deployment of Japanese troops sent to participate in an eventual invasion of Australia.

### The Battle of Midway

The United States achieved another major victory over the Japanese at the **Battle of Midway** in June 1942. After American cryptologists had uncovered a secret Japanese plan to invade Hawaii, U.S. Navy commanders decided to intercept the Japanese fleet before it could attack. The Japanese lost all four of the aircraft carriers they brought to Midway, while the United States lost only one. The Japanese did not win another significant battle in the Pacific for the rest of the war.

### U-BOATS AND THE BATTLE OF THE ATLANTIC

The United States also faced naval challenges in the Atlantic. "Wolf packs" of German submarines began menacing American shipping after the U.S. had declared war. U-Boats sunk hundreds of ships along the United States Atlantic coast and in the Caribbean throughout 1942. By the middle of 1943, the Allies effectively neutralized the dangers posed by U-Boats and won the Battle of the Atlantic.

## THE ALLIED STRATEGY IN EUROPE

In Europe, the Allies had to decide when and where to strike the Germans and Italians. Stalin wanted the British and Americans to stage a cross-channel invasion of France as soon as possible in order to open a second major front and pull troops away from the Eastern. On the other hand, Churchill argued for smaller offensives around the edges to eventually build up to a full-scale invasion of Germany. After meeting with Churchill in Washington in 1942, Roosevelt opted for the British plan, which would get American troops into battle more quickly.

## THE NORTH AFRICAN CAMPAIGN

American ground forces faced their first real test in the deserts of North Africa. German forces under **General Erwin Rommel** had penetrated British-controlled Egypt in the hope of capturing the Suez Canal. In October 1942, the British halted Rommel's advance at **el-Alamein** in Egypt. They then began pushing the Germans back across Libya. On November 8, 1942, **General Dwight D. Eisenhower** landed American troops in French Morocco to join British forces attacking Rommel. By May 1943, the Allies had forced the Germans out of North Africa and cleared the way for the invasion of Italy.

## CASABLANCA

In January 1943, Roosevelt and Churchill met again in **Casablanca**, Morocco, to further discuss war plans. Both the Americans and British ultimately decided they needed more time to prepare for an invasion of France. However, they did agree to invade Italy via Sicily and accept only unconditional surrender from the Axis powers. They also agreed to launch major offensives in the Pacific.

CHAPTER 6
1939–1945

# War on the Home Front

World War II had a significant impact on the lives of all Americans. Over 15 million men and women served in the armed forces. Even though the fighting never directly affected civilians at home, it nonetheless transformed their lives. The demands of war production brought about a return to prosperity after a decade-long depression, increased membership in labor unions, ended many of the reform programs of the New Deal, and provided new opportunities for women and minorities.

## WAR PRODUCTION AND THE ECONOMY

Most historians agree that World War II effectively ended the Great Depression. The demand for war materials drove up production, which in turn created jobs and put money in the hands of American workers. At the same time, the draft removed millions of men from the workforce. To meet the needs of the growing economy and conserve resources, the U.S. government poured money into war production, as well as established agencies to manage the **economic conversion** of industry. Additionally, the government established **price and wage controls** to prevent runaway inflation, rationed vital resources, and worked with **labor unions** to prevent slowdowns in production.

### Government Spending During the War

By funneling money into war industries, the American government played an important role in the economic boom. The federal budget rose from $9 billion in 1939 to $100 billion in 1945. Roosevelt wanted to fund the war solely with tax increases, but conservatives in Congress would not comply. They reached a compromise by agreeing to pay for half of the war with revenue raised from increased taxes and the remainder by borrowing from the public. The federal government did this by issuing **War Bonds** throughout the war, and Americans purchased over $150 billion worth of bonds. Additional money came from banks and other financial institutions.

### Economic Conversion

In order to manage the economic conversion, the United States moved quickly to organize and direct the national economy. In 1942, the government created the **War Production Board** to manage the conversion of private industry to war production. **"Dollar-a-year men,"** businessmen who moved to Washington, D.C., to work without pay, led a multitude of new agencies designed to oversee war production. As a result of these efforts, larger companies grew stronger because they could better handle mass production.

### Price and Wage Controls

Americans had more money in their pockets, but the industrial commitment to war production meant that people could not spend their money on new housing, automobiles, or appliances. Because officials feared that scarcity of goods would create inflation, Congress created the **Office of Price Administration (OPA)** to set caps on prices, wages, and rents in 1942. By the end of the war, prices had risen 31 percent—only half as much as they had risen during World War I.

### Rationing and Shortages

Consumer items such as sugar, gasoline, and meat also came in short supply. The government addressed these shortages by instituting a **rationing** program. Officials also encouraged the public to conserve precious resources for the good of the war effort. Some Americans, for example, planted **"victory gardens,"** in which they grew their own food. Others gathered old rubber and scrap metal to be recycled and reused as war materials.

### Labor Unions

The government ensured that all new workers would automatically join unions. In exchange, labor leaders agreed to accept limits on wage increases and made a **"no-strike" pledge** for the duration of the war. As a result, membership in labor unions rose from about 10.5 million in 1941 to 15 million just four years later.

Cooperation between the government and labor occasionally broke down. Sometimes workers would strike without the approval of their unions. In 1943, a United Mine Workers strike led by **John L. Lewis** prompted Congress to pass the **Smith-Connally Act**. The law required a thirty-day cooling-off period before unions could strike and gave the president authority to seize war plants if necessary. States also passed additional laws to curtail the power of unions.

## POLITICS DURING WARTIME

The federal government gradually became more and more conservative as the American economy improved. With the Great Depression over, New Deal reforms seemed less pressing and less necessary, and as a result, the 1942 elections led to the repeal of some Depression-era programs.

### The End of Reform

Soldiers and war workers who had moved away from home could not cast their traditionally Democratic votes in 1942. This, plus general annoyance with wartime shortages and controls, helped increase Republican numbers in Congressional elections. Conservatives grabbed the opportunity to end or cut back popular New Deal programs, including:

- The Works Progress Administration (WPA)
- The Farm Security Administration
- The National Planning Resources Board

By the end of 1943, Roosevelt had acknowledged the changing priorities of Americans and announced that winning the war would take precedence over the New Deal.

### The Election of 1944

Roosevelt sought reelection once again in 1944, and he ran against Republican Thomas E. Dewey from New York. Bowing to pressure from Democratic leaders, Roosevelt agreed to drop his vice president, Henry Wallace, and ran with the more moderate

**Harry S Truman**, who had chaired a Senate committee to investigate fraud and waste in war production. Roosevelt won with 432 electoral votes to Dewey's ninety-nine.

## WOMEN AND THE WAR

The war emergency produced new opportunities for women in the workplace and the military. Women experienced unprecedented economic and social freedom as a result.

Approximately 350,000 women served in the armed forces during the war. Roughly 200,000 of these women served in the **Women's Army Corps (WAC)**, the Navy's **Women Accepted for Volunteer Emergency Service (WAVES)**, and other military auxiliaries. The rest joined the Nurse's Corps.

### Women in War Industries

During the Great Depression, women had been discouraged from seeking work for fear that they would steal jobs from men. But the new demand for labor during the war prompted the government and industries to recruit women to increase war production. The government's publicity campaign encouraged women to enter traditionally male manufacturing positions by producing famous images of **Rosie the Riveter**.

Their campaign was successful, and about 6 million women entered the workforce during the war, an overall increase of more than 50 percent. The number of women working in manufacturing increased 110 percent, and the percentage of married women in the workforce rose from 15 percent in 1940 to 24 percent in 1945.

## AFRICAN AMERICANS AND THE WAR

The war also had a profound social impact on African Americans. Many joined the military and saw other parts of the country and the world for the first time. The demand for labor in northern and western industrial cities also prompted more than 5 million blacks to move out of the agricultural South and to the cities during the 1940s.

CHAPTER 6
1939–1945

### African Americans in the Military

One million African Americans served in the U.S. military during World War II. Most served in segregated units due to a military policy that remained largely intact throughout the war. The Red Cross even maintained separate blood supplies for whites and blacks. In 1940, however, the government ended segregation in all officer candidate schools except for those training air cadets. About 600 black pilots received their training at a special military flight school established at Tuskegee, Alabama. Many of these **Tuskegee Airmen** went on to serve in decorated combat units.

### African-American Employment

In 1941, **A. Philip Randolph**, the head of the Brotherhood of Sleeping Car Porters, announced plans for a massive **March on Washington**. This march was to demand that the government require defense contractors to integrate their workforce and open more skilled-labor jobs to African Americans. Afraid of racial violence, Roosevelt convinced Randolph to cancel the march in exchange for creating the **Fair Employment Practices Commission**. During the war, the commission helped reduce black unemployment by 80 percent.

### The Double V Campaign

Because the war against fascism implicitly criticized the racial theories of Nazi Germany, African Americans seized the opportunity to fight all forms of prejudice at home. The NAACP started launched the "victory at home, victory abroad" campaign, also known as the **Double-V Campaign**. As a result, NAACP membership during the war increased from 50,000 members to roughly 450,000. A new civil rights group founded in 1942, the **Congress of Racial Equality (CORE)**, also campaigned for desegregation by staging demonstrations and sit-ins around the country.

### Race Riots

The influx of African Americans into the workforce and cities, combined with growing demands for equal rights, created serious tensions with white Americans. During 1943, 242 separate incidents of racial violence occurred in forty-seven different American cities, the most serious being the **Detroit Race Riots**, in which twenty-five African Americans and nine whites died.

## NATIVE AMERICANS AND THE WAR

More than 25,000 Native Americans served in uniform during World War II, often in integrated units. Some of the most famous were the Native American **"Code-talkers"** who used their native languages to encode important military messages. Many Native Americans also worked as laborers alongside whites in various war industries. Those who left their reservations for military service or war work acquired new skills, came into close contact with whites for the first time, and discovered new opportunities in American society.

## INTERNMENT OF JAPANESE AMERICANS

After Pearl Harbor, Americans grew deeply distrustful of Japanese Americans, many of whom lived on the West Coast. Although no Japanese American ever committed treason during the war, Roosevelt authorized the **internment** of all Americans of Japanese descent in "relocation centers" in early 1942.

Internment camps in the western interior of the United States eventually housed about 100,000 Japanese Americans, two-thirds of whom were American citizens. Prisoners had little time to make arrangements for their property before being deported to the camps, so many people lost homes and businesses. The Supreme Court upheld the order in 1944.

*After much debate, in 1988, Congress decided to award $20,000 and an official apology to each of the roughly 60,000 surviving Japanese American internees.*

# Victory in Europe

In 1943, the Allies began their campaign to roll back the Axis in earnest. Churchill and Roosevelt ignored Stalin's request to engage the Germans on a second front and instead followed up on their success in North Africa by invading Italy. But a year later, the United States and Great Britain did attack in the West when they invaded France. The Allies pressed in on Germany from both sides, meeting in the spring of 1945 and forcing Germany's surrender.

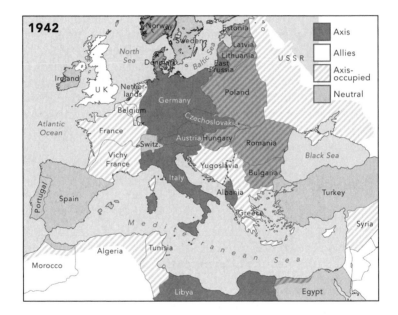

### THE ITALIAN CAMPAIGN

In July 1943, roughly 160,000 American and British troops invaded the island of Sicily. Unprepared to fight, the Italians quickly retreated to the Italian mainland. By the end of the month, the fascist regime had collapsed and Mussolini had fled to northern Italy. The Italian government soon surrendered unconditionally and even joined the Allies. Despite Hitler's eleventh-hour campaign to restore Mussolini to power, the Allies finally captured Rome in June 1944.

## CAIRO AND TEHRAN

In November 1943, Roosevelt, Churchill, and Stalin met face to face for the first time. After conferring with Chinese leader **Chiang Kai-shek** in Cairo, Egypt, the Allies issued the **Declaration of Cairo**, which reaffirmed the demand for Japan's unconditional surrender, promised to return all Chinese territory occupied by Japan to China, and declared that the Korean peninsula would become an independent state free from outside control.

The **"Big Three"** leaders then proceeded to **Tehran**, Iran, to plan their final assault on the Axis powers. In Tehran, they agreed that the United States and Great Britain would invade France the following May, that the Soviet Union would begin fighting Japan once Germany had surrendered, and that all three countries would occupy Germany at the end of the war and establish a postwar security organization.

## STRATEGIC BOMBING OVER EUROPE

American and British planes conducted a lengthy bombing campaign against military and industrial targets in Germany. By targeting cities such as Dresden and Berlin, bombers delayed German war production and disrupted transportation. These attacks also depleted the German air force, distracted the German military's attention from other fronts, and reduced Hitler's popularity amongst the German people.

## D-DAY

In the middle of 1944, the Americans and British finished preparations to open a second front with a cross-channel invasion of France, dubbed **Operation Overlord**. The Germans prepared for an assault, but they mistakenly believed that the Allies would cross at the narrowest point in the English Channel and land at Pas de Calais, near the French-Belgian border. Instead, the roughly 150,000 Allied soldiers landed on the beaches of **Normandy**, France, on **D-Day**: June 6, 1944. Poor landing conditions, logistical errors, and German gun emplacements made the invasion difficult, but the Allies eventually secured the beach with the help of paratroopers dropped behind enemy lines the night before. Within two weeks, a million more Allied troops had landed in France.

### THE ALLIED ADVANCE FROM THE WEST

The Allies pushed through France and toward Germany over the summer of 1944. The only real resistance posed by the Germans occurred at the **Battle of the Bulge**. By the end of the year, the Americans, British, and French in the West and the Russians in the East had effectively surrounded the Germans.

### THE SURRENDER OF GERMANY

After successfully breaking through German lines at the Battle of the Bulge, American **General Omar Bradley** led his troops toward Berlin through central Germany, while the British swept through the North and the Russians approached from the East. Meanwhile, Adolph Hitler retreated to his underground bunker in Berlin and committed suicide on April 30. On May 2, Berlin fell to the Soviets, and within a few days, the Germans had unconditionally surrendered.

### THE DEATH OF PRESIDENT ROOSEVELT

Even though he had conducted the war through an unprecedented three presidential terms and part of a fourth, Franklin Roosevelt did not live to see Germany defeated. After a lengthy illness, he died of a massive stroke on April 12, 1945. The nation's grief for the beloved president cast a shadow over the otherwise jubilant celebration for the victory in Europe. Roosevelt's vice president, **Harry S Truman**, immediately assumed office.

### THE HOLOCAUST

The defeat of Germany also uncovered disturbing revelations about Hitler's **"final solution."** Even though the Nazis had announced their belief in the racial inferiority of Jews to "pure" Germans, American anti-Semitism and isolationism during the 1930s had prevented Roosevelt from changing immigration policies to welcome European refugees. As early as 1942, the U.S. government had received reports that Germany had detained Jews and other "impure" peoples in concentration camps, with the intention of systematically exterminating them. But many officials had dismissed such reports as preposterous. When the Allies liberated the camps in 1945, they found incontrovertible proof of genocide. As many as 10 million Jews and other minorities died in the **Holocaust**.

# *Victory in the Pacific*

The Americans finally went on the offensive against the Japanese in the Pacific in mid-1942. The victories at Coral Sea and Midway had damaged the Japanese fleet and marked the start of an American campaign to roll back Japanese gains. U.S. forces succeeded every step of the way, despite intense and extremely bloody opposition from the Japanese at Guadalcanal, Iwo Jima, and Okinawa. The anticipation of a costly invasion of Japan inspired support for President Truman's decision to ultimately end the war by dropping two **atomic bombs**.

## GUADALCANAL

The first major American offensive in the Pacific occurred in the Solomon Islands, east of New Guinea. On August 7, 1942, the First Marine Division attacked a Japanese installation building on an airfield on the island of **Guadalcanal**. It took American forces six months of brutal fighting to push the Japanese off the island and prevent them from building air bases from which to attack Australia and New Zealand.

## THE AMERICAN OFFENSIVE IN THE PACIFIC

After Guadalcanal, the American military leaders put into action a two-pronged strategy that combined the recommendations of General MacArthur and **Admiral Chester Nimitz**. American troops in the South Pacific would move northward through New Guinea and retake the Philippines while naval forces would simultaneously sweep westward through the Pacific from Hawaii toward Japanese island outposts. The two would eventually meet and prepare for an invasion of Japan.

### MacArthur in the South Pacific

American forces in Australia and New Guinea approached the Philippines by attacking Japanese-controlled territory in the South Pacific. In the **Battle of the Bismarck Sea**, which lasted from March 2 to March 3, 1943, U.S. forces sank eighteen enemy ships and discouraged the Japanese from shipping future rein-forcements to besieged islands. The victory allowed MacArthur's forces to reclaim the western Solomon Islands and the northern coast of New Guinea with the help of Australian troops.

### Nimitz in the Central Pacific

Meanwhile, the Navy moved westward from the central Pacific. In November 1943, Admiral Nimitz began his **island-hopping campaign** by attacking Japanese bases in the Gilbert Islands. Over the next year, Nimitz moved westward across the Pacific. In 1944, he conquered the Marshall Islands in February, the Mariana Islands in June, and the western Caroline Islands in September.

### Battle of Leyte Gulf

MacArthur met with Nimitz in October of 1944 at Leyte Gulf near the Philippines. In the **Battle of Leyte Gulf**, the largest naval battle in history, American forces effectively decimated what remained of Japan's navy. Japanese pilots in **"kamikaze"** units attacked U.S. battleships and aircraft carriers in suicide attacks.

### Iwo Jima and Okinawa

Fighting grew more intense and more costly as American forces inched closer toward Japan. On February 19, 1945, U.S. Marines landed on the island of **Iwo Jima** only 750 miles from Tokyo. In roughly six weeks, U.S. troops secured the island at a cost of 7,000 dead and nearly twice that number wounded. On April 1, 1945, the Americans landed on the island of **Okinawa**, 370 miles from Tokyo. For nearly three months, 300,000 U.S. servicemen fought to secure the island. Once again, kamikaze pilots flew their planes into American ships. In the end, over 100,000 Japanese soldiers and about a third as many Okinawans died in the fighting. American troops suffered 50,000 casualties.

### THE ATOMIC BOMB

The dropping of the terrifying atomic bomb marked the end of the war in the Pacific. President Truman's decision to drop two atomic bombs hastened an inevitable Japanese defeat and arguably saved thousands of American lives. His decision also ushered in the atomic age and changed the nature of modern warfare.

### The Manhattan Project

The United States worked on developing an atomic bomb throughout the war. In 1939, famous physicist **Albert Einstein** warned Roosevelt that the Germans had experimented with nuclear fission in the hope of creating their own atomic bomb. Roosevelt therefore diverted military funds into a secret nuclear research program called the **Manhattan Project** in order to develop the weapon first.

Over 100,000 people worked on the secret project in thirty-seven locations throughout the United States. **Dr. J. Robert Oppenheimer** led the theoretical research team based in Los Alamos, New Mexico. On July 16, 1945, scientists witnessed the first explosion of an atomic bomb in the desert near Alamogordo, New Mexico.

### Truman's Ultimatum

After becoming president, Harry Truman had little time to contemplate the ramifications of using a nuclear weapon to end the war, because he and military commanders feared that as many as 250,000 Allied troops would die in the invasion of Japan. Upon hearing of the successful test at Alamogordo, Truman issued an ultimatum to the Japanese by demanding that the Japanese surrender unconditionally before August 3, 1945, or face "utter devastation."

### Hiroshima and Nagasaki

When the Japanese still failed to surrender, Truman authorized dropping the bomb. On August 6, 1945, the B-39 bomber **Enola Gay** dropped an atomic bomb on **Hiroshima**, Japan. The explosion flattened the city and killed 78,000 people instantly. By the end of the year, 70,000 more had died from radiation exposure. On August 9, the United States dropped a second atomic bomb on **Nagasaki**, Japan, killing more than 100,000 civilians.

*Once the United States had established air bases within striking distance of Japan, American bombers had dropped thousands of conventional bombs over major Japanese cities. By the end of the war, U.S. forces had firebombed over sixty cities, destroyed Tokyo, and killed approximately 500,000 Japanese civilians. Still, Japanese rulers steadfastly refused to surrender, forcing Truman to consider using the atomic bomb to end the war.*

### Japanese Surrender

Truman's decision to use the bomb succeeded in averting an Allied invasion. After the bombing of Nagasaki, a peace faction assumed control of the Japanese government and surrendered unconditionally. On September 2, 1945, Japan signed a formal surrender on the deck of the battleship **Missouri** in Tokyo Bay.

**If the United States had acted differently, could it have prevented World War II in Europe?**

From the moment Adolf Hitler assumed power in Germany in 1933, he set in motion a plan to conquer all of Europe and, eventually, the rest of the world. Many historians believe that nothing short of war could have stopped him. However, a closer look at the causes of World War II tells a different story. Before the Nazis controlled Germany, the American government had the power to positively affect the European economy and to cooperate with other countries to address potential conflicts. Even after the European crisis began, the United States could have played a stronger role in international affairs instead of retreating into isolationism. Had America acted differently, World War II might have been averted.

The Nazi Party came to power in large part because of crisis conditions in Germany. It had suffered a humiliating defeat in World War I, and its economy was in shambles, largely due to the burden of paying war reparations. The German populace resented the terms of the 1920 Versailles Treaty, which they felt had imposed inordinately harsh terms upon them. Hitler and the Nazis fed on their resentment and amassed political power by exploiting economic hardship, pandering to feelings of national pride, and fostering xenophobia and racism. When they finally captured the government, they were able to undermine the weak democratic institutions established in the wake of the country's defeat in 1918.

If the United States recognized the vital importance of stability in Europe, it could have worked in the 1920s to prevent the collapse of the democratic Weimar Republic. As creditor to Great Britain and France after World War I, the United States could have forgiven some of those war debts in exchange for a greater relaxation of German war reparations. If the Americans had been able to soften the economic impact of war reparations on Germany, the Weimar Republic might have thrived and the Nazis might not have been able to exploit public discontent and assume

# Student Essay

control. At the same time, by joining the League of Nations, the United States could have strengthened that organization and the entire international community. The intervention of an international body including all the world's major powers, like the U.N. of today, might have averted the collapse of democracy in Germany.

Even if one assumes the rise of the Nazis to be inevitable, American isolationism certainly allowed problems in Europe to escalate. When Franklin D. Roosevelt ran for the presidency in 1932, he abandoned his earlier support of the League of Nations and the restructuring of European war debts. Roosevelt's early foreign policy initiatives in the 1930s signaled a reluctance to engage in military intervention and a preference to let trade foster good relations. While the "Good Neighbor" Policy was effective in opening Latin America to exports, Nazi Germany only responded to force, which Roosevelt was not willing to engage in. The Germans' eventual allies, the Japanese, were even more belligerent, invading China in 1937 and discarding the 1922 Nine-Power Treaty—intended to prevent war in the Pacific—when the agreement no longer served their purposes.

Yet despite the clear presence of danger on the international scene, in both the European and Pacific arenas, the United States did its best not to exert influence on brewing world conflicts. The Neutrality Acts of 1935–37 aimed to keep the United States out of foreign wars in Ethiopia, Spain, and the Pacific. As a result, Great Britain and France did not feel they could rely upon American help in the event of war with Germany. With more confidence in their ally across the Pacific, the British and French might have been able to respond to Hitler's aggression early on with a better show of force. The British and French instead adopted the American policy of nonintervention, allowing the Italians and Germans to help fascists overrun Republican Spain. While Roosevelt had to respect the desires of Congress and the public, his later efforts to break down American neutrality demonstrated that Roosevelt was able to use his leadership to move the country toward internationalism.

The question of whether the United States could have prevented World War II can never truly be answered. Still, the United States avoided nearly every opportunity it had to stop Germany's march to war until it was too late to preserve peace. Struggling with the hardships of the Great Depression, Americans thought they could isolate themselves from the problems of the outside world. But in the end, they only allowed those problems to grow inescapably large.

# Test Questions and Answers

1. *Describe the steps the United States took to try and prevent involvement in another world war during the 1920s and 1930s.*

   • The United States refused to join the League of Nations.

   • American leaders pursued the Five-Power Naval Treaty, the Four-Power Treaty, and the Nine-Power Treaty in order to prevent conflicts in the Pacific.

   • In the Neutrality Act of 1935, Congress forbade the sale of arms to countries at war and warned American citizens to travel in war zones at their own risk.

   • In 1936, Congress revised the Neutrality Act to forbid loans to warring countries.

   • From 1936 to 1939, the United States refused to intervene in the Spanish Civil War.

   • In the Neutrality Act of 1937, Congress prohibited the arming of American ships trading with nations at war.

2. *In a sense, the Allies in World War II fought against Nazi theories of racial supremacy. In what ways did the United States "fail" in this war?*

   • The United States government interned Japanese Americans, many of whom were American citizens, solely because they were of Japanese descent.

   • In 1943, whites attacked African Americans in urban race riots, including a riot in Detroit that lasted two days and killed thirty-four people.

   • The U.S. government refused to come to the aid of European refugees before the war. When confronted with evidence of the Nazi Holocaust in 1942, the government made only modest efforts to rescue European Jews and denied requests that Allied bombers disrupt the activity at Auschwitz.

### 3. How did World War II benefit Americans?

- President Roosevelt's secret deal with Winston Churchill secured new American bases in the western hemisphere.

- War production provided jobs, increased wages, and ended the Great Depression.

- Many industries employed women and minorities in jobs once limited to white men.

- America expanded its military power in order to meet the threat of the Axis powers.

- The United States exited the war with the atomic bomb, a weapon that gave it a distinct advantage over potential rivals.

### 4. In the election of 1940, Wendell Willkie accused President Roosevelt of leading the country into war. Is there any evidence to support Willkie's claim?

- Roosevelt pressed for the Neutrality Act of 1939, which once again permitted the United States to sell arms to warring nations.

- After the passage of the Neutrality Act, Roosevelt made a secret deal with Great Britain that went outside the bounds of the cash-and-carry policy for arms and linked American interests to British concerns.

- When Congress passed the Lend-Lease policy in 1941, Roosevelt applied it to Great Britain and China, both enemies of the Axis powers.

- In 1941, Roosevelt extended the scope of American shipping, putting American vessels in danger of attack from German U-Boats.

- In 1941, Roosevelt signed the Atlantic Charter with Great Britain's Winston Churchill. The Charter called for the destruction of Nazi tyranny.

- In addition to sending aid to China, Roosevelt placed an embargo on Japan, which relied on the United States for important resources.

## 5. How did the United States justify dropping the atomic bomb on civilians in Japan?

- Americans' firebombing of dozens of Japanese cities had had no effect.

- Fighting in the Pacific proved that an invasion of the Japanese mainland would have cost more in American lives alone than the number who died in the bombings.

## 6. What measures did American civilians and the government take to meet the demands of war production?

- President Roosevelt created the War Production Board to manage economic conversion.

- The Office of Price Administration capped wages and prices in order to control inflation.

- The government rationed vital resources such as sugar and gasoline.

- American citizens conserved scarce commodities.

- "Dollar-a-year" men worked for no compensation for government agencies to oversee war production.

- Labor unions agreed to wage freezes and made a "no-strike" pledge.

- Women took traditionally male jobs in manufacturing.

# Timeline

| | |
|---|---|
| **1921** | Congress collaborates with the international community on disarmament with the Five-Power Naval Treaty, the Four-Power Naval Treaty, and the Nine-Power Naval Treaty. |
| **1924** | The United States provides loans to Germany in the Dawes Plan. |
| **1931** | Japan invades Manchuria. |
| **1933** | Roosevelt announces the Good Neighbor Policy. |
| **1935** | Italy invades Ethiopia. |
| | Congress passes the Neutrality Act of 1935. |
| **1936** | Congress passes the Neutrality Act of 1936. |
| | Spanish Civil War begins. |
| | Roosevelt is reelected. |
| **1937** | Congress passes the Neutrality Act of 1937. |
| | Japan invades China. |
| **1938** | Germany invades Austria. |
| | The Munich Conference is held in Germany. |
| **1939** | Germany invades Czechoslovakia. |
| | Hitler signs a nonaggression agreement in the Nazi-Soviet Pact. |
| | Germany invades Poland to begin World War II. |
| | Congress passes the Neutrality Act of 1939. |
| **1940** | Germany invades France, Denmark, Norway, the Netherlands, and Belgium. |
| | The British Royal Air Force counters the German attack in the Battle of Britain. |
| | The United States makes the Bases-for-Destroyers Deal with Great Britain. |
| | Roosevelt is reelected. |

| 1941 | Congress passes the Lend-Lease Act. |
| | Germany invades the Soviet Union. |
| | Roosevelt and Churchill sign the Atlantic Charter. |
| | Japan attacks Pearl Harbor. |
| | The United States enters the war. |
| | Randolph prepares the March on Washington. |
| | Roosevelt establishes Fair Employment Practices Commission. |
| 1942 | Japanese-Americans are forced into internment camps. |
| | Japan invades the Philippines. |
| | The Battle of the Coral Sea occurs. |
| | The Battle of Midway occurs. |
| | The United States invades North Africa. |
| | Congress of Racial Equality is founded. |
| | The first major American offense in the Pacific occurred at the Battle for Guadalcanal. |
| 1943 | Roosevelt and Churchill hold the Casablanca Conference. |
| | Allies invade Italy. |
| | The United States achieves victory at the Battle of Bismarck Sea. |
| | The "Big Three" plan their final assault on the Axis powers at the Tehran Conference. |
| 1944 | Allies invade Normandy on D-Day. |
| | Roosevelt is reelected. |
| | The Battle of the Bulge begins. |
| 1945 | Roosevelt dies. |
| | Truman becomes president. |
| | Germany surrenders. |
| | U.S. Marines invade Iwo Jima. |
| | Thousands die in the battle at Okinawa. |
| | The United States drops atomic bombs on Hiroshima and Nagasaki. |
| | Japan signs a formal surrender on the *Missouri* in Tokyo Bay. |

# Major Figures

**Winston Churchill**  As prime minister of Great Britain between 1940 and
1945, Churchill helped Franklin Roosevelt conduct the war for the Allies
against Nazi Germany.

**Albert Einstein**  The most prominent physicist of his time, Einstein propsed
the Theory of Relativity, changing the way scientists conceived of the relationship between space and time.

**Dwight D. Eisenhower**  Commander in chief of Allied forces in Western
Europe during World War II, Eisenhower led the massive D-Day invasion
of Normandy in 1944 and directed the conquest of Nazi Germany. He
later served as president from 1953 until 1961.

**Adolph Hitler**  Chancellor of Germany and leader of the fascist Nazi Party,
Hitler tried to conquer all of Europe during World War II. He also ordered
the execution of as many as 10 million Jews and other minorities in the
Holocaust. He committed suicide in 1945 as Allied forces entered Berlin.

**Douglas A. MacArthur**  American General McArthur served as Allied supreme
commander in the Southwest Pacific and supervised the conquest of Japan
during World War II. He later directed American forces against communist
North Korean and Chinese forces in the Korean War until President Harry
S Truman fired him for insubordination.

**Benito Mussolini**  As leader of the Italian fascist party, Mussolini fought
alongside Germany in the early years of the war to conquer Europe, North
Africa, and much of the Near East.

**Dr. J. Robert Oppenheimer**  The directory of the team of scientists under the
Manhattan Project, Oppenheimer helped devise the atomic bomb.

**A. Philip Randolph**  An African-American labor leader, Randolph convinced
Roosevelt to eliminate racial discrimination in defense industries and federal bureaus during the war.

**Franklin Delano Roosevelt**  First elected president in 1932 and reelected in the following three presidential elections, Roosevelt led the nation during the Great Depression and World War II.

**Joseph Stalin**  The Soviet leader, Stalin had initially signed a non-aggression treaty with Adolph Hitler at the beginning of the war, he quickly joined the Allies after the Germans invade Russia.

**Harry S Truman**  President after Roosevelt's death in 1945, Truman made the decision to drop the atomic bomb on Japan to end World War II.

# Suggested Reading

- Dower, John. *War Without Mercy: Race and Power in the Pacific War*. New York: Panetheon Books, 1986.

This study explores the role and significance of Japanese and American racism in the Pacific theater during World War II.


- Keegan, John. *The Second World War*. New York: Penguin Books, 1990.

Arguably the best single volume to date on World War II, this book proceeds chronologically through the war and provides a detailed factual analysis as well as extensive commentary. Keegan sheds light on the motivations of the Allied and Axis powers.


- Specter, Ronald. *Eagle Against the Sun: The American War with Japan*. New York: Vintage Books, 1985.

Specter's book examines the war in the Pacific from both Allied and Japanese perspectives.


- Weinberg, Gerhard L. *A World at Arms: A Global History of World War II*. New York: Cambridge University Press, 1994.

Weinberg's award-winning study bypasses the military details of the war to focus on overall strategy and diplomacy.

# The Cold War: 1945–1963

- The Yalta Conference
- The Cold War Begins
- The Korean War
- The Cold War at Home
- Prosperity and Consumerism
- The Civil Rights Movement Begins
- The Cold War in the Fifties
- Kennedy and the Rise of Liberalism

Japan's surrender in 1945 brought World War II to a close, but Joseph Stalin threatened that peace when he seized control of most Eastern European states in the immediate postwar years. The Soviet Union's desire to spread communism alarmed American leaders, who willingly accepted the mantle of world leadership. Rivalry with the Soviet Union turned into an ongoing global confrontation known as the Cold War. And with the new technology of nuclear weapons, fear of total global destruction intensified.

Americans were also worrying about changes closer to home. They desperately wanted to avoid another Great Depression. Minorities in the United States, many of whom had joined the war effort against tyranny and oppression overseas, hoped to achieve freedom and equality at home by launching the civil rights movement. In the decades after World War II, American's focus was on fighting communism abroad, achieving prosperity, and winning freedom at home.

# The Yalta Conference

As the Allies prepared for victory in Europe and Japan, they also laid plans for the postwar world. In separate conferences at **Yalta** and **Potsdam**, the United States, Great Britain, and Soviet Russia sought to avoid the mistakes of the post–World War I negotiations and prevent another world war in the future. These powers created a new organization more powerful than the League of Nations: the United Nations. Still, disagreements among the three produced mixed results over the postwar fates of both Germany and Poland.

## PLANNING THE POSTWAR WORLD

In February 1945, Roosevelt, Churchill, and Stalin met in the Russian town of Yalta to discuss the postwar world. Stalin agreed to side against Japan in exchange for authority over areas controlled by China and Japan. At the end of the **Yalta Conference**, the three leaders released the **Yalta Declaration of Liberated Europe**, which affirmed the promises in the Atlantic Charter to ensure free democratic systems in postwar Europe. In addition, there were three points of discussion:

1. The establishment of a new international organization
2. The plans for occupied Germany
3. The fate of a liberated Poland

### The United Nations

Roosevelt, Churchill, and Stalin endorsed a plan for the establishment of a new world body called the **United Nations (UN)**. Every nation would have a seat in the organization's General Assembly, but real power would reside with the smaller **UN Security Council**. The United States, the Soviet Union, Great Britain, France, and China would each have a permanent seat on the Security Council as well as veto power. At the end of April 1945, fifty nations met at the **UN Conference in San Francisco** to draft the charter for the United Nations. The U.S. Senate ratified the charter in July 1945.

### The Partition of Germany

Discussions at Yalta also determined the fate of occupied Germany. Roosevelt, Churchill, and Stalin agreed to temporarily divide occupied Germany into four zones to be controlled by the United States, Great Britain, France, and the Soviet Union. The city of Berlin, located in the Soviet zone, would consist of four similar zones. The agreement, which anticipated the eventual reunification of Germany, provided no specific plan or timeline. Stalin requested that Germany pay $20 billion in reparations to the Allies, half of which would go to the Soviets, although the Reparations Committee never resolved the issue.

### Poland

The Allies also discussed the future of Poland. At the Tehran Conference, Roosevelt and Churchill had agreed to let the Soviet Union annex eastern sections of Poland but refused Stalin's proposal to install a procommunist government. Instead, the pair wished to return the Polish government-in-exile that had operated out of London since Hitler's invasion in 1939. At Yalta, they agreed to allow both the old government and communists form a new provisional government for the duration of the war. Stalin promised free elections in Poland, but he set no specific deadline. Poles ultimately waited forty-five years before they could vote in free democratic elections.

### POTSDAM

Shortly after Roosevelt's death, **President Truman** attempted to revisit the unresolved issues of the Yalta Conference. In April 1945, he met with the Soviets and accused them of breaking the agreements set at Yalta. That July, he met with Churchill and Stalin in Potsdam, Germany, in Russian-controlled territory. There, Truman accepted Stalin's proposed borders for Poland but refused to agree to reparations from the other Allied zones of Germany. In 1949, the Russian zone became the republic of East Germany, and the three remaining zones joined together to form the separate state of West Germany.

Not long after the war, Europe grew divided between democracy and communism. President Franklin D. Roosevelt had anticipated that rivalries between nations would lead to conflict. To compensate, he developed a plan for the **United Nations (UN)** that would force nations to cooperate and maintain peace. Both the United States and the Soviet Union agreed to join the UN. But, as members of the UN Security Council, both countries held a veto over UN actions. Thus, the Cold War held the UN hostage and rendered the organization relatively powerless.

> Winston Churchill described the division between the democratic west and the communist east as an **"iron curtain."** In the mid-1940s, no one knew if the iron curtain would remain in a fixed position or if it could change its location.

# The Cold War Begins

As soon as World War II ended, soldiers and their families anticipated a quick return to normality. Instead, the United States found itself in a new kind of war: the **Cold War**. In the aftermath of World War II, the United States and the Soviet Union stood alone as the two great world powers. While the Soviet Union appeared eager to spread communism across the globe, the United States sought to defend democracy.

### UNITED STATES–SOVIET UNION RIVALRY

President Franklin D. Roosevelt hoped to work with Soviet leader Joseph Stalin, but Roosevelt's death prevented such a partnership. When Truman succeeded Roosevelt as president, he brought with him a reluctance to deal with Stalin, and soon Cold War tensions cooled relations between the United States and the Soviet Union. The Truman administration drastically expanded its role in the postwar world order. With the atomic bomb and a country relatively undamaged by World War II, American leaders created a new foreign policy based strictly on anticommunism.

### The Berlin Airlift

Stalin's actions in Poland led many U.S. policymakers to believe that the Soviet Union would also try to expand into Western Europe. Therefore, the Truman administration took immediate steps to confront the Soviet empire. Truman authorized the creation of an intelligence organization called the **National Security Agency** as well as the **National Security Council** to advise him. When Stalin cut off western access to Berlin, Truman refused to back down. He ordered the Air Force to drop thousands of pounds of food, clothing, and other goods to West Berlin in the **Berlin Airlift**.

### Containment

Truman built his foreign policy around U.S. diplomat **George Kennan**'s containment theory. Kennan believed that the Soviet Union wanted to expand, and that if the United States kept the Soviets within their current borders, communism would eventually collapse. Kennan argued that a patient policy of containment would allow the United States to defeat the Soviet Union without having to suffer any loss of life on the battlefield. The Truman administration quickly applied the containment theory as follows:

- Pledging to assist other countries fighting communist armies or revolutionaries in the **Truman Doctrine** in 1947. The first aid payments supported democratic governments in Greece and Turkey.

- Giving billions of dollars in aid to Western Europe according to the **Marshall Plan** in 1948. This aid improved the tattered economies of Western Europe and quieted communist movements. The plan also ensured that Western Europe would spend much of its aid money buying American goods.

- Forming the **North Atlantic Treaty Organization (NATO)**. NATO allied the United States with Canada, France, Great Britain, and other countries in Western Europe. Each NATO member pledged to support the others in the event of a Soviet invasion.

When Germany joined NATO in 1954, the Soviet Union formed its own treaty with the nations of Eastern Europe known as the **Warsaw Pact**.

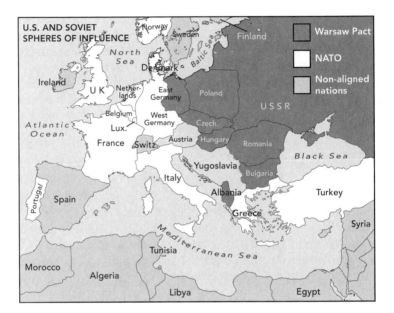

## THE FOUNDING OF ISRAEL

Jews across the world had long sought their own independent state. In the twentieth century, they focused their effort on creating a state in British-controlled Palestine, their spiritual home. After the Holocaust, world sentiment began to increase in favor of a Jewish state in Palestine. Eventually, Palestinian Jews founded the independent Jewish state of Israel in 1948, and Truman offered diplomatic recognition. Despite some criticism, Truman believed in the Jewish right to a home state and also knew that the decision would prove popular during the upcoming presidential election.

# The Korean War

Even though the Truman administration applied its containment strategy primarily in Europe, the first major battle in the Cold War occurred in East Asia as the Soviet Union and the United States backed different factions in the Korean civil war.

## THE WAR BEGINS

After World War II, the United States and the Soviet Union had their own areas of influence on the Korean peninsula. Stalin installed a Soviet-friendly government in the north, while the American-backed **Syngman Rhee** controlled the southern half below the **Thirty-eighth Parallel**.

### North Koreans Invade the South

In June 1950, North Korea launched an attack on the South. In accordance with containment and the Truman Doctrine, Truman immediately sent troops to protect South Koreans and managed to garner UN support for the mission. The initial fighting proved disastrous for the U.S. military, and by mid-September, the North Korean army had nearly conquered the entire peninsula.

*Although Truman strongly advocated civil rights, Congress ignored or struck down many of his legislative proposals. After World War II, many African American soldiers remained bitter about having fought a war for freedom while serving in segregated units and reporting to racist officers. As president, Truman strongly believed that the military should be fully integrated. In July 1948, Truman issued an executive order banning racial discrimination in the armed forces. During the Korean War, African Americans fought side by side with white soldiers for the first time.*

## MACARTHUR'S INCHON LANDING

On September 15, 1950, General **Douglas A. MacArthur** launched a daring amphibious assault at Inchon near Seoul and then proceeded to drive back communist forces north of the Thirty-eighth Parallel. When U.S. troops reached the border between North and South, Truman ordered MacArthur to invade the North, hoping to wipe out communism in Korea altogether. In early October, MacArthur's troops entered North Korea and quickly trounced the communist forces.

### Disaster on the Yalu River

As the U.S. army approached the Yalu River, which separated North Korea from China, Chinese troops swarmed into North Korea and quickly drove the U.S. soldiers back southward well into the territory MacArthur had just regained. U.S. General Matthew Ridgway eventually halted the U.S. retreat and pushed the Chinese forces back to the Thirty-eighth Parallel. By 1951, it was apparent both sides had stalemated each other, even though fighting continued for another two years.

### TRUMAN FIRES MACARTHUR

After Ridgeway and American forces drove the Chinese north of the Thirty-eighth parallel, Truman decided to negotiate a peace settlement. But MacArthur couldn't stand the idea of cutting a deal with communists after so many men had died for so little gain. The general therefore ignored Truman's orders and demanded that China surrender or face a United States invasion.

Moreover, General MacArthur publicly criticized the president's decisions in the American press, especially since Truman refused to use nuclear weapons in Korea or in China. MacArthur's threats ended the peace negotiations and forced the stalemated war to drag on for almost two more years. Truman fired Mac-Arthur for his insubordination.

### THE AFTERMATH OF KOREA

The Korean War finally ended after Eisenhower negotiated an armistice. After almost four years of war, North and South Korea had the same boundaries as before the war. Even though historians have dubbed the conflict America's "forgotten war," the Korean War killed roughly 33,000 Americans and injured more than 100,000. North Korea and China had over 1.5 million casualties.

The Korean War prompted the United States to implement **NSC-68**, a National Security Council report that called for a massive military buildup to wage the Cold War. NSC-68 tripled defense spending, as well as fueled anticommunism both at home and abroad.

# The Cold War at Home

Truman had to balance his attention between the Cold War overseas and demobilization at home. However, just as life began to return to normal, fears of communist infiltration in the United States gripped American society.

### DEMOBILIZATION

**Demobilization** from war to peace proved to be an uneasy process, as millions of G.I.s returned home hoping to find work. They wanted the millions of women who had joined the workforce during World War II to give up their jobs. Business leaders meanwhile pressured Truman to remove the government regulations Congress had enacted during the war, such as price controls and pro-labor laws. Workers, on the other hand, refused to give up their rights. A series of strikes broke out in the years following the war, including a railroad strike that almost completely paralyzed the nation.

The postwar turmoil eventually settled down. The Truman administration gradually ended price controls, and Americans began to spend the money they had saved during the war. The **GI Bill** provided veterans with money for education, housing, and job training. However, organized labor suffered when Congress passed the **Taft-Hartley Act** in 1947, which placed harsh restrictions on unions and limited the right to strike. Truman vehemently opposed the law, but Congress passed it over his veto.

## TRUMAN'S FAIR DEAL

Truman's support of organized labor made up just one part of his domestic agenda that sought to expand Franklin Roosevelt's New Deal. His support was dubbed the **"Fair Deal,"** and included the following stipulations:

- Stronger civil rights laws, including a ban on racial discrimination in the hiring of federal employees

- A higher minimum wage

- Extension of Social Security benefits

- Funding of low-income housing projects

The Republican-dominated Congress rejected other more radical aspects of Truman's Fair Deal. Several Democrats, mostly from southern states, disagreed with Truman over his stance on civil rights. When Truman ran for reelection in 1948, a group of southern Democrats broke from the party. Calling themselves **Dixiecrats**, they nominated Senator **Strom Thurmond** for president. Although Truman won the election, he continued to face opposition from the Republican Congress and the southern wing of his own party.

## THE SECOND RED SCARE

The fear of communism also spawned a **Second Red Scare** in the mid-1950s. Ordinary people began to believe that communist insurgents had infiltrated American institutions and suspected Hollywood actors, government officials, and even their own neighbors of being communist spies. Politicians capitalized on these fears and used anticommunism in their favor as a political tool to purge their enemies from office. Americans had grown more and more afraid of communism since the end of World War II for the following reasons:

- Communist forces under **Mao Zedong** had taken control of China in 1949. The so-called **Fall of China** meant that communists ruled the two largest nations on earth.

CHAPTER 7
1945–1963

- Espionage trials had concluded that **Klaus Fuchs** and **Julius and Ethel Rosenberg** had given information about the atomic bomb to the Soviet Union.

- The Soviet Union had developed nuclear weapons.

- Communist forces had nearly overwhelmed American troops in Korea.

- U.S. officials had convicted former State Department official **Alger Hiss** of perjury.

### Growing Suspicion

Although only a few hundred people belonged to the American Communist Party, government authorities began a comprehensive campaign to eradicate socialist influences in the United States. The **Federal Bureau of Investigation (FBI)** under the direction of J. Edgar Hoover, for example, began spying on people suspected of being communists. In Congress, the **House Un-American Activities Committee (HUAC)** also held widely publicized investigations of labor unions and other organizations suspected of harboring communist sympathizers.

*HUAC hearings hunting for communists in the Hollywood film industry prompted a group of ten Hollywood screenwriters to cry out that HUAC violated the First Amendment. In response, Hollywood film executives placed the writers, who came to be known as the* **Hollywood Ten**, *on a* **blacklist,** *or a list of suspected communists who shouldn't be hired. This blacklist grew over the next few years to include hundreds of Hollywood writers, directors, actors, producers, and other employees. Famous screen actor and future president Ronald Reagan helped authorities hunt suspected communists in the industry.*

**CHAPTER 7** 1945–1963

### Government Action

Upon realizing that anticommunism played well with the American people, the Republican party criticized the Truman administration for being "soft on communism." As a result, Republicans in Congress passed two acts:

- **The Loyalty Acts**, which required federal employees to remove any worker who had any connection to a communist organization

- **The McCarran Act**, which forced communist groups to register their names with the attorney general and restricted immigration of potential subversives. Truman vetoed this, but Congress overruled him.

### McCarthyism

Senator **Joseph McCarthy** from Wisconsin took anticommunism to new heights by holding public hearings in which he badgered witnesses and accused people of being communists. He never proffered any evidence and branded anyone who disagreed with him a communist. Despite this, his tactics made him extremely popular and won him national fame and reelection to the Senate.

McCarthy finally overstepped his reach in 1954 when he accused the U.S. Army of harboring communists. Aired on national television, the **Army-McCarthy Hearings** revealed McCarthy's vindictive behavior to millions of Americans across the country. The Senate censured McCarthy for his misconduct shortly after the hearings and effectively ended his career.

# Prosperity and Consumerism

Domestic politics settled into a tame routine after the tumult of the Second Red Scare. An economic boom muted political divisions, and American society embraced an exploding consumer economy.

### EISENHOWER'S DOMESTIC AGENDA

President **Dwight D. Eisenhower** loomed over the 1950s as the central political figure of the age. The economy soared, creating a level of affluence not seen before in American history. Additionally, Eisenhower worked to maintain the essential elements of the New Deal.

### Dynamic Conservatism

In the 1952 election, Eisenhower defeated Democrat Adlai Stevenson. A moderate conservative, Eisenhower appealed to members of both parties, and partisan tensions decreased during his two terms in office. "Ike" Eisenhower championed **dynamic conservatism**, a philosophy that combined conservative fiscal policies with the social reforms of the New Deal. Policies included:

- Closer ties between government and business

- Reduction of federal spending, balancing the budget, ending wage and price controls, and lowering farm subsidies

- Expandsion of Social Security benefits and raising the minimum wage

- Funding of public works programs, including the **St. Lawrence Seaway** and the **Interstate Highway system**

### Economic Boom

The **Gross National Product (GNP)** more than doubled between 1945 and 1960 as the economy grew stronger and stronger in the postwar years. Inflation stayed low, and the income of the average American household rose, allowing more people to buy expensive consumer goods. The economy thrived, for such reasons as:

- Government spending encouraged economic growth. Federal funding of schools, housing, highways, and military expenditures created jobs.

- Europe offered little competition to American levels of production. As the rest of the world recovered from World War II, the United States exported goods across the globe.

- New technologies like computers boosted productivity in many areas, including heavy industry and agriculture.

- Consumption increased. After the lean years of the Great Depression and World War II, Americans bought goods they couldn't previously afford. The **baby boom** also increased consumer needs.

The rising level of affluence in America left some people behind. Small farmers and residents of rural areas, for example, suffered hardship. The total number of farmers fell as prices steadily dropped. Many city dwellers, including African Americans and other minorities, often lived in poverty. Many industries cut jobs for unskilled workers, and racial discrimination often kept minorities out of other jobs.

## CONSUMER CULTURE

Although rural and urban areas suffered during the 1950s, the suburbs boomed. Meanwhile, the postwar prosperity gave birth to a new consumer culture.

### The Growth of Suburbs

As middle-class Americans grew wealthier, every family wanted a home of their own. Americans began spreading out of the cities and into the suburbs. Builders rapidly constructed suburbs like New York's Levittown, which consisted of nearly identical houses. Levittown and other suburban developments often excluded African Americans.

### The Consumer Culture

During the 1950s, industrial jobs began to disappear, while white-collar jobs in industries like advertising and finance increased. The newly expanded industry of advertising encouraged Americans to buy new goods such as televisions, cosmetics, and frozen TV dinners. The consumption of consumer goods soon became one of the driving forces behind the American economy. Shopping malls consequently sprouted in suburbs across the United States. When Americans could not afford a purchase, they relied on credit, a psychology that differed greatly from the thrift and financial conservatism of the previous generation that had come of age during the Great Depression.

### Critics of the Postwar Culture

Not everyone approved of the changing American culture. Some artists and writers began to challenge the culture of suburbs,

> The United States also became a nation of automobile owners. Americans could buy cars on credit, and auto manufacturers introduced new models every year to encourage people to replace their old cars. The **Interstate Highway Act** of 1956 created a uniform system of roads across the country. As a consequence, countless fast food restaurants and hotel chains popped up along the nation's highways.

nonindustrial jobs, and interstates. For example, William H. Whyte's *The Organization Man* argued that American business had lost its enterprising spirit. Whyte believed that instead of encouraging innovation, white-collar jobs stifled creativity by forcing workers to conform to company norms. Many Americans extended this argument to apply to the suburbs. Critics argued that the suburbs lacked the cultural institutions and ethnic diversity of the cities; rather, suburbanites focused on matching the consumption of their neighbors.

A literary group known as the **Beats** challenged the conformity of the times. The Beats rejected mainstream culture and embraced spontaneity and individuality in personal behavior. "Beatnik" Jack Kerouac and his 1957 novel *On the Road* typified the movement.

> American youth began to challenge conformity during this time period. Young people embraced **rock 'n' roll**, a sexually charged type of music that crossed racial boundaries by blending African-American rhythm and blues with white country music. Top performers included Chuck Berry, Elvis Presley, and Bill Haley.

# The Civil Rights Movement Begins

Although many Americans prospered during the 1950s, African Americans experienced few benefits from the economic boom. **Jim Crow laws**—laws that enforced segregation throughout the South—continued to exist, while the Eisenhower administration expressed little interest in civil rights. A landmark Supreme Court decision in the mid-1950s, however, sparked a massive **civil rights movement** that ultimately reshaped American society. Historians identify several factors that led to the rise of African-American protest during the 1950s and 1960s:

- Experiences in World War II had offended many African Americans' sense of justice. The United States had fought a war for freedom abroad but had ignored civil rights at home.

- A black middle class began to emerge. This class consisted of doctors, ministers, lawyers, and teachers, who also acted as community leaders. The civil rights movement relied heavily on these men and women.

- University enrollment began to increase after World War II. African-American college students formed networks of activism that eventually helped end segregation.

### BROWN V. BOARD OF EDUCATION

For decades, the **National Association for the Advancement of Colored People (NAACP)** had issued court challenges against segregated schooling. In 1954, the Supreme Court, under the stewardship of Chief Justice **Earl Warren**, unanimously struck down segregated education with its landmark decision in **Brown v. Board of Education of Topeka, Kansas**. The decision overturned the notion of "separate-but-equal" previously established by **Plessy v. Ferguson** in 1896.

Unfortunately, very little changed after the ruling. The predominantly black schools still lacked the resources and money of white schools. President Eisenhower refused to voice support for the *Brown* v. *Board of Education* decision.

### School Desegregation

Across the South, racist whites campaigned vigorously against the Court's decision. Many school districts desegregated as slowly as possible, and some whites even shut down their schools rather than admit black students. A showdown over school integration occurred in Little Rock, Arkansas, in 1957, when an angry mob of whites prevented a group of nine African Americans from entering Little Rock's Central High School. Arkansas Governor Orval

Faubus supported the mob but eventually backed down after Eisenhower reluctantly sent army troops to escort the **"Little Rock Nine"** to class. Eisenhower's decision demonstrated that federal government supported desegregation.

## THE MONTGOMERY BUS BOYCOTT

Having won desegregation in schools, African-American activists began to challenge other Jim Crow laws as well. The first major burst of activism occurred in Montgomery, Alabama, after police had arrested black resident **Rosa Parks** for refusing to give up her seat on a city bus to a white man in December 1955. NAACP attorneys immediately filed a lawsuit against the city, while the African-American community boycotted the bus service.

### The Rise of Martin Luther King, Jr.

A young, charismatic preacher named **Martin Luther King, Jr.,** who empowered the civil rights movement with powerful rhetoric and skillful, nonviolent tactics, mobilized Montgomery's religious community behind the bus boycott. King's eloquence eventually won the movement national support. Within a year, Montgomery city officials agreed to desegregate its bus system.

*The Montgomery movement exposed the potential power of ordinary African Americans. Consequently, communities throughout the South began mobilizing to end Jim Crow laws. Racists organized themselves as well, hoping to stem the tide of social change.*

**CHAPTER 7
1945–1963**

# The Cold War in the Fifties

The Cold War moved in two directions during the 1950s. On the one hand, the United States and the Soviet Union moved closer together. After Stalin died in 1953, Eisenhower reached out to the new, more moderate Soviet leader **Nikita Khrushchev.** Eisenhower and Khrushchev began a dialogue about ending the arms race and reducing nuclear weapons. In other ways, however, Cold

War tensions increased. The development of new technologies and weapons threatened the peace with new methods of destruction. As a result, Eisenhower's administration adopted a newer and more aggressive foreign policy.

### THE NEW LOOK AND MASSIVE RETALIATION

Eisenhower and his secretary of state, **John Foster Dulles**, promised a new type of foreign policy. They sought to contain the Soviet Union, but they also wanted to "roll back" communism and liberate Eastern Europe. The new foreign policy also relied on covert CIA operations to prevent communist groups from taking power in strategic countries. Additionally, Eisenhower sought to reduce spending on conventional weapons and increase spending on nuclear weapons, believing that nuclear weapons provided "more bang for the buck," a policy known as the **New Look**. Dulles promised to respond to Soviet aggression with **massive retaliation**, i.e., a devastating nuclear attack.

### THE COLD WAR IN THE THIRD WORLD

The Eisenhower administration devoted much attention to preventing communism in the third world, or areas outside of American or Soviet spheres of influence. In fact, Eisenhower and Dulles often used the **Central Intelligence Agency (CIA) to** topple unfriendly governments or combat communist revolutionaries. For example, the CIA prevented a coup from deposing the corrupt shah, or king, of Iran in 1953; engineered a coup against a popularly elected socialist government in Guatemala in 1954; and invaded Cuba in 1961 after communist Fidel Castro seized power.

#### The Suez Crisis

In 1956, Dulles froze American aid in Egypt when Egyptian president **Gamal Abdel Nasser** voiced his intention to accept aid from communist countries. Nasser responded to Dulles's actions by seizing the **Suez Canal**, jointly owned by Great Britain and France. When Great Britain, France, and Israel attacked Egypt in order to take back the Suez Canal, an outraged Eisenhower refused to sell them the oil they needed to maintain their economies. Unable to risk angering the United States and thus endanger their oil supply, they withdrew and allowed UN peacekeeping forces to stabilize the region.

### Vietnam Troubles

Eisenhower also faced a growing crisis in Southeast Asia, where France had struggled to maintain control of their colonies since the end of World War II. In Vietnam, for example, rebels led by procommunist **Ho Chi Minh** declared their independence from France after seizing the strategic French army garrison at **Dien Bien Phu**. Although the United States provided France with plenty of aid to support its war in Indochina, Eisenhower refused to commit U.S. troops to the conflict.

### THE ARMS RACE

The arms race continued to escalate during the 1950s. In 1957, advances in rocketry allowed the Soviet Union to launch an artificial satellite called **Sputnik** into orbit around the earth. This event sparked fears in the United States that Soviet science and technology had surpassed America. Sputnik's flight also meant that the Soviets might soon be able to launch **intercontinental ballistic missiles (ICBMs)** that could travel from silos in the Soviet Union to destroy targets in the United States. Suddenly, the threat of nuclear attack became a real possibility for Americans.

### The Space Race

In response, the Eisenhower administration accelerated its own space program. Soon, the United States had ICBMs of its own, while the **National Aeronautics and Space Administration (NASA)** blazed a trail in the exploration of space. Eisenhower soon became concerned about the increased militarization of American life. In his 1961 farewell address, he warned Americans to defend against the influence of the **military-industrial complex**. He feared that a powerful military linked to wealthy defense industries would negatively influence "every city, every state house, every office of the federal government."

*During Eisenhower's term, the CIA developed a spy plane known as the **U-2**. The U-2 flew over the Soviet Union high enough to avoid Soviet fire but close enough to snap photos of a car's license plate. These flights angered the Soviets. As relations between the United States and Soviet Union warmed during the 1950s, Eisenhower hoped to stop the U-2 flights. But just before a meeting with Khrushchev in 1960, Eisenhower approved one final U-2 flight that Soviet defenses managed to destroy. When Eisenhower refused to apologize for the flight, Khrushchev called off the summit.*

# Kennedy and the Rise of Liberalism

Americans in the 1960s anticipated that the new decade would bring a sharp break with the past. A new generation came of age and attempted to distance itself from what it regarded as a stagnant 1950s. Instead of merely accumulating wealth, Americans began to envision using their wealth for something meaningful. During the 1960s, President John F. Kennedy established a powerful liberal state that extended some of the vast resources of the United States to people who needed them. At the same time, Kennedy promised a new approach to the Cold War.

### THE ELECTION OF 1960

The election of 1960 featured many remarkable twists and turns. At first, many observers predicted Republican Vice President **Richard Nixon** would win because his Democratic opponent **John F. Kennedy** lacked Nixon's experience and national exposure. But Kennedy overcame these obstacles and narrowly won by just over 100,000 votes. Rather than challenge the results, Nixon gracefully accepted his surprising defeat.

*Kennedy won the election of 1960 primarily thanks to television. In the nation's first televised debates, Kennedy projected a youthful confidence that contrasted sharply with Nixon's countenance. Although radio listeners judged the debates to be about even, television viewers believed Kennedy prevailed.*

### THE NEW FRONTIER

In his inaugural address, Kennedy challenged the American people to accept the nation's role as a world power and outlined his **New Frontier** program for the United States. "Ask not what your country can do for you," he stated. "Ask what you can do for your country." During his campaign, Kennedy promised changes toward economic equality and civil rights. With time, he grew increasingly frustrated as Republicans and southern Democrats joined together to defeat most of his domestic programs. As a result, Kennedy abandoned the New Frontier at home and refocused his attention on foreign policy.

Many of the liberal reforms of the 1960s originated from the Supreme Court, still led by Chief Justice Earl Warren. For example, the Warren Court:

- Forced states to redefine electoral districts to match the population
- Provided the right to counsel for accused criminals who could not afford lawyers
- Required law-enforcement officials to read suspected criminals their rights
- Worked to limit religion in schools

### KENNEDY AND "FLEXIBLE RESPONSE"

At first, Kennedy's foreign policy appeared to share the same idealism as his domestic agenda. He founded the **Peace Corps,** which sent volunteers on humanitarian missions in underdeveloped countries. But the centerpiece of Kennedy's foreign policy was on anticommunism.

Whereas Truman had fought communism by giving money to fight communist insurgents and Eisenhower had threatened the U.S.S.R. with "massive retaliation," the Kennedy administration devised the doctrine of **"flexible response."** Developed by Defense and State Department officials like Robert S. McNamara, the containment doctrine of "flexible response" gave Kennedy a variety of military and political options to use depending on the situation.

### The Bay of Pigs Invasion

Kennedy chose to fight **Fidel Castro**'s revolutionary army in Cuba by allowing the CIA to train an anticommunist invasion force comprising 1,500 Cuban expatriates. The small invasion army landed at the Bay of Pigs in Cuba in spring 1961 only to find the Cuban revolutionaries waiting for them. The failed **Bay of Pigs Invasion** evolved into a major political embarrassment for the United States, and it ruined American-Cuban relations.

### Commitment in Southeast Asia

Kennedy also sent approximately 30,000 troops to South Vietnam in 1961 as "military advisors" to prevent South Vietnamese from toppling **Ngo Dinh Diem**'s corrupt regime in Saigon. These troops served as the first American ground forces in Vietnam and thus marked the beginning of American military commitment in the region that would plague future administrations.

### The Berlin Crisis

Relations between Kennedy and Khrushchev proved to be just as difficult. In 1961, Khrushchev erected the **Berlin Wall** between the eastern and western sections of Berlin. The wall quickly became a symbol of Cold War divisions.

CHAPTER 7 1945–1963

### The Cuban Missile Crisis

The most intense confrontation between the two leaders occurred in October 1962 when Kennedy learned that Khrushchev had sent nuclear missiles to Cuba. The drama of the **Cuban Missile Crisis** played out as follows over thirteen days:

- U.S. intelligence photos showed Soviet workers constructing nuclear missile silos in Cuba on October 14, 1962.

- Kennedy then announced a blockade of Cuba on October 22. He stated that U.S. forces would fire on any ships that attempted to pass through the blockade.

- Soviet ships approached the blockade, but stopped just short of entering Cuban waters on October 24.

- Kennedy and Khrushchev finally reached an agreement on October 28 in which Khrushchev agreed to remove the missiles in exchange for Kennedy's promise not to invade Cuba.

Never before had the Cold War powers come so close to nuclear war. In 1963, the United States and the Soviet Union agreed to the first arms control measure of the Cold War, when they signed the **Nuclear Test Ban Treaty**, limiting the testing of nuclear weapons.

### JFK'S ASSASSINATION

On November 22, 1963, a gunman shot and killed President Kennedy in Dallas, Texas, as he was riding in an open car. The Kennedy assassination continues to puzzle Americans to this day. Soon after the assassination in November 1963, authorities arrested **Lee Harvey Oswald** for the murder. Days later, during transport between jails, Dallas nightclub owner **Jack Ruby** murdered Oswald. An investigation headed by Supreme Court Chief Justice Earl Warren concluded that Oswald had acted alone, but the mysterious circumstances surrounding his death have left some questions unanswered. Books, films, and other media have kept different conspiracy theories alive.

Would you characterize the Eisenhower Era (1953–1960) as tame or turbulent? Take a position and support your argument with historical facts.

The predominant cultural images of the 1950s are ones of placid domesticity: nuclear families, suburban homes, and wholesome lives. These images held true for much of the U.S. population during the 1950s. At the same time, many radical changes and movements—including the Civil Rights movement, the second wave of feminism, and the Beat movement—began during this era. The 1960s are often remembered as the most turbulent era of the twentieth century in America, but in fact the seeds of this turbulence were planted in the 1950s.

Plenty of evidence exists to support the tameness of the 1950s. For example, books like *The Organization Man* showed how the business culture of the 1950s discouraged businessmen to think of innovative solutions to issues. Instead, companies expected their employees to adhere to established procedures and rules of conduct. Additionally, most businessmen lived in the suburbs, where Americans faced the pressure to conform to societal norms. They often lived around people with the same values and social status and felt pressure to conform to the mainstream. A dark undercurrent to this strain of American life was the persistence of the Jim Crow segregation laws in the South and the spawning of suburbs like Levittown that excluded African Americans.

Though television programs of the era, like *Leave It to Beaver* (1957–1963), might portray this period as serene and normal for the American family, its literature shows darker forces at work. Two novels published in 1960 that illuminate 1950s family life, Richard Yates's *Revolutionary Road* and John Updike's *Rabbit, Run*, both end with tragic family deaths, brought on in part by the ennui of 1950s suburban conformity. The wife in Yates's book, who has been plotting to escape the suburbs for Paris until she discovers her own pregnancy and her husband's adultery, dies while attempting to perform an abortion on herself. In Updike's book, the wife, plunged into an alcoholic stupor by the idea that her husband has left her for a second time, accidentally drowns

# *Student Essay*

her infant daughter. While these characters are undone by boredom, the heroes of a parallel literary movement, the Beats, set off on road trips and experimented with drugs and sex to ward off the suburban doldrums, anticipating the ethos of the 1960s hippie counterculture.

Some of the turbulence of the 1950s, especially that of the nascent Civil Rights movement, transpired in public and eventually led to progressive changes in American society. In 1954, the Supreme Court struck down segregated schooling in the *Brown v. Board of Education* decision. Racial barriers were broken, and when President Eisenhower sent U.S. troops to enforce integration in Little Rock, Arkansas, he set a precedent for government support of the Civil Rights movement. After hundreds of years of oppression, the government finally began to grant the rights of the Declaration of Independence to African Americans. After the Montgomery bus boycott (1955–56), the Civil Rights movement became front-page news. Jim Crow laws dating from the end of the Civil War began to be overturned.

The Cold War also contributed to the turbulence of the era and brought about great changes in American society. The Soviet Union developed new long-range nuclear weapons, putting the United States at great risk, and launched the first satellite, Sputnik, into space. This event caused many Americans to fear that the United States lagged behind the U.S.S.R. in the arms race and the Cold War. Much of the American economy came to be based on military and defense spending. Even President Eisenhower warned of this danger in his military-industrial complex speech, a concern shared by Americans at the time.

Though we usually think of the 1950s as a quiet interlude between the war of the 1940s and the civic upheavals of the 1960s, this decade was actually as turbulent as any era of the past hundred years.

# Test Questions and Answers

*1. How did Truman, Eisenhower, and Kennedy wage the Cold War differently?*

- All believed that communism and the Soviet Union had to be contained.

- The Truman Doctrine pledged the United States to helping other countries like Greece and Turkey fight communist insurgents.

- Eisenhower and Dulles's New Look threatened to retaliate against Soviet aggression with "massive retaliation," or nuclear war.

- Kennedy's doctrine of "flexible response" allowed him to respond to Soviet moves with a variety of measures including money, troops, or nuclear strike.

*2. How was the Supreme Court's ruling in* Brown v. Board of Education *so significant?*

- It reversed the Court's 1896 ruling in *Plessy v. Ferguson* by striking down the concept of "separate but equal."

- It was the first major federal blow against Jim Crow laws in the South.

- It helped launch the civil rights movement.

*3. Describe the social trends of the 1950s.*

- Postwar economic prosperity increased the size of the middle class.

- Americans began purchasing more expensive consumer items like refrigerators and televisions.

- More Americans purchased cars and began to move out of the cities to live in the suburbs.

- The growing African-American middle class began challenging white supremacy in the early years of the civil rights movement.

- Some Americans like the Beats resisted these changes and the rise of mass consumerism.

# Timeline

| | |
|---|---|
| **1945** | Roosevelt, Churchill, and Stalin discuss the postwar world at the Yalta Conference. |
| | The Potsdam Conference ends with an ultimatum for Japan to unconditionally surrender. |
| | The United Nations is formed. |
| **1947** | Truman announces his Truman Doctrine. |
| | Congress sends $400 million to Greece and Turkey. |
| | The United States gives Europe aid under the Marshall Plan. |
| | Congress passes the Taft-Hartley Act. |
| | Congress passes the National Security Act. |
| | House Un-American Committee hunts for communists. |
| **1948** | Israel is founded. |
| | Truman orders the Berlin Airlift. |
| | Truman is elected. |
| **1949** | North Atlantic Treaty Organization is created. |
| **1950** | Senator McCarthy begins hunting for communists. |
| | NSC-68 is put into effect. |
| | The Korean War begins. |
| | Congress passes the McCarran Act. |
| **1951** | Truman fires General MacArthur. |
| **1952** | Dwight D. Eisenhower is elected president. |
| **1953** | Julius and Ethel Rosenberg are executed. |
| **1954** | The Army-McCarthy Hearings are aired on national television. |
| | Segregated education is struck down in *Brown v. Board of Education*. |
| **1955** | The Warsaw Pact is created. |
| | Montgomery Bus Boycott begins. |
| **1956** | Eisenhower is reelected. |

| | |
|---|---|
| **1957** | U.S.S.R. launches Sputnik. |
| | Southern Christian Leadership Coalition (SCLC) forms. |
| **1960** | The U-2 Incident angers the Soviets. |
| | John F. Kennedy is elected president. |
| | The Student Nonviolent Coordinating Committee (SNCC) forms. |
| **1961** | Bay of Pigs Invasion tranishes Kennedy's image. |
| | Freedom Rides occur throughout the South. |
| **1962** | The Cuban Missile Crisis brings the Cold War powers close to war. |
| **1963** | The Nuclear Test Ban Treaty is signed. |
| | Martin Luther King, Jr., leads the March on Washington. |
| | Kennedy is assassinated. |

# Major Figures

**John Foster Dulles**  As secretary of state under President Dwight D. Eisenhower, Dulles's strong anticommunism and reliance on nuclear deterrence drastically altered U.S. foreign policy during the 1950s.

**Dwight D. Eisenhower**  President Eisenhower's restrained style of leadership helped create nearly a decade of economic growth but was slow to support social change. In foreign policy, Eisenhower showed a willingness to coexist with the Soviet Union, while simultaneously building up the U.S. nuclear arsenal.

**George Kennan**  An American diplomat who served in the Soviet Union during the 1940s, Kennan outlined the strategy of containment that called for the United States to thwart communist advances abroad in order to prevent more countries from falling under the influence of the U.S.S.R.

**John F. Kennedy**  President John F. Kennedy's exuberance and charisma energized the nation after the conformity of the 1950s. While Congress stalled his domestic initiatives, Kennedy's foreign policy proved to be risky and dramatic. Under his leadership, the Cold War intensified in underdeveloped countries.

**Martin Luther King, Jr.**  As a civil rights leader, King's passionate oratory and skillful civil disobedience tactics helped end legal racial segregation in the United States. His assassination in 1968 sparked riots across the country and caused a rift in the civil rights movement.

**Douglas A. MacArthur**  General of the U.S. Army during World War II and the Korean War, MacArthur's masterful landing at Inchon reversed a series of dramatic U.S. defeats. His later departure from President Truman's conduct of the war led to his controversial dismissal.

**Joseph McCarthy**  A Wisconsin senator made famous by his controversial anticommunism, McCarthy accused people of being communists with little or no evidence and labeled any political opponent as procommunist. His combative tactics proved popular and successful during the Red Scare of the 1950s.

**Richard M. Nixon**  A member of the House Un-American Activities Committee during the Red Scare of the late 1940s, Nixon lost the presidential election in 1960. He won the presidency in 1968.

**Rosa Parks**  Parks's 1954 arrest sparked a grassroots protest in Montgomery, Alabama. The subsequent victory for Parks's supporters helped launch the civil rights movement.

**Harry S Truman**  As thirty-third president of the United States, Truman earned admiration for his strong stand against the Soviet Union at the start of the Cold War. His initiatives in Europe bolstered democratic governments and restrained communist aggression. On the other hand, Truman faced high opposition at home as he attempted a smooth transition from war to peace.

**Earl Warren**  As chief justice of the Supreme Court from 1953 to 1969, Warren helped decide one of the most dramatic Supreme Court rulings in U.S. history when he orchestrated the unanimous verdict in *Brown v. Board of Education* (1954) that ended school segregation in the United States. During the 1960s, Warren presided over a Supreme Court that dramatically expanded civil liberties in the United States.

# Suggested Reading

- Gaddis, John Lewis. *We Now Know: Rethinking Cold War History.* New York: Oxford University Press, 1997.

Eminent Cold War historian Gaddis delivers an eye-opening reappraisal of the key events of the 1950s and '60s.


- Halberstam, David. *The Fifties.* New York: Ballantine Books, 1994.

A sweeping cultural, economic, and political history of an often misunderstood decade. The book was a national bestseller.


- Weisbrot, Robert. *Freedom Bound: A History of America's Civil Rights Movement. New York.* Norton, 1990.

This book provides a fast-paced chronicle of the civil rights movement in the United States.

CHAPTER 7
1945–1963

# Civil Rights and Vietnam: 1963–1975

- The Civil Rights Movement
- Johnson in the 1960s
- Nixon Abroad
- Nixon at Home
- Watergate, Resignation, and Ford

**8**

Protest, defeat, and progress defined the United States in the 1960s and 1970s. While the civil rights movement and the war on poverty dominated the agenda at home, President Lyndon B. Johnson drastically escalated the Vietnam War to prevent the spread of communism. Nixon's administration further expanded the war in Vietnam in 1973.

Liberal and conservative critics alike expressed their disappointment with the government and the war, and this distress fueled the American public's growing distrust of the government, spurring the development of the counterculture that rose to prominence in the late 1960s and 1970s. Americans were starting to question the values and norms of the previous generation and challenge the social and political structure of the nation. For the first time, the youth of America began to emerge as a significant culture, a voice that rebelled against the regularity of the 1950s mentality. Ultimately, this backlash against rigidity would give birth to one of the country's most fascinating eras and a new generation of innocents with a utopian vision of universal brotherhood.

# The Civil Rights Movement

Across the South, African Americans waged campaigns of civil disobedience that often proved effective enough to bring about social change. As the movement gained momentum, however, white racists increased their efforts to stop it. The conflict between social change and hatred drew national attention to civil rights.

## STUDENT ACTIVISM

Students, including the **Student Nonviolent Coordinating Committee (SNCC),** waged some of the more powerful campaigns of the civil rights movement. SNCC organized a number of events that had far-reaching consequences. In 1960, African-American college students and other activists seated themselves at white-only lunch counters, refusing to leave until served. The demonstrators frequently suffered abuse from white onlookers and ended up in jail. Additionally, members of SNCC and the **Congress of Racial Equality** embarked on a series of bus rides across the South in 1961. The rides aimed to integrate traveling facilities across the South. White mobs greeted the riders with violence in Alabama. Finally, in 1964, northern college students went to Mississippi to register African Americans to vote. By the end of the summer, many activists had been severely beaten by the police, and a few lost their lives.

### Major Civil Rights Organizations

| Acronym | Name | Major Accomplishments |
|---------|------|----------------------|
| CORE | Congress of Racial Equality | Freedom Rides |
| NAACP | National Association for the Advancement of Colored People | *Brown v. Board of Education* |
| SCLC | Southern Christian Leadership Conference | Birmingham, Alabama, civil rights campaign;  March on Washington |
| SNCC | Student Nonviolent Coordinating Committee | Freedom Summer |

## THE KING CAMPAIGNS

In 1963, **Martin Luther King, Jr.,** began a civil rights campaign in Birmingham, Alabama, to pressure the municipal government to end segregation in the city. King and his fellow activists staged sit-ins and marches. When authorities arrested demonstrators, including King himself, more demonstrators simply took their places. The city jail soon filled up and the city's bureaucracy became overwhelmed. A series of economic boycotts of downtown businesses also brought the city's economy to a halt.

As demonstrations grew in number and power, white resistance to the movement increased. Vigilante bombers attempted to kill King and his family and city police attacked demonstrators with fierce dogs and fire hoses. Pictures of the violence ended up in newspapers across the country, turning public opinion in favor of the civil rights activists. Eventually, city officials capitulated and ended segregation.

### The March on Washington

Months after the successful Birmingham campaign, King led more than 200,000 civil rights activists in a **March on Washington**, D.C. Standing in front of the Lincoln Memorial, King gave his **"I Have a Dream"** speech, one of the key speeches of his career.

### Selma

The next major civil rights campaign occurred in Selma, Alabama, in 1965. Civil rights activists planned a march from Selma to Montgomery to publicize whites' disenfranchisement of Alabama blacks. But Alabama state troopers attacked the activists as soon as they began their march. When the protestors demonstrated their determination to march again a few days later, President **Lyndon Johnson** sent the Alabama National Guard to protect them.

## GOVERNMENT ACTION

Johnson supported the civil rights movement and succeeded in getting Congress to pass the **Civil Rights Act of 1964**. The act effectively ended legal segregation and discrimination. Racial discrimination in all public places, including hotels, restaurants, and schools was outlawed. The Equal Employment Opportunity Commission was also created, which prevented racial and gender discrimination in the workplace.

After the Selma campaign demonstrated the degree of disenfranchisement among southern blacks, Johnson and Congress also passed the **Voting Rights Act of 1965**, which allowed African Americans to register to vote quickly and easily, without fear of violence.

## THE MOVEMENT SPLITS

Most civil rights activism during the 1950s and 1960s occurred in the South. Racism existed in the North, of course, but ghettoes and urban poverty made civil disobedience far less effective there. Pent-up rage over black poverty and racial injustice eventually exploded across northern cities in the mid- to late-1960s.

### Riots

For some African Americans, social change occurred too slowly. Outside the South, certain black Americans concerned themselves more with fighting poverty than with voting rights or desegregation. Beginning in 1964, riots erupted across major U.S. cities, the largest occurring in Watts, Detroit, and Washington, D.C. Rioters often had no specific goals other than expressing rage and frustration over the racial and economic inequality in American society.

### Malcolm X

For decades, the **Nation of Islam** advocated black independence in the United States and drew a large African-American following in many northern cities. In the 1960s, **Malcolm X**, who promoted black pride and self-reliance, became one of the most eloquent and widely followed black Muslims. At times, he called for active self-defense against white violence. He was assassinated in 1965.

### Black Power

Some African-American activists concluded that laws and speeches would not change the deep-rooted causes of racism and oppression. In the mid-1960s, these activists embraced a more radical approach to civil rights. SNCC leader **Stokely Carmichael** began to use the term **Black Power** to describe his cause. Black Power expressed many of the themes advocated by Malcolm X, and its supporters encouraged African Americans to become independent of white society.

Advocates of the movement formed all-Black schools, organizations, and political groups such as the **Black Panthers**. Above all, Black Power expressed pride in African-American culture. Mainstream press coverage of Black Power often emphasized its aggressive side, leading to a severe backlash among whites.

# Johnson in the 1960s

After taking office in 1963, **Lyndon Johnson** pledged himself to righting the nation's social wrongs. In his State of the Union Address in January 1964, he informed Congress of his plans to build a **Great Society** by waging a **War on Poverty**.

### THE GREAT SOCIETY

Author **Michael Harrington**'s 1962 national bestselling book, *The Other America,* exposed middle-class suburbanites to the hunger, poverty, homelessness, and disease that afflicted as many as 50 million Americans. In response, Johnson and Democrats in the House and Senate passed the **Economic Opportunity Act** in the summer of 1964 to help the poorest Americans, especially urban blacks. Johnson and the Democrats promised a revolution with over $2 billion in social welfare reform and hailed the Great Society as the beginning of a new tomorrow.

CHAPTER 8
1963–1975

## THE WAR ON POVERTY

**The Economic Opportunity Act** created the Office of Economic Opportunities to spearhead the various projects aimed at creating jobs, improving education and housing, and providing medical care to those who could not afford it. OEO Programs included:

- **The Job Corps**, which offered vocational training to thousands of young inner-city black men
- **Project Head Start,** which educated more than 2 million of the poorest preschool-age children
- **Medicaid,** which offered federally funded health benefits to the poor
- **Medicare**, which offered health benefits to the elderly

Johnson also helped immigrants by passing the **Immigration and Nationality Act of 1965** to eliminate the national quota system. As a result, the number of yearly immigrants, especially from East Asia, skyrocketed.

> *Eventually, the quest for civil rights became a quest for better housing and better jobs. In launching the War on Poverty, Johnson revived the belief that government had a responsibility to help the less fortunate. Not since Roosevelt's New Deal had Congress spent so much money on social welfare programs.*

The War on Poverty had only limited success in helping the poor. This was primarily because none of the new government programs tackled the root problem of enormous income inequality. Although the government did redistribute roughly $1 billion, most of this money went to Americans who already earned middle-class incomes—not those in poverty. Blacks in particular saw very little of this money, even though they had been among the first to demand more social welfare spending. The Job Corps, for example, taught obsolete skills and provided only temporary unskilled work that offered no future. The war in Vietnam also siphoned the most money away from the War on Poverty, because Congress simply couldn't afford to fund both an antipoverty campaign and a major war abroad. Johnson's semiutopian vision of a Great Society had all but died by the mid-1970s.

## TONKIN GULF

As the War on Poverty moved forward, Johnson pledged to honor John F. Kennedy's limited troop commitments in Vietnam. More specifically, he promised not to send any more "American boys nine or ten thousand miles away from home to do what Asian boys ought to be doing for themselves." The president's policy changed dramatically, though, just a few months later when several **North Vietnamese Army (NVA)**, gunboats allegedly attacked two U.S. Navy destroyers in the **Gulf of Tonkin** off the coast of North Vietnam.

In response, Johnson requested from Congress the authority to take "all necessary steps" to protect U.S. servicemen in South Vietnam. Congress complied and passed the **Tonkin Gulf Resolution** in August 1964. Out of the 535 total members of Congress, only two voted against this resolution. Many policymakers considered this to be a de facto declaration of war.

## THE ELECTION OF 1964

Johnson easily won the support of the Democratic nominating convention on a Great Society platform. The attack in the Gulf of Tonkin and the congressional resolution only helped him in his election bid. LBJ's Republican opponent **Barry M. Goldwater** argued that much more needed to be done in Vietnam to contain communism; he even advocated using nuclear weapons. A self-proclaimed extremist, he also denounced the Great Society, the War on Poverty, and the civil rights movement in favor of near-radical conservatism. Not surprisingly, Johnson won the presidency that year with more than 60 percent of the popular vote and with 486 electoral votes to Goldwater's fifty-two.

## ESCALATION IN VIETNAM

In February 1965 procommunist **Viet Cong** guerillas in South Vietnam attacked Marine barracks on an American base in the hamlet of Pleiku. Eight soldiers died, and more than a hundred more suffered casualties. Newly endowed with a blank check from Congress, Johnson capitalized on the **Pleiku Raid** and immediately ordered the air force and navy to begin an intense series of air strikes called **Operation Rolling Thunder**. He hoped that the bombing campaign would demonstrate his commitment to the South Vietnamese and his resolve to halt the spread of communism. Ironically, the air raids seemed only to increase the number of NVA and Viet Cong attacks.

### Operation Rolling Thunder

Operation Rolling Thunder set the gears in motion for a major escalation of the war. Johnson believed that he could convince the NVA to withdraw by slowly increasing the number of American troops in Vietnam. He ordered more and more troops to South Vietnam in the next two years, bringing the total number to a staggering 400,000 men by the end of 1966. By 1968, the total number of troops had further jumped to more than 500,000. Sadly, as the number of in-country troops increased, so too did the number of casualties. More than 100,000 American men were killed or wounded by 1968.

*At the height of the Cold War, many believed that if the United States allowed one country to fall to communism, then many more would follow suit like a row of dominos. This **domino theory** led the United States to support anticommunist regimes throughout the world, whether or not they upheld democratic ideals. The domino theory also provided the primary rationale for Johnson's massive escalation of the conflict in Vietnam to full-scale war.*

### The Destruction of South Vietnam

Although Johnson hoped the 500,000 American troops would save South Vietnam, his policy of escalation effectively destroyed the country. By 1968 alone, the military had used 3 million tons' worth of bombs on Vietnam, more than all the bombs dropped in Europe during World War II. The United States also used **napalm**, a slow-burning chemical agent dropped with bombs to maximize destruction. The military also used 20 million gallons of another chemical weapon called **Agent Orange** to kill forest-lands and drive out the Viet Cong.

*The Vietnam War was so destructive because neither Johnson nor the military leadership knew how to fight a **guerilla war**. Having always fought professional armies in previous wars, Americans had no experience fighting an enemy like the Viet Cong. U.S. leaders failed to recognize that they had become involved in a civil war in which most civilians supported the NVA. As a result, American servicemen often found themselves fighting uncooperative or hostile civilians just as much as enemy forces.*

## COLLEGE STUDENT ACTIVISM

By 1968, the war had drastically divided society. College students made up one of the more vocal segments of the antiwar movement. On campuses across the nation, students held teach-ins, marches, and other forms of civil disobedience in protest of the war. Some of the more radical activists initiated student strikes and violently occupied campus administration buildings. At the same time, many Americans continued to support the war. These **"hawks"** opposed the peace-advocating **"doves"** and tried to brand their antiwar activities as un-American.

### The Tet Offensive

In 1968, the Vietnamese communists launched a major offensive against the South's major cities on the Vietnamese New Year, or Tet. Nightly news broadcasts showed the increasing violence and seemingly endless numbers of dead U.S. soldiers. Although American forces repelled the attackers and inflicted serious damage on the Viet Cong, most Americans at home interpreted the **Tet Offensive** as evidence that America was losing.

Consequently, criticism of the war increased sharply, and massive demonstrations occurred on college campuses and in Washington, D.C., while Johnson's popularity plummeted. With the situation in Vietnam becoming ever more hopeless, Johnson announced a bombing halt in March 1968. He then added that he would not seek reelection in the upcoming presidential election.

> Johnson's request to send hundreds of thousands more troops to
> Vietnam while simultaneously declaring victory prompted many
> Americans to question the president's honesty in the late 1960s.
> This **"credibility gap"** widened further when Johnson authorized
> the CIA and FBI's **"Cointelpro"** (Counter Intelligence Program) to
> spy on antiwar activists. The credibility gap also made the
> president a political liability for the Democratic Party, ruining his
> chance to run for reelection in 1968.

### The Assassinations of King and Robert F. Kennedy

As the war raged, tumultuous events continued to upset the
nation. In April 1968, an assassin gunned down Martin Luther
King, Jr., in Memphis, Tennessee. Riots broke out across America,
an expression of tremendous rage and grief over the loss. Later
that summer, an assassin killed **Robert F. Kennedy** at a California
campaign rally. The younger brother of John F. Kennedy, Robert Kennedy had been running for president on a platform of
opposition to the Vietnam War and support for civil rights.

### The Election of 1968

In the summer of 1968, thousands of protestors traveled to Chicago for the Democratic National Convention. As the convention proceeded, massive demonstrations took place around the
city. While most of the demonstrations remained peaceful, certain radical factions made more provocative statements. Chicago
police forces started to attack the demonstrators, and a full-scale
riot broke out.

The divisions in society caused by the war played out in the 1968
presidential election. Democrats nominated Vice President **Hubert
Humphrey**, but Humphrey's refusal to denounce the Vietnam War
divided the party. Republicans meanwhile nominated **Richard
Nixon**, who campaigned on a platform of "law and order." **George
Wallace** also ran on the third-party American Independent ticket.
Nixon's campaign appealed to many Americans who believed in the
war or thought that the antiwar and Black Power movements had
gotten out of hand. Nixon won with 301 electoral votes to Humphrey's 191 and Wallace's 46.

# Nixon Abroad

Soon after entering the White House, Nixon announced his new policy of **"Vietnamization"**—a slow withdrawal of the more than 500,000 American soldiers from Vietnam and a simultaneous return of control of the war to the South Vietnamese. He still intended to fund and train the South Vietnamese Army, but hoped that slow troop withdrawals would appease voters at home and reduce casualties in the field. He also announced the **Nixon Doctrine**: America would honor its current defense commitments but would not commit troops anywhere else to fight communism.

## THE SECRET INVASION OF CAMBODIA

Nixon sought instead to defeat the North Vietnamese by destroying their supply lines and base camps in neighboring Cambodia. Although Cambodia officially remained neutral during the war, the NVA ran weapons and troops through the country to circumvent American bombers and raiding parties. In the spring of 1970, Nixon authorized the invasion of Cambodia. The order shocked Congress and the American public. Renewed public outcry and waves of protests convinced Nixon to renege the order later that summer.

> When criticized by antiwar protestors, Nixon and his vice president, **Spiro Agnew**, always responded that the **"silent majority"** of Americans still supported the war in Vietnam. In other words, the president claimed that noisy activists constituted only a small percentage of the American public.

## MY LAI AND THE PENTAGON PAPERS

Other scandals sparked protest against the military and the president. In 1971, the U.S. Army court-martialed Lieutenant William Calley for ordering the rape, torture, and murder of more than 350 women and children in the 1968 **My Lai Massacre**. Other soldiers anonymously confessed that dozens of similar incidents had taken place over the course of the war. The military came under fire again that year when the *New York Times* published a series of leaked documents called the **Pentagon Papers**, which accused the army, John F. Kennedy, and Lyndon Johnson of deceiving the public during the war.

## CONGRESS CHECKS UNLIMITED POWER

Outraged by the unauthorized invasion of Cambodia and by the double scandal of the My Lai Massacre and the Pentagon Papers, many in Congress took steps to exert more control over the war and to appease an equally angry public. For example, the Senate (but not the House of Representatives) voted to repeal the Tonkin Gulf Resolution to reduce the military's unchecked spending power. Congress reduced the number of years drafted soldiers needed to serve in the army, and they also ratified the **Twenty-Sixth Amendment** in 1971 to lower the voting age from twenty-one to eighteen on the grounds that young soldiers in Vietnam should help elect the politicians who sent them to fight.

## DÉTENTE

Nixon decided the only solution rested on improving relations with the Soviet Union; this policy came to be known as **détente**. He believed détente would divert attention from the growing failures in Vietnam and allow the United States to eventually withdraw on more graceful terms. Nixon's national security advisor **Henry Kissinger** supported the plan.

### Nixon Goes to China

The president chose to approach Russia by opening relations with China in 1972. Although both communist countries, Maoist China and the Soviet Union were deeply suspicious of each other. Consequently, they had one of the most heavily fortified borders in the world. Nixon hoped dialogues with China would spark fear in Russia over a possible American-Chinese alliance. After visiting Beijing in 1972, Nixon and Kissinger then flew to Moscow, where they played their so-called **"China card"** to bring the Soviets to the negotiating table.

## ABM and SALT I

Even though the tactic outraged liberals and conservatives alike back in the United States, Nixon's ploy worked. While in the U.S.S.R., Nixon managed to smooth tensions with Soviet leader **Leonid Brezhnev** and usher in a new era of "cooler" American-Soviet relations called détente. He agreed to sell the Soviets $1 billion worth of badly needed American grain. This arrangement both helped Brezhnev feed his starving people and boosted Nixon's popularity with farmers in the Midwest.

In 1972, Nixon signed the **Anti-Ballistic Missile (ABM) Treaty** to limit the missile defense system, and the **Strategic Arms Limitation Talks Treaty (SALT Treaty)** to prevent both sides from developing any more nuclear weapons for the next five years. Washington enjoyed improved relations with Beijing as an added benefit.

## NIXON'S LANDSLIDE IN 1972

Nixon's successful trip to China and Russia gave him the advantage he needed in Vietnam. When the NVA crossed the demilitarized zone and invaded South Vietnam in 1972, Nixon authorized an intense bombing campaign of Hanoi without fear of retaliation from Moscow or Beijing. Nixon also secretly sent Kissinger to meet with North Vietnamese diplomats in Paris that year to discuss peace.

As the presidential elections of 1972 approached, Nixon clearly had the upper hand: he had initiated détente, reduced the number of American troops in Vietnam from 500,000 to 30,000, and had halted a major NVA advance. As a result, he easily defeated peace Democrat **George McGovern** in a landslide victory with 520 to thirteen electoral votes and nearly 20 million more popular votes.

## THE CHRISTMAS DAY BOMBING AND CEASE-FIRE

Nixon authorized the **Christmas Day Bombing**, an intense two-week bombing campaign of North Vietnam that he hoped would end the war. Kissinger and North Vietnamese officials finally announced a cease-fire in January 1973. Nixon accepted and agreed

*Hoping to win reelection by a landslide in the election of 1972, Richard Nixon employed his **"southern strategy"** to make himself as appealing as possible to white voters in the South. He promised to take a hardliner's stance against civil rights and to oppose Great Society social welfare spending, even though he proved to be supportive to both causes during his tenure as president.*

to withdraw the remaining American troops, despite the fact that the NVA controlled more than a quarter of South Vietnamese territory. In exchange, the North Vietnamese promised that an election in Saigon would determine the fate of the country.

# Nixon at Home

Although Nixon focused most of his attention on Vietnam and détente, he could not avoid contending with domestic issues, particularly the stagnant economy at home. Beginning in the early 1970s, both inflation and the cost of living crept skyward, while wages remained the same. Worker productivity was declining for the first time since before World War II. To make matters worse, cheaper and better foreign products from Japan started entering the market. On top of all this, Congress paid roughly $22 billion a year to fund Lyndon Johnson's social welfare programs and the war in Vietnam.

### THE NEW LEFT

The war in Vietnam and continuing racial strife in the United States spurred the radicalization of American youth during the 1960s and 1970s. In the early 1960s, idealistic young white Americans involved in the civil rights movement and other liberal endeavors expanded their efforts to other issues, forming what collectively became known as the **New Left.**

### COUNTERCULTURE

Students and other radical young people created a new **counterculture** in America. This counterculture flouted the values and conventions of middle-class society and embraced a new style that defied traditional standards. Many young Americans grew their hair long, wore shabby clothing, and exhibited rebellious disregard for the old manners and rules. Rock, folk music, and drugs, such as marijuana and LSD, came into vogue as well as new attitudes about sexuality. The ascendancy of the counterculture reflected wider currents in American society at large, as growing numbers of Americans became distrustful of the American government and official rhetoric during the Vietnam era.

*In the summer of 1969, about 400,000 people gathered on a farm in upstate New York for a three-day rock and folk music festival called the* **Woodstock Music and Art Fair***. Performers included many who would become the most celebrated musicians of the counterculture movement, including Joan Baez, Janis Joplin, Jimi Hendrix, the Grateful Dead, and Carlos Santana.*

## NIXON AND RACE RELATIONS

Even in 1969, fifteen years after the Supreme Court ruled in favor of mandatory desegregation in *Brown v. Board of Education,* the majority of southern schools were not racially integrated. Backed by a supportive Supreme Court, civil rights advocates pushed through a number of policies that fostered integration in schools across the entire country. The Nixon administration placed severe limits on the methods schools used to achieve integration goals. One of the most controversial integration measures involved busing students across cities and school districts in order to achieve desegregation.

Some of Nixon's policies furthered the goals of the civil rights movement. He enacted several initiatives intended to motivate contractors and unions to hire more minorities, offered incentives to minority businesses, and expanded the power of the Equal Rights Employment Opportunity Commission. While Nixon never supported racial quotas in hiring or education, his administration did support certain forms of affirmative action.

## WOMEN'S LIBERATION

The women's liberation movement gained new momentum in the 1970s. Engaging in peaceful protests for equality, these activists voiced their dissatisfaction with women's rights in the United States. Although women gained the right to vote in the 1920s, structural and cultural factors maintained inequality. The **National Organization for Women (NOW)** emerged as the primary group representing the concerns of mainstream feminists. NOW initiated strikes and protests to demand equality in employment, education, childcare, and reproductive control. Many smaller groups also fought for the passage of the **Equal Rights Amendment (ERA)** to the Constitution.

### The ERA

The proposed Equarl Rights Amendment to the Constitution would have required equal treatment of men and women in all domains. Although the amendment passed Congress and was ratified in a number of states, it failed to receive the three-fifths majority required to make it part of the Constitution. As a result, women continued to generally receive lower wages for comparable work in the ensuing decades.

> The Supreme Court's landmark decision in **Roe v. Wade** in 1973 granted constitutional protection to women seeking abortions. It also prohibited individual states from passing legislation that would ban abortions during the first three months of pregnancy.

## NIXON AND THE ENVIRONMENT

Although the Nixon administration generally prioritized economic interests over environmental concerns, Congress passed several protective acts in the 1970s. The administration supported the **Occupational Safety and Health Act (OSHA)**, the **Clean Air Act**, and the **Endangered Species Act**. At the same time, Nixon also created the **Environmental Protection Agency (EPA)** to protect air and water quality and to monitor the use of pesticides.

## NIXON'S SOCIAL WELFARE PROGRAMS

Nixon publicly advocated decreased government participation in social welfare. He cut key programs such as Medicare, Head Start, and legal services as part of his commitment to "Middle America." In spite of these cuts, Nixon also increased Social Security benefits, subsidized low-income housing, expanded the food stamp program, and established a government assistance program for low-income students.

## ECONOMIC POLICY

The Arab **oil embargo of 1973** combined with inflation at home created the nation's first energy crisis. Inflation rose steadily, as did the unemployment rate. The United States gradually lost its predominant place in the world economy as foreign countries such as Japan and Germany finally rebounded from post–World War II depressions. Nixon temporarily improved the economy by taking steps to increase exports while freezing wages and prices. Yet by 1974, the United States faced a severe economic crisis.

*Several of the world's leading oil-producing countries formed the **Organization of Petroleum Exporting Countries (OPEC)**, in 1960 to monopolize the sale of oil on the global market. OPEC began the **energy crisis** in the 1970s when it embargoed the sale of oil to the United States in retaliation for the American-backed Israeli defeat in the 1973 Yom Kippur War. Throughout the 1970s, OPEC punished the United States and other Western powers that supported Israel with a combination of oil embargoes and unannounced rate hikes. These retaliatory **"oil shocks"** damaged the American economy by raising prices and aggravating inflation.*

# Watergate, Resignation, and Ford

On June 17, 1972, local police officers apprehended five men during an early-morning break-in at the national Democratic Party headquarters in the **Watergate** apartment and office complex. Police soon discovered that the men worked for the **Committee to Reelect the President (CREEP)**. The burglars had attempted to repair a bugging device that they had installed during a previous forced entry. Over the next two years, the investigation brought the Nixon administration's worst secrets to light.

### THE NIXON TAPES

In April 1973, Nixon appeared on television to publicly accept responsibility for the Watergate events. He adamantly denied any direct knowledge of the break-in and cover-up and announced the resignations of several of his subordinates. The Senate investigative committee uncovered more incriminating evidence against the president and added charges concerning the misuse of federal funds and tax evasion. The committee subpoenaed some of the president's audiotapes of White House conversations, but Nixon refused to relinquish them.

### NIXON'S RESIGNATION

In July 1974, the Supreme Court unanimously decided that the president had to present his White House tapes to congressional investigators. These tapes clearly established Nixon's guilt in the Watergate cover-up. Armed with damning evidence, the House Judiciary Committee gained majority support on three charges of impeachment against Nixon:

- Obstruction of justice
- Abuse of power
- Contempt of Congress

Faced with imminent impeachment, Nixon chose instead to resign. In a dramatic, nationally televised speech on August 8,

1974, he accepted responsibility for his poor judgment in the Watergate scandal but continued to defend his good intentions.

## FORD: THE UNELECTED PRESIDENT

Following Nixon's resignation, Nixon's vice president, **Gerald Ford**, became president of the United States. Congress had recently appointed Ford to office after Vice President Agnew had resigned in the wake of a corruption scandal in 1973. As a result, Ford became the nation's first and only unelected president. Highlights of the Ford presidency include:

- **Nixon's presidential pardon**. Only a month into his presidency, Ford granted a formal pardon to Nixon for all his purported crimes, sparing the ex-president and the nation the embarrassment of a trial and likely conviction. The decision angered many Americans and ruined Ford's political and public credibility.

- **Evacuating Vietnam**. Ford pulled the last remaining troops out of Vietnam in 1975 which marked the end of American involvement in the Vietnam War. U.S. forces helped approximately 150,000 South Vietnamese flee the country.

- **The Continuing Economic Crisis**. Ford faced a number of liabilities during his brief term in office that proved insurmountable. He lacked the resources, knowledge, and political clout to tackle the stagnant economy. He also vetoed thirty-nine bills Congress had passed to improve domestic affairs and reduce taxes, and at the same time, he increased government spending. As a result, Americans faced the deepest recession since the Great Depression by the end of his two years in office.

Although the 1970s could be seen as an era of progress in terms of civil rights and social reform, undercurrents of conservatism became increasingly apparent and would fully emerge by the 1980s. Write an essay linking the relevance of an event or movement in the 1970s to the resurgence of conservatism in the 1980s.

The American Feminist Movement, which began in the nineteenth century and hit full stride with the winning of women's suffrage in 1920, peaked in its powers in the late 1960s and 1970s. However, like many progressive movements that flowered in the 1960s and 1970s, the Feminist Movement faced a conservative backlash in the 1970s that hardened into what some have termed the "radical" conservatism of the 1980s to the present. The dynamics of this backlash can be observed in the fate of the Equal Rights Amendment (ERA).

The National Women's Party (NWP) introduced the ERA to Congress in 1923, but the amendment failed to gain the required two-thirds majority in both houses of Congress. Finally, in 1972, with the support of Republican President Richard Nixon and the National Organization for Women (NOW), both houses of Congress approved the amendment. Yet the amendment failed to gain backing by the necessary three-fifths of the states. This failure reflected the well-organized opposition that the amendment faced from emboldened conservatives. These conservatives sought to preserve the traditional roles of women, opposed the expansion of the federal government's powers, and defended the prolife position on abortion, which had been undermined by the 1973 legalization of abortion by the Supreme Court.

The most conservative opposition to the amendment argued that ratification of the ERA would cause women to forgo protection of their God-given differences. This faction championed the financial dependence implicit in the role of the housewife and felt that the government should protect that role. The amendment's more mainstream opponents agreed there was a need for protective

# *Student Essay*

legislation to address issues unique to women, including wage differentials, exemption from Selective Service and the draft, health issues, and motherhood. Phyllis Shlafly, a conservative Republican and founder of the anti-ERA organization STOP (Stop Taking Our Privileges), vocalized support for such protective legislation. She organized women, including large numbers of housewives, to persuade legislators to share her perspective. Most historians agree that Shlafly's efforts were vital to the ultimate failure of the amendment.

Opponents of the ERA also argued for a limited federal government. They felt that the amendment would unduly increase governmental powers and decrease the rights of the individual. The widespread popularity of Reagan's drastic cuts in social spending in the 1980s demonstrated that a significant proportion of Americans feared a potentially intrusive big government. Such Americans wanted individuals to be self-regulating and represented by smaller, more accessible state governments. If Congress were granted the power to enforce the ERA, opponents felt that the federal government would be required to intervene in individual matters to an unprecedented extent.

Americans who opposed abortion represented another major faction of ERA opposition. They worried that the equality advocated by the amendment would preclude future governmental anti-abortion legislation. To that end, they argued that the possibility of differential treatment had to be maintained. Without the ability to legislate on a case-by-case basis, opponents feared that the government would be forced to eliminate all legislation and action that would recognize differences in gender. Such opponents worried about outcomes ranging from women being drafted for the military to women being denied maternity leave to the compulsory integration of single-sex educational institutions and sports teams.

Although less conservative individuals opposed the ERA—including Democratic Party activist Dorothy Smith McCallister, who argued for the protection of women in the workplace—the substantial opposition to the ERA reflected the conservative strains of public thought in the 1970s. Although the ERA was ultimately defeated in Congress in 1982 by a narrow margin, the conservatism associated with opposition to it would be fed by the Reagan administration in the 1980s. This combination of promoting tradition and limiting government power ensured the long-term suppression of the amendment and dominated American political culture for the next three decades.

# Test Questions and Answers

### 1. In what ways did the civil rights movement succeed?

- Martin Luther King, Jr., succeeded in bringing the civil rights movement to national attention by organizing a series of boycotts and protests.

- The Civil Rights Act of 1964 ended legal segregation and discrimination in the United States.

- The Voting Rights Act of 1965 eliminated southern voting restrictions on blacks.

### 2. Assess the presidency of Lyndon Johnson.

- He enacted the far-reaching reforms of the Great Society.

- The civil rights movement gained ground during his presidency.

- The Vietnam War plagued his administration, inciting division among Americans.

### 3. What factors contributed to the failure of American involvement in the Vietnam War?

- In spite of superior military resources, American troops were not able to successfully combat the Vietcong and other opposition, due in part to the guerilla tactics employed by those groups.

- The American public grew increasingly discouraged over the costs of the war, including steep American casualties.

- The United States had no clear goal in Vietnam except for the containment of communism.

- Bombing proved ineffective, since Vietnam lacked major urban centers to destroy.

### 4. How did the protection of women's rights progress during the 1970s?

- *Roe v. Wade* guaranteed a woman's right to abortion.

- Women gained more political power through organizations such as NOW.

- Women's rights activists gained congressional support of the ERA.

# Timeline

| 1963 | Lyndon Johnson becomes president. |
|------|-----------------------------------|
| 1964 | Tonkin Gulf Resolution authorizes military action in Souteast Asia. |
|      | Johnson launches War on Poverty. |
|      | Freedom Summer marks the climax of intensive voter-registration activities in the South. |
|      | Congress passes the Civil Rights Act of 1964. |
| 1965 | Johnson begins "escalation" in Vietnam. |
|      | The Pleiku Raid sparks off an intense series of airstrikes called Operation Rolling Thunder. |
|      | Peace protestors march on Washington D.C. |
|      | Congress passes the Voting Rights Act. |
| 1967 | Rallies, riots, and protests erupt throughout the United States. |
| 1968 | The Tet Offensive incites massive demonstrations on college campuses throughout the United States. |
|      | Paris peace talks begin. |
|      | Robert Kennedy is assassinated. |
|      | Martin Luther King, Jr., is assassinated. |
|      | Riots erupt outside the Democratic convention in Chicago. |
|      | Richard Nixon is elected president. |
| 1969 | The Woodstock Music and Art Fair attracts 400,000 people. |
|      | Nixon begins "Vietnamization" withdrawl of U.S. troops. |
| 1970 | The United States bombs Cambodia. |
|      | Student protests turn violent throughout the country. |
| 1971 | The New York Times publishes the Pentagon Papers. |
|      | The Twenty-Sixth Amendment is ratified. |
|      | Lieutenant William Calley is court-martialed for the My Lai Massacre. |

| | |
|---|---|
| *1972* | Nixon and Henry Kissinger visit China and the Soviet Union. |
| | Nixon signs the SALT and ABM treaties to reduce nuclear weapons. |
| | Nixon is reelected. |
| | Nixon authorizes the Christmas Day Bombing in North Vietnam. |
| *1973* | Congress passes the War Powers Act. |
| | The Watergate scandal erupts. |
| | *Roe v. Wade* gives women the right to an abortion. |
| | Arab oil embargo begins an oil/energy crisis. |
| *1974* | The House of Representatives prepares to impeach Nixon. |
| | Vice President Spiro T. Agnew resigns. |
| | Nixon resigns. |
| | Gerald Ford becomes president. |
| | Ford pardons Nixon. |
| *1975* | The Helsinki Accords reduces tension between Soviet and western blocs. |
| | Communists declare victory in South Vietnam. |

# Major Figures

**Spiro Agnew**  Elected vice president under Richard Nixon in 1968, Agnew resigned in 1973 after journalists discovered he had accepted several bribes while in office. Congress selected Congressman Gerald Ford to be the new vice president later that year. His resignation was merely one of the many scandals that soured public opinion against Nixon and politics in the 1970s.

**Stokeley Carmichael**  Radical civil rights leader in the mid-1960s, Carmichael coined the phrase "black power." He served as chairman of the Student Nonviolent Coordinating Committee (SNCC) and was a leading member of the Black panthers. He took the name Kwame Ture in 1968 and died in 1998.

**Gerald Ford**  Congress selected Ford from the House of Representatives in 1973 to replace Richard Nixon's vice president Spiro Agnew after Agnew had resigned in the wake of a bribery scandal. Ford became the first "unelected" president the next year after Nixon himself resigned. He unfortunately ruined his squeaky-clean image after he pardoned Nixon within days of taking office. Ford continued the policy of détente by signing the Helsinki Accords in 1975. That year he also withdrew the final remaining troops from South Vietnam. Hoping to win the presidency in his own right, he ran on the Republican ticket in 1976, but lost to Democrat James "Jimmy" Carter.

**Barry M. Goldwater**  An ultra-conservative senator from Arizona, Goldwater ran against Democrat Lyndon Johnson in the election of 1964. He hated Johnson's vision of a Great Society and the War on Poverty, despised the notion of equal rights for blacks, and advocated the use of nuclear weapons in Vietnam. He received 40 percent of the popular vote, but lost with only fifty-two electoral votes to Johnson's 486.

**Michael Harrington**  Author of the widely read *The Outer America*, Harrington was a prominent socialist during the 1960s. He served as a memember of the League for Industrial Democracy and became an advisor to Martin Luther King, Jr., in 1965. *The Outer America* revealed that in spite of the postwar economic boom, many Americans remained trapped in poverty. President Kennedy used the book to help shape his War on Poverty.

**Hubert Humphrey**  Vice president under Lyndon Johnson, Humphrey ran for president against George Wallace and Richard Nixon in 1968 on a platform to continue the War on Poverty and the war in Vietnam. The split in the Democratic party between Humphrey and Wallace and the Chicago riots at the nominating convention, however, gave Nixon an easy victory.

**Lyndon Johnson**  Vice president under John F. Kennedy, Johnson became president after JFK's assassination in 1963. In January 1964, he launched several new social welfare programs such as Head Start, Medicare, and Medicaid as part of his War on Poverty to create a Great Society. A nearly unanimous vote in Congress passed the Tonkin Gulf Resolution that gave Johnson a free hand to escalate the war in Vietnam. After soundly defeating Republican Barry M. Goldwater in the election of 1964, he authorized Operation Rolling Thunder in February 1965, hoping to bomb North Vietnam into peace. When this failed, Johnson sent more than 500,000 troops to South Vietnam and ultimately converted the conflict into a protracted and bitter war.

**Martin Luther King. Jr.**  Civil rights leader King's passionate oratory and skillful civil disobedience tactics helped end legal racial segregation in the United States. His assassination in 1968 sparked riots across the country and caused a rift in the civil rights movement.

**Robert Kennedy**  A former attorney general and younger brother to president John F. Kennedy, Democrat "Bobby" Kennedy campaigned in the 1968 presidential primary on a pro-civil rights and antiwar platform. He posed a serious threat to candidate Hubert Humphrey until a deranged American Muslim named Sirhan Sirhan assassinated him that summer.

**Henry Kissinger**  A former political science and history professor from Harvard, German-born Kissinger first served as Richard Nixon's national security advisor and then as Nixon's and Ford's secretary of state. Many historians believe he first proposed making a trip to China to scare the Soviets into détente. Although he has since retired from politics, his essays and works on diplomatic history and foreign policy are still highly regarded.

**George McGovern**  A Democratic senator from South Dakota, McGovern ran against incumbent Richard Nixon for the presidency in 1972 on an anti-Vietnam War platform. Nixon defeated him in a landslide victory with 520 electoral votes to McGovern's seventeen and with almost 20 million more popular votes.

**Richard Nixon**  A former communist-hunter and vice president under Dwight
D. Eisenhower, Nixon defeated Hubert Humphrey and George Wallace for
the presidency in 1968. Despite his policy of Vietnamization to withdraw
American troops from Vietnam, Nixon nevertheless intensified the Vietnam War by bombing Cambodia and North Vietnam. By opening relations
with China, he and Henry Kissinger forced the Soviet Union into negotiating a new era of eased tensions known as détente. Surprisingly, he
expanded and improved Lyndon Johnson's Great Society social welfare
programs and helped eliminate racial discrimination in the federal government. After defeating George McGovern in a landslide victory in 1972,
Nixon increased bombing raids in Vietnam and forced a peace settlement
out of North Vietnam. The Watergate scandal and his unwillingness to
hand over several incriminating audio tapes eventually forced him to
resign in 1974 rather than face unfavorable impeachment proceedings and
trial in Congress.

**George Wallace**  Wallace ran for president on the American Independent
Party ticket against Democrat Hubert Humphrey and Republican Richard
Nixon in 1968. A former governor from Alabama, he had vehemently
opposed the civil rights movement and desegregation. In his bid for the
presidency, Wallace campaigned for segregation and intensified bombing
in Vietnam. He carried only five states in the Deep South on Election Day.

**Malcom X**  Malcolm X's powerful rhetoric and calls for black self-reliance drew
many supporters from urban areas. His ideas of black pride signaled a split
with the mainstream civil rights movement. He was murdered in 1965.

# Suggested Reading

• Andrew, John A., III. *Lyndon Johnson and the Great Society*. Chicago: Ivan R. Dee Publishers, 1998.

Andrew's study recounts the rise and fall of Johnson's various Great Society Programs and discusses the War on Poverty's impact on present-day politics.

• Garthoff, Raymond. *Détente and Confrontation: American-Soviet Relations and the End of the Cold* War. Washington D.C.: Brookings Institute, 1994.

Garthoff exhaustively considers a balanced experience of both sides of the Cold War conflict including détente and reasons for the extended struggle over it.

• McQuaid, Kim. *The Anxious Years: America in the Vietnam and Watergate Era*. Philadelphia: Basic Books, 1990.

McQuaid examines the antiwar movement and Nixon's presidency in an effort to make sense of the social and cultural upheaval in America during the period.

• Summers, Anthony. *The Arrogance of Power: The Secret World of Richard Nixon*. New York: Penguin Books, 2000.

Summers's biography examines Nixon's early political career, banishment from politics in the early sixties, subsequent comeback in 1968, and resignation.

# Carter and Reagan: 1976–1988

9

- The Presidency of Jimmy Carter
- The Reagan Revolution
- Reagan Abroad

In spite of his honesty, faith, and good intentions, President Jimmy Carter appeared to lack the clout and political knowledge to resolve the numerous crises that plagued his presidency. He had no political experience in Washington, which proved problematic. A devout, born again Christian, Carter hoped to bring a smile and warmth to government with his southern-style, humanitarian politics, and support for human rights. This left many cynics to proclaim in later years that Carter was simply too nice to accomplish much in Washington.

Carter's successor, Ronald Reagan, made a powerful impact upon the country. With almost unprecedented popularity, he completely transformed the federal government. Reagan's promise to reduce the size and the role of the government killed Lyndon Johnson's Great Society and marked the end of New Deal liberalism, ushering in a new era for the United States.

# The Presidency of Jimmy Carter

After defeating **Gerald Ford** in 1976, **Jimmy Carter** assumed the presidency with promises to improve the economy, strengthen education, and provide assistance to the aging and the poor. Carter began his term in office with confidence and enthusiasm. A variety of obstacles and unexpected events prevented the new president from achieving many of his goals.

## THE ELECTION OF 1976

Gerald Ford received the Republican party's official nomination in the summer of 1976 and was desperate to win the presidency in his own right. Unfortunately for him, Americans had a tainted image of Washington politics, the White House, and anything even remotely tied to Richard Nixon. Instead, they turned to a surprise presidential contender, James "Jimmy" Carter. A Democrat, peanut farmer, and former governor of Georgia, Carter had almost no political experience in Washington, D.C., and was therefore "clean" in the eyes of many Americans. His down-to-earth demeanor and truthfulness only made him more likeable and refreshing to American voters.

During the campaign, Carter vowed to clean up Washington, cut taxes, and end the energy crisis. Thanks largely to enormous support from southern and black voters, Carter received slightly more than 50 percent of the popular vote and 297 electoral votes to Ford's 240.

## DOMESTIC POLICY

Unlike most of his Democrat predecessors, Carter increased taxes for the lower and middle classes and cut taxes for wealthier individuals. In the face of soaring inflation, slow economic growth, and high levels of unemployment, Carter also made minimizing federal spending and preserving Social Security two of his top priorities. Additionally, he protected struggling big businesses by reducing capital gains taxes and deregulating the banking, airline, trucking, and railroad industries.

## THE ENERGY CRISIS

Carter tried to reduce domestic oil consumption and American dependence on foreign crude oil, but he lacked the necessary support from consumers and Congress. As a result, none of the initiatives that Carter successfully launched had any real effect.

### "Stagflation"

The president's inability to tackle the **energy crisis** damaged his reputation, especially considering voters had elected him to do just that. Americans were forced to wait in long lines or buy gasoline only on certain days, just as they had under Nixon and Ford. Moreover, soaring gas prices made it more expensive to transport goods across the country. Manufacturers and retailers compensated for the increased transportation costs by raising retail prices so that, on average, inflation increased by 10 percent *per year* between 1974 and 1980 without any economic growth or change in wages. In other words, a product that cost $100 in 1974 cost over $180 in 1980. It thus became more expensive to drive, buy a house, buy consumer goods, and even buy groceries.

> After a nearly two-week hiatus from any public appearances, Carter made a televised address to the nation in which he blamed inflation and the energy crisis on morally and spiritually bankrupt Americans concerned only with money and consumerism. This **"Malaise Speech"** shocked the nation and led many to question Carter's ability to lead.

### CARTER'S FOREIGN POLICY

Carter made the protection of human rights through diplomacy his highest foreign policy priority. He slapped economic sanctions on countries like Argentina, Chile, and South Africa, infamous for rampant human rights violations. Critics argued that the president's human rights policies displayed inconsistencies. For example, he overlooked human rights violations in strategically important countries such as China, Iran, and South Korea. Others charged that Carter's human-rights-centered foreign policy distracted the United States from facing Cold War concerns, like the communist revolution in Nicaragua. Outside of America, many leaders around the world lauded his morally grounded foreign policy.

Carter attempted to extend his moral principles to amend some of America's past imperialist actions. In 1977, Carter signed a new treaty with Panama regarding the control and use of the **Panama Canal**. Until this point, the United States enjoyed sole control of the isthmian canal, but the new treaty granted Panama joint control until the year 2000 (at which point Panama would assume complete control). Many Americans perceived this action as compensation for the "big stick" tactics the United States had utilized to secure the land to build the canal in the first place. At the same time, critics became concerned with Carter's willingness to forgo control of such an economically and strategically vital waterway.

### Peace in the Middle East

Carter's successful leadership during negotiations between Egyptian president **Anwar el-Sadat** and Israeli prime minister **Menachem Begin** proved to be one of his greatest international achievements. After inviting the two men to the presidential retreat at Camp David, Maryland, Carter spent days guiding the discussion between the bitter rivals, who often refused to even meet face to face. Largely thanks to Carter, both men signed the **Camp David Accords** in 1978 to agree to end several decades of war. As a result, Egypt also became the first Arab nation to formally recognize Israel, and Israel agreed to withdraw from the Sinai Peninsula.

### SALT II

Carter hoped to end his first term on a high note before the 1980 elections by reducing the threat of Soviet aggression and nuclear holocaust. In 1979, he met with Soviet premier Leonid Brezhnev to sign the **Second Strategic Arms Limitation Talks (SALT II Treaty)**, to reduce the number of both countries' nuclear warheads.

Although a treaty would have significantly eased American-Soviet relations, conservatives in the Senate bitterly opposed it out of fear that the treaty would leave Americans vulnerable to attack. They pointed to Russia's support of the Cuban interventions in Ethiopia and Angola and the Soviet invasion of Afghanistan in

December 1979. Carter denounced the invasion and stopped all grain shipments to the U.S.S.R., but party leaders in Moscow refused to withdraw.

### The Iran Hostage Crisis

Carter's greatest international policy challenge came from Iran. Although the Shah of Iran, **Mohammad Reza Pahlavi**, had long been a U.S. ally, Carter criticized the shah's autocratic rule and refused to provide military aid to support him against an armed insurrection. In 1979, Carter allowed the shah to flee to the United States for medical treatment and political asylum. Iranian militants—who were enraged by American support of the ousted leader—broke into the U.S. embassy in Tehran and took fifty-three hostages.

The militants demanded that the United States return the shah for trial and possible execution in return for the release of the hostages. The new Iranian government, headed by the Shi'ite cleric **Ayatollah Khomeini**, actively participated in the hostage situation. Khomeini established a Shi'ite theocracy in Iran that remains in power.

Carter's attempts to deal with the hostage crisis were ineffective. After a year of failed negotiations, he authorized a military rescue operation. The rescue turned out to be a complete disaster, however, when eight American soldiers died in a helicopter crash in the Iranian desert. Khomeini refused to sign an agreement for the release of the hostages. Carter's inability to resolve the **Iran hostage crisis** weakened American confidence in the administration and contributed to his defeat in the election of 1980.

*Carter's inability to curb inflation, prevent Soviet aggression, or save the American hostages in Iran damaged his reputation at home and abroad. The Malaise Speech worsened matters. Many people in the United States expressed outrage over the president's attempt to blame them for his own shortcomings. With so much controversy, anger, and resentment clouding Carter's four years, Reagan's victory in 1980 came as no surprise.*

**CHAPTER 9** **1976–1988**

# The Reagan Revolution

Americans elected **Ronald Reagan**, a former movie actor and governor of California, to the presidency in 1980. Reagan swept into the White House in 1981 on a mission to reduce the size of the federal government and shift the balance of political power back to the individual states. A die-hard conservative Republican, he abhorred most social welfare programs, hated affirmative action, and felt that policymakers in Washington had overstepped their mandate by exerting too much control over the lives of average Americans.

Reagan managed to overcome opposition and pass most items on his agenda by cajoling southern conservative Democrats in Congress to vote with his Republican allies. He also received support from the so-called **Religious Right**, a prominent group of conservative Protestant ministers who opposed homosexuality and abortion, among other things. More important, he had the support of the vast majority of Americans.

## "REAGANOMICS"

Reagan immediately set out to balance the budget and curb the growing deficit that had plagued Jimmy Carter's administration. He proposed to slash social welfare programs in order to reduce the budget deficit to just under $40 billion a year. Then, he slashed tax rates across the board by nearly 25 percent. Corporations received even more benefits from Washington, D.C., in the hopes that their prosperity would "trickle down" to the average American worker. Although most conservatives praised Reagan's **"supply-side economics,"** a few Republicans dissented including Vice President **George H. W. Bush**, who had previously denounced Reagan's fiscal agenda as **"voodoo economics"** because it simply made no sense.

### The Recession of 1982

By 1982, **"Reaganomics"** had taken its toll as several banks failed, the stock market plummeted, and unemployment soared in the worst economic recession since the Great Depression. Eventually the economy pulled out of the pit, thanks in part to sound policies from the Federal Reserve Board. Prosperity eventually came, but at a steep price as the gap between the very rich and the very poor widened considerably. With reduced government welfare programs to alleviate the hunger and homelessness, the poor had nowhere to turn for help. The recession hit women, children, and blacks especially hard.

*The Reagan administration angered many women by openly opposing the **Equal Rights Amendment** and abortion rights. Additionally, Reagan's social-spending cuts had a disproportionate effect on women, who often earned less than men and sometimes carried the burden of raising families alone. The women's movement worked hard to improve public knowledge of the needs of lower-income women and children, who outnumbered lower-income men.*

### Deficits and Debt

Although Reagan entered the White House promising to reduce government spending and return more power to the states, he ironically became the biggest spender in American history. Not even Roosevelt's New Deal during the Depression or Johnson's Great Society had dumped so much money into the economy as Reaganomics. Between 1980 and 1988, Congress overspent its budget by more than $200 billion every year, while the national debt soared from roughly $1 trillion to $2.5 trillion.

Moreover, almost all of Reagan's spending went into the military and defense; very little actually "trickled down" to the average American. Still, Americans continued to support the president. For many citizens, his charisma and his unwavering stance against Soviet aggression abroad translated to a sense of safety. In the wake of Vietnam, social unrest, the energy crisis, and the Iran hostage crisis, Americans sought strength and protection above all else.

*By raising the national debt to astonishing and unprecedented proportions, Reagan ensured that no future Congress, for at least several generations, would be able to afford major social welfare programs either. In this sense, the staggering deficit thus became an incredible, long-term political victory.*

CHAPTER 9
1976–1988

### The Savings and Loan Crisis

Reagan also deregulated many aspects of the banking industry, which allowed the traditionally local, financially conservative **savings and loan** institutions to enter the arena of high-yield, high-risk corporate investments. As a result, hundreds of savings and loans across the country had gone bankrupt by the late 1980s. Congress's decision to rescue failing institutions saved many families from financial ruin, but it also further increased the federal budget deficit.

### The Stock Market Crash of 1987

Though a bull market ruled for much of the decade, Americans indulged in several imprudent financial practices that ultimately caused a stock market crash. Following the cue of the federal government's increased deficit spending, both consumers and businesses ran up huge debts. The United States also had a very high trade deficit, importing much more than it exported. Again, borrowed money often paid for these imports.

A shaky stock market finally buckled on October 19, 1987, or **Black Monday**, when the Dow Jones Industrial Average lost nearly 23 percent of its value in a single day. $560 billion in paper assets disappeared. Reagan reassured the nation that the economy would remain stable and tried to help the economy by reducing some deficit spending and increasing some taxes. These measures could not prevent stock markets around the world from buckling.

## CONSERVATISM IN THE COURT

Reagan's long presidency altered the composition of the federal courts. Reagan tended to appoint judges and justices who held politically conservative views and focused less on protecting individual rights. Reagan's most high-profile appointment was **Sandra Day O'Connor**, a middle-of-the-road conservative who became the first female Supreme Court justice.

While many critics expected Reagan's appointments to signal a profound change in the federal court system, the new conservative judges tended to maintain the status quo. Even when given the opportunity, they rarely overturned long-standing decisions on controversial issues (e.g., abortion). Instead, the justices began to defer to state-government decisions regarding rights issues.

### LANDSLIDE REELECTION IN '84

Democrats prayed that the recession would ruin Reagan's chances for reelection in 1984. But the president's popularity held steady. Democrats nominated Jimmy Carter's former vice president **Walter Mondale**, who surprised everyone by choosing a woman, **Geraldine Ferraro**, as his vice-presidential running mate. In the end, Reagan and Bush easily defeated Mondale and Ferraro with approximately 17 million more popular votes and 525 electoral votes to their thirteen.

# Reagan Abroad

A former "red" hunter in Hollywood during the McCarthy era, Reagan also took a hard stance against the "evil empire" of the Soviet Union. He believed that a **"window of vulnerability"** had temporarily weakened the United States.

### STAR WARS

Tired of détente and outraged by Soviet aggression in Afghanistan, Regan proposed to dramatically boost defense spending based on the belief that a crippled Russian economy wouldn't be able to keep up with American military development. His plan culminated with the proposal of a futuristic orbital laser defense system called the **Strategic Defense Initiative (SDI)**. Most scientists agreed that **"Star Wars,"** as pundits called it, would never work. Still, Reagan hoped the proposal would strong-arm the Soviet Union to the bargaining table on American terms.

### THE REAGAN DOCTRINE

The **Reagan Doctrine** stated that the United States had to combat any Marxist revolutions abroad in order to counter Soviet advances. The president employed this doctrine in several developing Latin American countries. For example, Reagan denounced the communist **Sandinista** revolutionaries in Nicaragua and gave tens of millions of dollars to the pro-American **"contra"** rebels to take back the country. He dumped even more money into neighboring El Salvador and sent military advisors to prevent a revolution there too. On top of this, Reagan ordered the invasion of the tiny island nation of Grenada in the Caribbean in 1983 to oust communist usurpers.

> The Reagan Doctrine served as the principle tenet of Reagan's foreign policy. He incorrectly assumed that all instability in the third world stemmed from Marxist revolutionaries or Soviet aggression and committed the United States to preventing the spread of communism even in the farthest corners of the world. In doing so, he ended détente, reversed the Nixon Doctrine, and revived the policy of containment. In other words, the United States would do and spend whatever it took to maintain the status quo and keep communism contained. Reagan's pledge and the renewed Cold War cost Americans hundreds of millions of dollars for very little gain.

## THE IRAN–CONTRA AFFAIR

Even though the vast majority of Americans supported Reagan's tough stance against communism, Congress did not. This was primarily because upholding the Reagan Doctrine simply cost too much money. The United States had poured hundreds of millions of dollars into fighting communist revolutions abroad—most notably in Nicaragua, to help the "Contra" rebels fight the Marxist Sandinistas. Finally, the invasion of Grenada had proven that Reagan would not hesitate to use troops to fight these insurgents.

### The Boland Amendment

Hoping to avert a Vietnam-esque war in Nicaragua, Congress passed the **Boland Amendment** in 1983, which forbade the federal government from further assisting the Contras with either troops or money.

### Illegal Arms Sales

Scandal erupted when journalists discovered that the White House had ignored the amendment and funneled secret money raised from arms sales in Iran and other Middle Eastern countries into Nicaragua. After a lengthy investigation, a congressional committee indicted several officials on the president's National Security Council, including Admiral Poindexter and Marine Corps colonel **Oliver North**. Both Poindexter and North claimed they acted in the interests of national security. Essentially, they argued that the ends justified the illegal means. The investigation implicated Reagan and Bush, but their involvement was never proven.

### REFORM IN RUSSIA

Although Reagan had taken an incredibly harsh stance against the Soviet Union, he actually played a key role in ending the Cold War. In 1985, reform-minded **Mikhail Gorbachev** came to power in the Soviet Union with some radical new ideas about politics, the economy, and society as a whole. Soon after taking office, he initiated **glasnost**, or "openness," to relax some political controls, including restrictions on the press, and **perestroika**, or "restructuring," to slowly convert the Soviet Union into a more capitalist economy.

In order to transition to capitalism, Gorbachev drastically reduced the amount the U.S.S.R. spent on its military, which effectively meant ending the Cold War. He met with Reagan at four different summit meetings between 1985 and 1988 and signed the **INF Treaty** at the final summit in Washington, D.C., to remove all nuclear weapons aimed at Europe and effectively end the Cold War.

How did President Ronald Reagan revive the Cold War during his first term? Can he be credited with helping to end the Cold War?

Ronald Reagan was elected president in 1980. Reagan advocated a return to a hard-line policy in dealing with the U.S.S.R. after a decade of *détente*, or reduced tension, between the two superpowers. He hoped to cause the U.S.S.R.'s collapse from within by stepping up anti-Soviet rhetoric, forcing the U.S.S.R. to overextend itself by building up a nuclear arsenal to compete with the United States. In many ways this was true, but perhaps a greater share of credit for ending the Cold War belongs to Mikhail Gorbachev, the reforming Soviet leader who came to power in 1985. Both Reagan and Gorbachev were able to cast aside their ideological differences and finally put the Cold War to rest.

The first and most prominent aspect of Reagan's Cold War policy was a heightening of anti-Soviet rhetoric after a decade of more friendly relations. Reagan referred to the U.S.S.R. as an "Evil Empire" and promised in 1983, "Freedom and democracy . . . will leave Marxism-Leninism on the ash heap of history." Reagan's fighting words caused fear both in the Soviet Union, which had grown used to milder relations with the United States, and in America's European allies, who feared they would be caught in the middle of an armed conflict between the super powers. Most of all, it stirred patriotism and pro-Reagan sentiment on the home front, where he came to be seen as a hero confronting a sinister enemy in Russia and won landslide election victories.

The most crucial of Reagan's policies was the heightening of the arms race. Reagan's goal was to cripple the Soviet economy by forcing the U.S.S.R. to overextend itself by building a nuclear arsenal to compete with the United States. Negotiations on the SALT II treaty for limiting nuclear arms, begun in 1972, were abandoned, and Reagan spent over $1 trillion on the military in his first three years in office. This stockpiling proceeded despite the fact that both powers had, by the mid-1980s, approximately 25,000 nuclear warheads—enough to accomplish any foreseeable military goals several times over. Additionally, there had been no

# Student Essay

military crises involving the two powers at once since the 1962 Cuban Missile Crisis and the 1973 Middle East War. Reagan pressed on and drove the federal government into a budget deficit because he believed that the Soviet Union's planned Communist economy could not compete with the free-market economy of the West. He went even further by announcing the Strategic Defense Initiative (SDI), a.k.a. the "Star Wars" program, which proposed to use satellites in space to defend the United States from ballistic missile attacks. Many scoffed that the science of the program was unworkable, but it proved intimidating to the Soviets.

The faltering of the Soviet economy coincided with the rise to executive office of genuine reformers in Mikhail Gorbachev and Foreign Minister Edward Schevardnadze. The former inaugurated an era of *perestroika* (restructuring) and *glastnost* (openness) in the U.S.S.R. unseen since before the revolution of 1917. When Reagan encountered Gorbachev and Schevardnadze at the negotiating table, he found people he could deal with. Consequently, his second term was marked by a series of arms reduction treaties. Still, the rhetoric remained heated: even as Reagan was in Berlin imploring, "Mr. Gorbachev, tear this wall down," he was working behind the scenes to improve United States-Soviet relations. The single term of his successor, George H. W. Bush, was marked by the breakup of the Soviet Union, the arrival there of democracy and free market capitalism, and the fall of the Berlin Wall.

Reagan was often referred to as the "Great Communicator" during his two terms of the presidency. But although he made bold, provocative statements about the Cold War, he never seriously wielded American power to the extent that he could have. The Cold War was a product of mutual distrust as much as feuding ideologies, and when leaders in both powers were finally able to put aside their ideologies in favor of realism and trust, it ended. When Reagan died in 2004, the United States counted Russia among its allies and trading partners.

# Test Questions and Answers

## 1. Why did Carter's immense popularity plummet in just four years?

- Carter was unable to resolve the energy crisis as he had promised during his campaign in 1976.

- The Senate refused to ratify the SALT II Treaty.

- His "Malaise Speech" alienated many voters.

- He was unable to resolve the 444-day Iran hostage crisis.

## 2. How did Reagan revive the Cold War during his first term?

- He revived the theory of containment by declaring the U.S.S.R. an "evil empire" that had to be stopped.

- His Reagan Doctrine announced that the United States would take action to prevent communist insurgency abroad, effectively reversing the Nixon Doctrine of the early 1970s.

- He fought communism with money and troops in Grenada, Nicaragua, and El Salvador.

- His Strategic Defense Initiative, or "Star Wars" program, sought to outspend the Soviets and bring them to the negotiating table to prevent economic collapse.

## 3. How did Reagan help end the Cold War during his second term?

- He supported Gorbachev's glasnost and perestroika reform initiatives.

- He met with Gorbachev at four different summits to discuss arms reduction.

- He signed the INF Treaty that removed all Soviet warheads aimed at Western Europe, effectively ending the Cold War.

## 4. Describe Reagan's fiscal policies.

- Even though Reagan championed limited government, he spent more money than all previous presidents combined.

- He cut funding to most social welfare programs in favor of financing defense and military programs.

- He drastically slashed corporate taxes, hoping that the extra money would "trickle down" to the average worker.

- He deregulated the banking industry.

- His enormous deficit spending ensured that Congress would not be able to fund more social welfare programs for a very long time.

# *Timeline*

| | |
|---|---|
| **1976** | James "Jimmy" Carter is elected president. |
| **1978** | Anwar Sadat and Menachem Begin agree to end hostility and sign the Camp David Accords. |
| **1979** | Carter delivers his Malaise Speech. |
| | Carter meets with Lenoid Brezhnev to sign the SALT II Treaty (never signed by the Senate). |
| | The Iran hostage crisis begins. |
| | The Soviet Union invades Afghanistan. |
| **1980** | Ronald Reagan is elected president. |
| **1981** | The Iran Hostage crisis ends. |
| | Reagan slashes taxes but increases government spending. |
| **1982** | Recession hits. |
| **1983** | Reagan announces SDI, or "Star Wars." |
| | 241 American troops are killed in Lebanon. |
| | The United States invades Grenada. |
| **1984** | Reagan is reelected. |
| **1985** | Mikhail Gorbachev initiates reform in the U.S.S.R. |
| | Nuclear disarmament is discussed at the first Reagan-Gorbachev summit meeting. |
| **1986** | The Iran-Contra Affair erupts. |
| | Congress passes the Immigration Reform and Control Act. |
| | The second Regan-Gorbachev summit meeting is held. |
| **1987** | The third Reagan-Gorbachev summit meeting is held. |
| | Reagan signs the INF Treaty at the fourth Reagan-Gorbachev summit meeting in Washington, D.C., to remove all nuclear weapons. |

# Major Figures

**George Bush**  A former director of the CIA and ambassador to China and the UN, Bush attacked Ronald Reagan's supply-side economic policies during the 1980s. He even referred to "Reaganomics" as "voodoo economics" during the 1980 presidential primaries. Ironically, however, he accepted Reagan's invitation to be his running mate. He served as vice president throughout Reagan's two terms, and defeated Michael Dukakis for the presidency in 1988.

**James "Jimmy" Carter**  A former peanut farmer and Georgian governor, Carter defeated incumbent President Gerald Ford for the presidency in 1976 with promises to clean up Washington, D.C. He revised the tax system and gave Americans $18 billion in tax cuts, but failed to curb rising inflation or resolve the energy crisis. Public opinion of the president soured after he blamed the crises on over-consumption and the degradation of society in his infamous Malaise Speech in 1979. Although he successfully negotiated a lasting peace between Israel and Egypt with the Camp David Accords, the rest of his humanitarian-oriented foreign policy floundered, especially after he bungled the Iran hostage crisis. He ran for reelection in 1980, but lost to Republican Ronald Reagan.

**Geraldine Ferraro**  A Congresswoman from New York, Ferraro was the first woman nominated for the vice presidency by a major political party. She unsuccessfully ran with Walter Mondale on the Democratic ticket against Ronald Reagan in 1984.

**Mikhail Gorbachev**  Selected to lead the Soviet Union in 1985, Gorbachev initiated sweeping reforms that drastically changed the U.S.S.R. His policy of glasnost, or "openness," for example, introduced free speech and some degree of political liberty to the country. Gorbachev also initiated perestroika, or "restructuring," to revive the stagnant Soviet economy with capitalist market principles. He met with Ronald Reagan at four summits between 1985 and 1988 to discuss improved Soviet–American relations and signed the INF Treaty with Reagan to remove nuclear warheads from Europe. Gorbachev's reforms shook the U.S.S.R. to its core and contributed both to the collapse of the Soviet Union in 1991 and the end of the Cold War.

**Ayatollah Ruholla Khomeini**  A fundamentalist Muslim cleric, Khomeini led the radical revolutionary forces that overthrew the American-backed shah of Iran in 1979. As the new religious ruler of Iran, he cut off all oil exports to the West, which sent the United States into a second oil crisis. In November 1979, his forces took several Americans hostage at the U.S. embassy in Tehran and demanded the return of the escaped shah. President Jimmy Carter refused to negotiate and instead ordered an unsuccessful military rescue operation. His failure to end the Iran hostage crisis helped lead to his defeat in the 1980 presidential election. Khomeini released the hostages on Ronald Reagan's inauguration day in 1981 after holding them for 444 days.

**Walter Mondale**   A Democrat, Mondale ran against incumbent Ronald Reagan for the presidency in 1984. Even though he lost badly, with only thirteen electoral votes to Reagan's 525 and with 20,000,000 fewer popular votes, he nevertheless distinguished himself as the first presidential candidate to choose a woman, Geraldine Ferraro, as his vice-presidential running mate.

**Oliver North**   A lieutenant colonel in the Marine Corps and staffer on the National Security Council, North testified at a congressional hearing in 1987 about his role in the Iran-Contra Affair. He freely admitted that he and his superiors on the council had destroyed evidence of their illegal actions, arguing that he had acted honorably, in the best interests of the United States. A court convicted him for blatantly defying the Boland Amendment, but North was eventually acquitted. Still, his actions cast a pall on Ronald Reagan's presidency and integrity.

**Ronald Reagan**   A former movie star from the 1930s, '40s, and '50s and governor of California, Reagan defeated incumbent Democrat Jimmy Carter for the presidency in 1980 with promises to drastically downsize the federal government. His election ushered in a new era of political conservatism. Reagan cut almost all federally funded social welfare programs in an effort to shift the balance of power back to the individual states. Ironically, he spent more than all previous twentieth-century presidents combined in an effort to bolster national defense against Soviet attack. Reagan declared the Soviet Union an "evil empire" and proposed the Strategic Defense Initiative, also known as SDI or Star Wars, to build a laser defense shield. He spent millions of dollars funding the anti-communist Contras in Nicaragua and El Salvador and sent troops to Grenada, though the Iran-Contra Affair proved that he didn't always have control over his foreign policy advisors. Reagan's supply-side economic theories, dubbed "Reaganomics" or "voodoo economics," meanwhile made wealthy Americans wealthier and poor Americans poorer. He participated in four debates with Soviet leader Mikhail Gorbachev, cosigned the INF Treaty, and thus helped end the Cold War.

# Suggested Reading

- Edwards, Lee. *The Conservative Revolution: The Movement that Remade America*. New York: Free Press, 2000.

Edwards examines the lives of four key players in the "conservative revolution": Robert Taft, Barry Goldwater, Ronald Reagan, and Newt Gingrich. Edwards admits that his writing is slanted toward his own conservative politics.


- FitzGerald, Frances. *Way Out There in the Blue: Reagan, Star Wars, and the End of the Cold War*. New York: Touchstone, 2000.

FitzGerald, a Pulitzer Prize–winner, provides a history of American missile development. FitzGerald's account spans both recent history and current events. Notably, she argues how Reagan's background as an actor heavily influenced his career.


- Kaufman, Burton I. *The Presidency of James Earl Carter, Jr.* Lawrence: University Press of Kansas, 1993.

Kaufman argues that Carter was quite intelligent but failed to articulate his purpose and direction as a president.


- Schulman, Bruce J. *The Seventies: The Great Shift in American Culture, Society, and Politics*. Cambridge: Perseus Books. 2001.

Schulman, the director of American Studies at Boston University, uses cultural examples to discuss politics.

# INDEX

**INDEX**

**INDEX**

**INDEX**

INDEX

**INDEX**

INDEX

and Native Americans, 187
Neutrality Act of 1939, 174
North African campaign, 181
Pearl Harbor, 177–178
and the Philippines, 180
politics during, 184–185
price and wage controls, 183
race riots, 187
rationing, 183
Roosevelt, death of, 190
and shipping in the Atlantic, 176–177
strategic bombing over Europe, 189
Tehran conference, 189
U.S. entry into, 178
victory gardens, 183
victory in the Pacific, 191–195
  American offensive in the Pacific, 192
  Guadalcanal, battle for, 192
  Iwo Jima, 193
  MacArthur in the South Pacific, 192
  Nimitz in the Central Pacific, 192
  Okinawa, 193
war production and the economy, 182–183
War Production Board, 183
women in war industries, 185

## Y

Yalta Conference, 208
Yalta Declaration of Liberated
  Europe, 208
Yamamoto, Admiral Isoroku, 178
Yates, Richard, 230
Yellow press, 63
Yom Kippur War (1973), 255
Young Men's Christian
  Association (YMCA), 54
Young Women's Christian
  Association (YWCA), 54

## Z

Zedong, Mao, 216
Zimmerman Note, 97
Zimmerman Telegram, 110

**INDEX**